HAYNES MAX POWER Vauxhall

nova

The definitive guide to **modifying**

by **Bob Jex** and **Em Willmott**

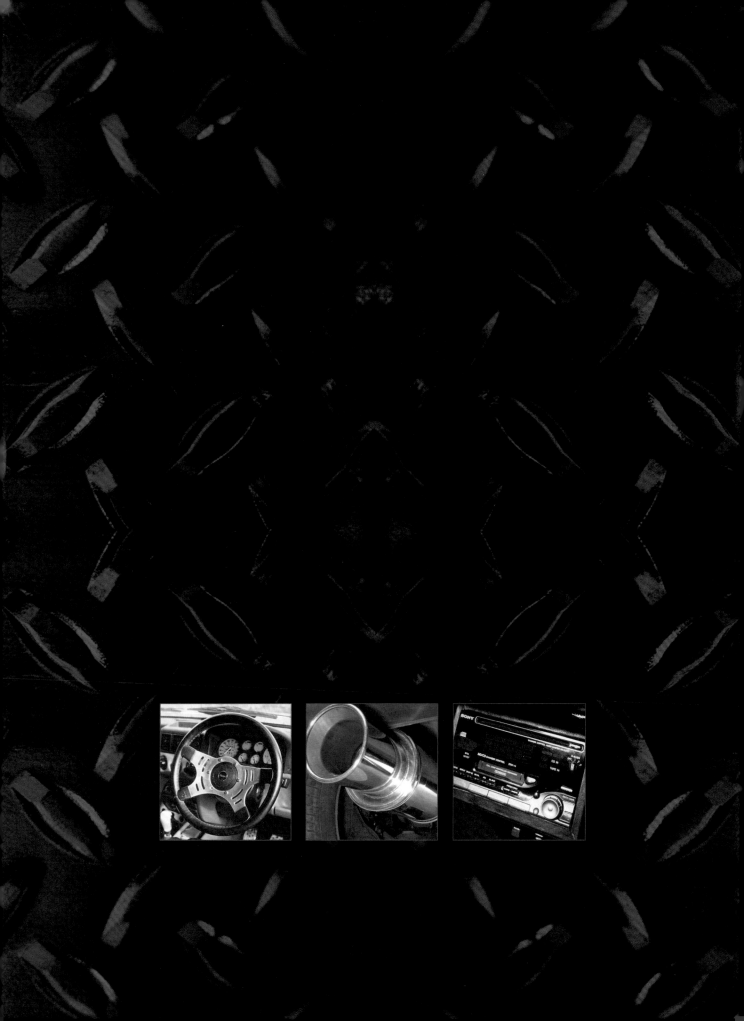

HAYNES MAX POWER Vauxhall

nova

The definitive guide to modifying
by **Bob Jex** and **Em Willmott**

Haynes Publishing

ISBN 1 84425 070 9

Printed by **J H Haynes & Co Ltd,**
Sparkford, Yeovil, Somerset BA22 7JJ, England.

Tel: 01963 442030 Fax: 01963 440001
Int. tel: +44 1963 442030 Fax: +44 1963 440001
E-mail: sales@haynes-manuals.co.uk
Web site: www.haynes.co.uk

Haynes North America, Inc
861 Lawrence Drive, Newbury Park, California 91320, USA

Editions Haynes
4, Rue de l'Abreuvoir
92415 COURBEVOIE CEDEX, France

Haynes Publishing Nordiska AB
Box 1504, 751 45 UPPSALA, Sweden

It wasn't my idea guv'nor!

1 Advice on safety procedures and precautions is contained throughout this manual, and more specifically on page 186. You are strongly recommended to note these comments, and to pay close attention to any instructions that may be given by the parts supplier.

2 J H Haynes recommends that vehicle customisation should only be undertaken by individuals with experience of vehicle mechanics; if you are unsure as to how to go about the customisation, advice should be sought from a competent and experienced individual. Any queries regarding customisation should be addressed to the product manufacturer concerned, and not to J H Haynes, nor the vehicle manufacturer.

3 The instructions in this manual are followed at the risk of the reader who remains fully and solely responsible for the safety, roadworthiness and legality of his/her vehicle. Thus J H Haynes are giving only non-specific advice in this respect.

4 When modifying a car it is important to bear in mind the legal responsibilities placed on the owners, driver and modifiers of cars, including, but not limited to, the Road Traffic Act 1988. IN PARTICULAR, IT IS AN OFFENCE TO DRIVE ON A PUBLIC ROAD A VEHICLE WHICH IS NOT INSURED OR WHICH DOES NOT COMPLY WITH THE CONSTRUCTION AND USE REGULATIONS, OR WHICH IS DANGEROUS AND MAY CAUSE INJURY TO ANY PERSON, OR WHICH DOES NOT HOLD A CURRENT MOT CERTIFICATE OR DISPLAY A VALID TAX DISC.

5 The safety of any alteration and its compliance with construction and use regulations should be checked before a modified vehicle is sold as it may be an offence to sell a vehicle which is not roadworthy.

6 Any advice provided is correct to the best of our knowledge at the time of publication, but the reader should pay particular attention to any changes of specification to the vehicles, or parts, which can occur without notice.

7 Alterations to vehicles should be disclosed to insurers and licensing authorities, and legal advice taken from the police, vehicle testing centres, or appropriate regulatory bodies.

8 The vehicle has been chosen for this project as it is one of those most widely customised by its owners, and readers should not assume that the vehicle manufacturers have given their approval to the modifications.

9 Neither J H Haynes nor the manufacturers give any warranty as to the safety of a vehicle after alterations, such as those contained in this book, have been made. J H Haynes will not accept liability for any economic loss, damage to property or death and personal injury arising from use of this manual other than in respect of injury or death resulting directly from J H Haynes' negligence.

Contents

Haynes
Max Power

Buyer's guide

Insurance

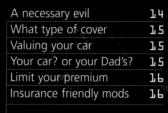

Suspension

Brakes

Interiors

Security

04

Body styling

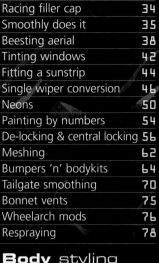

05

Lights & bulbs

06

Wheels & tyres

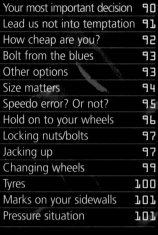

07

11

ICE

12

Engines

13

Exhausts

14

Reference

Haynes Max Power

What's that then?

Haynes Publishing have, for the last forty years, been helping people keep their cars on the roads in countries all over the world by publishing maintenance manuals. Chances are you've either got one of them yourself or you know somebody who has.

"Lights & bulbs" includes fitting high-power blue headlight bulbs, coloured rear light clusters, etc.

Before

After

Remember what it feels like on your birthday, or at Christmas, when you're faced by a pile of pressies? So do we, that gnawing feeling in your gut, what's in them? What did I get? Take that feeling and multiply it by twelve, that's how we felt when we started this project. When we decided that it was time to try something new, we couldn't wait. Because the same theories apply to modifying your car as servicing it, we reckoned we'd better get on and do it ourselves. We don't pay other people to do it for us, and we get the same dodgy instructions with kit as everybody else.

So if you've ever wondered how to fit a universal door mirror properly, smooth a tailgate or just bolt a seat in, this book is for you.

We've picked up a skip full of tips along the way, and they're all here for you to use. We haven't tried to set any trends, but we've covered every possible process we think you'll need. So where we've tinted a front door window, the same rules apply to a rear one, job done.

If you look in the magazines and want some of that, join us, 'cos so do we, and we'll show you how to get it.

Keeping it real

Modifying a car is not without its problems in the 'real world', as opposed to the seemingly fantasy world of the glossy mags. For instance, it's pretty silly to spend hours fitting illegal window tints or smoked lights if you get pulled the first time you're out afterwards. Of course, you can get pulled for all sorts of reasons (and just driving a modified car is reason enough sometimes), but keeping the car actually legal is one of the 'hidden' challenges with modifying. Throughout the book, our tips should give all the help you need to at least appear to be on the right side of the law. The annual MOT test is another favourite time for your mods to get panned, and again, we aim to give you all the help necessary to ensure at least that what you've changed doesn't lead to a fail.

Security is another major issue with a tweaked motor, and the perils of insurance cannot be taken lightly, either. We aim to give down-to-earth advice to help you keep the car in the first place, and to help you in not upsetting your insurers too much if the worst happens.

A word about fashion

In producing this book, we're aware that fashions change. What we show being fitted to our car might well be hideously out of date in 6 months time, or might not be your thing in the first place! Also, some of the stuff we've acquired from our various suppliers may no longer be available by the time you read this. We hope that, despite this, our approach of showing you step-by-step how to fit the various parts will mean that, even if the parts change slightly, the procedures we show for fitting will still be valid.

Our main project car was a 1.2 Luxe, 1991 J reg, with some additional work being carried out on other Novas.

*"Wheels & tyres"
takes a detailed
look at all the
options.*

*"Body styling"
shows you how
to fit universal
mirrors to full
body kits.*

*"Interiors"
includes seats,
painting trim,
gear knobs and
loads more.*

Super Nova - the lad's favourite

If you're shopping for your first car, you really can't go wrong with a Nova. The car's got such a huge following with the UK's young drivers, it's instant cred to be seen in one. Armies of fans have produced massively-detailed websites, photo galleries and chat forums devoted to this old 80s small hatch. So what's goin' on? This is the car that replaced the old Chevette, and that was rubbish - the Nova's got solid-gold cult status in comparison.

First of all, they're everywhere, and none are expensive - the youngest of them's over 10 years old, and there's TWO generations of replacement Corsa between it and the new-car forecourt.

Second, they look totally different to the roundy, curvy modern stuff out there now, so they achieve a certain cool classic style of their own, just because they've lasted so well. Third, and most important, the Nova's got just about the largest following of any modded motor out there - if you can't get something trick for a Nova, chances are, no-one's thought of making it yet.

Vauxhall have always been clever at playing a market, and realised early on there was a huge potential for a hot hatch version of the Nova. Like the Golf (that other icon of the modifying world) the Nova in standard trim was a plain, boxy-looking car, very under-stated and simple-looking - crying out to be tarted-up, in other words! By adding an air dam and rear spoiler, some smart alloys, stripes, and a decent Recaro interior, the humble shopping trolley was transformed into a very sharp-looking 1.3 SR with ease. This meant that the youngest of drivers could take an even more humble base-model Nova, and make it look totally wicked (on the cheap, if necessary) while keeping the insurance half-sensible - not too hard to figure out, is it?

Let's not forget the practical side of owning the little fella - if it wasn't easy on the wallet, the appeal to first-time drivers wouldn't exist. Insurance is cheap as chips (important when you're building up your no-claims) starting at Group 4 for the 'acceptable' 1.2 models, and even the 1.4 SR/SRi comes in an excellent-value Group 7. Parts won't strain the overdraft, and the car's dead easy to work on when things go wrong. Being easy to work on has other advantages too - the Nova's just like Meccano on wheels, because when your insurance allows it, you can just unbolt that poor little 1.2 engine, and drop in something a bit more fun. Like 150 bhp of 2.0 litre 16-valve Calibra power. Nova - the small car that grows with you.

Buyer's guide

What to buy

First of all, don't buy a 5-door Hatch, or a 4-door Saloon. The reason? NOBODY buys them for modifying purposes. If it doesn't say in the advert which it is, ask.

Novas with rear doors just don't look cool - you might have other ideas, but you'll be in a minority! We've not seen many modded 2-door Saloons either, but at least there's a glimmer of hope with one of those.

The lesser Novas make the best buys, especially if the insurance budget is tight. The real trick is finding one in half-decent condition. The cars will probably have had numerous owners, and finding one that hasn't been ragged or badly modified may be hard. One decision you'll have to make early on is whether you're after a 'Mk 1' or 'Mk 2' Nova. The change happened in September 1990, when the interior received a major overhaul, and the front end had a minor makeover. Less obviously, the rear arches on Mk 2s are apparently 5 mm wider than the Mk 1, meaning it's slightly easier getting big rims on a Mk 2 (this seals it for many modifiers).

Vauxhall created thousands of special edition Novas, yet sometimes the interior trim was the biggest thing they changed. Don't pay more just for nicer seats, if you're going to change everything anyway. The base models are fairly sad inside, with a dull dash and virtually no toys - smartening it up with a full interior makeover would be a priority on one of these babies. Levels of kit are pretty basic on all Novas, but if you can find one with tints, sunroof or central locking/electric windows, go for it - it's worth the extra. No power steering option for any Nova means you might be working hard at the wheel with your big rims on.

Although the 1.0 litre models are cheapest to insure (Group 3), there's a reason why, and it's the feeble little 1.0 litre pushrod engine under the bonnet. Pushing out a measly 45 bhp, it makes a particularly sad choice for the ambitious Maxer. Its only advantage over the rest of the range is there's no cambelt to worry about.

The most common engine's the 1.2, which at least is a modern overhead cam unit, with 54 bhp in carburettor form. Makes a fair job of hustling the Nova along, and in some ways it's more tuneable than some of the 1.4s which came along later. Group 4 insurance won't hurt the overdraft too much, either. After February 1992, the 1.2 models gained single-point fuel injection and a 'cat', reducing power to 44 bhp (that's less than a 1.0 litre), and dropping

insurance back to Group 3. We think the 1.2i models are well worth avoiding, for performance reasons alone.

The 1.3 motor packs 70 bhp, and we're starting to get into warm-hatch territory now, for just one group extra on insurance - no wonder the 1.3 SR was so popular. The 1.3 engine can be had in lesser trim levels too, and if you can find one, they make the best-value performance/insurance compromise. The 1.3s died in 1989, replaced by the 1.4 models.

With the 1.4 engines, you need to be careful what you're buying - they're not necessarily quicker than the 1.3s, yet they're all dearer to insure. The ones to avoid, performance-wise, are the 1992-on non-SR/SRi models with single-point fuel injection, known as the 1.4i models. These are afflicted with a 'cat', knocking the power down to just 60 bhp. The 1.4 carburettor engine has 72 bhp, which isn't much more than the 1.3 managed. Just to prove cats aren't always bad news, the later 1.4 SRi also has a 'cat', but with multi-point injection, it's packing 82 bhp. Bonus - with Group 7 insurance, decent kit and cheaper road tax, is it worth paying more for a 100 bhp GTE or GSi?

If insurance is no problem, the pick of the hot 1.6 Novas would be the 1990/91 GSi. Why? Well, the GSi has the obvious benefit of the 90-spec facelift over the earlier GTE, and models before 1992 didn't have a 'cat'. While the 'cat' didn't hurt the on-paper power, it certainly hit the on-road performance - if you're paying Group 11 premiums, you want the most from your money.

Finally, if you come across a Nova wearing a TD badge, don't be too quick to rule it out. While there's no getting round that diesel rattle, the 1.5 turbo-diesel motor's pretty lively (67 bhp) and there's excellent economy to be had as well. The last of them (after March 1992) even had a slightly sporty interior - Group 6 insurance is on a par with the 1.4 petrols.

Don't buy a **dog**

A well-looked-after Nova will stand the test of time - there's still some from 1983 running around out there, to back this up. But - Novas are often bought as first cars, get driven badly, and looked after worse. Treated like that, they soon fall apart. Your mission is to find a good one - and a cherished modded example can often be a good buy, so don't limit yourself to standards.

So what goes wrong? Let's start with the dreaded rust. Check the front wings for rust along the top edges, and the strut tops under the bonnet, where they're spot-welded to the inner wings. Tailgates rot out along the bottom edge (caused by not keeping the drain holes clear). Rear arches are another prime spot for major rust, especially if they've been badly trimmed for fitting big rims - look for signs of bodged repairs on the edges, and check inside, inboard of the rear shocks. On sports models with black vinyl lower door panels, the black can trap moisture behind it, which is game-over for the doors. Door bases are a weak spot on all later models in particular.

Engines are sound enough at the bottom end, but get rattly and smoky if oil changes are neglected (or if the car gets hunted to death). Check for blue smoke when starting up from cold (valve guides/oil seals), and for camshaft rattles when hot (worn cam/followers) - either of these means a large bill on the horizon. All engines except the 1.0 litre have a cambelt, which for safety should be changed every 3 years or 30 000 miles - if the belt snaps, the engine could be wrecked. Finished. Ruined. Knackered. It's an easy DIY job if you're confident under the hood, or budget for a £50 garage bill. Pull the dipstick, and look in the coolant bottle (engine cold) - if there's water on the dipstick, or brown sludge in the coolant bottle, run away. The cylinder head gasket's gone, or the head's cracked (another sign is a strange 'gurgling' noise heard inside the car on tickover).

The standard suspension's going to be shot by now, unless money's been spent - even uprated suspension could be getting tired if it's been on there a while. Expect to replace something, and haggle the price down. Listen out for rear wheel bearing wear (a drone at 40 - 50 mph), or worn CV joints (clicking noise on full-lock). Hard driving (or too many burnouts) might also have fried the Nova clutch - check for slipping by trying to pull away with the handbrake full on. Nova brakes never were that good - calipers seize up, which leads to rapid pad wear and warped discs (judder through the pedal). You'll uprate them of course, but haggle if the standards are no good. The interiors hold up quite well, but handles get very floppy with age, and sports seats suffer worn side bolsters.

General stuff

It's far better to buy your Nova privately, as long as you know what you're doing. Dealers still think they can charge over the odds for small cars, but all you'll get for the extra money is a full valet and some degree of comeback if the car's a dog. Buying privately, you get to meet the owner, and this can tell you plenty about how the car's been treated. Everyone's nervous when buying a car, but don't ignore your 'gut feelings' when you first see the car, or meet its owner. Also, don't make the common mistake of deciding to buy the car *before you've even seen it* - too many people seem to make up their minds before setting out, and blindly ignore all the warning

signs. Remember, there *are* other cars, and you *can* walk away! Think of a good excuse before you set out.

Take someone who 'knows a bit about cars' along with you - preferably, try and find someone who's either got a Nova, or who's had one in the past.

Never buy a car in the dark, or when it's raining. If you do have to view any car in these conditions, agree not to hand over any money until you've seen it in daylight, and when the paintwork's dry (dull, faded paint, or metallic paint that's lost its lacquer, will appear to be shiny in the rain).

One sign of a genuine car is a good batch of old MOTs, and as many receipts as possible - even if they're for fairly irrelevant things like tyres.

Check that the mileages and dates shown on the receipts and MOTs follow a pattern indicating normal use, with no gaps in the dates, and no sudden drop in the mileage between MOTs (which might suggest the mileage has been 'clocked'). If you are presented with a sheaf of paperwork, it's worth going through it - maybe the car's had a history of problems, or maybe it's just had some nice expensive new parts fitted (like a clutch, starter motor or alternator, for instance).

Check the chassis number (VIN number) and engine number on the registration document AND on the car. Any sign of welding near one of these numbers should be treated with suspicion - to disguise the real number, a thief will run a line of weld over the old number, grind it flat, then stamp in a new number. Other scams include cutting the section of bodywork with the numbers on from another car, then cutting and welding this section into place. The VIN number appears on a plate at the front of the engine compartment, or under a flap next to the driver's seat. If there's any sign this plate has been tampered with, walk away - the car could be a 'ringer' (a stolen car with a fake I.D.).

The engine number position varies by model, but it's stamped into the front of the engine block, on a raised section just below the cylinder head - shouldn't be difficult to spot. If the number's been removed, or if there's anything suspicious about it, you could be buying trouble.

Check the registration document very carefully - all the details should match the car. If buying privately, make sure that it's definitely the owner's name and address printed on it - if not, be very careful! If buying from a dealer, note the name and address, and try to contact the previous owner to confirm mileage, etc, before handing over more than a deposit. Unless the car's very old, it shouldn't have

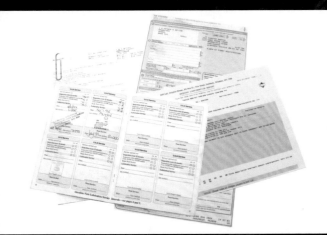

Full service history (fsh)

Is there any service history? If so, this is good, but study the service book carefully:

a *Which garage has done the servicing? Is it a proper dealer, or a backstreet bodger? Do you know the garage, and if so, would you use it?*

b *Do the mileages show a nice even progression, or are there huge gaps? Check the dates too.*

c *Does it look as if the stamps are authentic? Do the oldest ones look old, or could this 'service history' have been created last week, to make the car look good?*

d *When was the last service, and what exactly was carried out? When was the cambelt last changed? Has the owner got receipts for any of this servicing work?*

One sign of a genuine car is a good batch of old MOTs, and as many receipts as possible - even if they're for fairly irrelevant things like tyres.

had too many previous owners - if it's into double figures, it may mean the car is trouble, so checking its owner history is more important.

While the trim on a Nova is very durable, it should still be obvious whether the car's been abused over a long period, or whether the mileage showing is genuine or not (shiny steering wheels and floppy window winder/sunroof handles are a good place to start checking if you're suspicious). Okay, so you may be planning to junk most of the interior at some point, but why should you pay over the odds for a tat car which the owner hasn't given a stuff about?

Although you may feel a bit stupid doing it, check simple things too, like making sure the windows and sunroof open and shut, and that all the doors and tailgate can be locked (if a lock's been replaced, ask why). Check all the basic electrical equipment too, as far as possible - lights, front and rear wipers, heated rear window, heater fan; it's amazing how often these things are taken for granted by buyers! Instruments are pricey (even secondhand), so make sure they all work, especially the fuel gauge. Headlights give trouble if the dim-dip unit packs up, and the hazard warning light switch also breaks if it's been interfered with. If your chosen Nova already has alloys fitted, does it have locking wheel bolts? Where's the key? What about the code and removal tools for the stereo?

One thing to check on later Novas is that the catalytic converter ('cat') is working - this is a wickedly expensive part to replace, but the best way to ensure at least one year's grace is to only buy a car with a full MOT (the cat is checked during the emissions test).

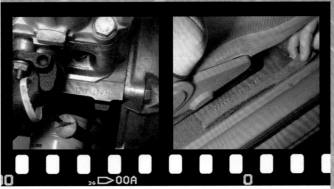

The engine number is stamped into the front of the engine block . . .

. . . and the VIN is stamped into the floorpan next to the driver's seat.

Sports models

Has it been treated well, or thrashed to death? We wouldn't pay top dollar for any sporty Nova without seeing evidence of careful maintenance, because any car will stand a good ranting much better if it's been properly serviced. Even a fully-stamped service book only tells half the story, though. Does the owner look bright enough to even know what a dipstick is, never mind how to check the oil level between services?

Remember that there's even more to look out for than on a lesser model. If the car's temptingly cheap (and even if it's not), never take anything just at face value - check everything you can about the car yourself. Getting your hands on a really good sporty Nova is not a simple task - dodgy dealers (and owners!) know there's a market for repaired write-offs and stolen cars ('ringers'), and gullible private punters get ripped every day.

More so than any other model, check for signs of accident damage, especially at the front end. Ask if it's ever been in a shunt - if the seller says no, but there's paint overspray under the bonnet, what's going on? Also check for paint overspray on the window rubbers, light units and bumpers/trim. With the bonnet open, check that the headlight rear shells are the same colour - mismatched or new-looking ones merit an explanation from the seller. Does the front number plate carry details of the supplying garage, like the back one? If not, why has a new plate been fitted?

Check the glass (and even the head and tail lights) for etched-in registration numbers - are they all the same, and does it match the car's actual registration? A windscreen could've been replaced for any number of innocent reasons, but new side glass indicates a break-in at least - is the car a 'stolen/recovered' (joyridden) example? Find the chassis and engine numbers, as described earlier in this Section, and satisfy yourself that they are genuine - check them against the "logbook" (registration document). An HPI check (or similar) could be well worthwhile, but even this won't tell you everything. If you're at all suspicious, or if the answers to your questions don't ring true, walk away. Make any excuse you like.

It's still worth a bit of discount if an approved (Thatcham Cat 1 or 2) alarm or immobiliser is fitted. Make sure that any aftermarket kit actually works, that it looks properly installed, with no stray wires hanging out, and that you get the Thatcham certificate or other paperwork to go with it. If possible, it's worth finding out exactly how it's been wired in - if it goes wrong later, you could be stranded with no chance of disabling the system to get you home.

Performance figures

(mph)	0-60 (sec)	Top speed
1.0	15.5	85
1.2	13.5	92
1.3	10.6	102
1.4 non-cat/SRi	10.2	100
1.4i cat	14.5	92
1.5 TD	12.1	102
1.6 GTE	8.4	115
1.6 GSi cat	9.1	114

Model history

Note: *Like many small-car ranges in recent years, the number of "special edition" models offered in the Nova's history has been enormous. The models listed below are a representative selection - to have listed them all would've taken half the book! Don't pay over the odds for a special edition, unless it's genuinely got some extra kit you're interested in having - most are just the 1.2 Merit with stickers and er… interesting seat trim!*

April 1983 (Y reg) - Nova range introduced. Spanish-built front-wheel-drive saloon or hatchback. New 1.0, 1.2, 1.3 engines. 1.3 SR has special spoilers/body mouldings, rally-style front seats, digital idle speed control, centre console and tinted glass.

January 1984 (A reg) - 1.2 GL hatchback added to range – spec includes tinted glass, rev counter and headlamp warning buzzer.

May 1984 (A reg) - Special edition 'Swing' launched. Removable sunroof, centre console.

January 1985 (B reg) - Limited edition 'Sport'. 1.3 engine, twin Weber 40s (89 bhp), SR suspension, sports seats and instruments.

May 1985 (B reg) - Front and rear suspension improvements. 'Merit' models become base spec, all other models have new cloth trim.

August 1985 (C reg) - New Pierburg 2E twin barrel carb fitted to 1.3. New brake servo/linkage for better 'feel', and corrosion-proof brake pipes.

May 1986 (C reg) - Special edition 'Antibes', based on Merit but with 5-speed gearbox, sunroof and rear spoiler.

August 1987 (E reg) - New grilles, front bumpers, new seats, revised instrument graphics and interiors.

May 1988 (E reg) - 1.6 GTE introduced. 3-door hatchback, fuel-injected engine, close-ratio 5-speed gearbox. Spec based on SR models but with added sunroof, spoiler, body-coloured bumpers, larger ventilated front brake discs, uprated suspension.

Sept 1988 (F reg) - All 1.2 models equipped with 5-speed gearbox.

Sept 1989 (G reg) - 'Merit' 1.5 turbo diesel added to range. New 'lean-burn' 1.4 litre engine (72 bhp, carburettor) replaces 1.3. 1.6 GTE gains electric windows.

Sept 1990 (H reg) - Revised Nova 'Mk 2' range introduced. All models have facelift - slimmer headlights, clear indicators, new grille, improved interior trim and new facia. 1.4 SR has new uprated suspension, electric front windows, close-ratio gearbox and central locking. GSi launched, replacing GTE .

June 1991 (H reg) - 'Sola' limited edition, with full-length electrically-operated canvas sunroof. Only 200 built, and primarily sold in 70 dealerships in the Greater London area.

February 1992 (J reg) - All models gain fuel injection and catalytic converter (carb models discontinued). 1.2i - 44 bhp, 1.4i - 60 bhp, 1.4 SRi - 82 bhp, 1.6 GSi - 100 bhp.

March 1992 (J reg) - 1.2 SX introduced, based on Merit, but with rear spoiler, sports interior and wheels.

March 1993 (K reg) - Nova range discontinued, replaced by Vauxhall Corsa.

Insurance
A necessary evil

Ah, insurance - loads of money, and all you get to show for it is a piece of paper you're not supposed to use! Of course, you must have insurance - you're illegal on the road without it, and you won't be able to get the car taxed, either. If you drive without insurance and are caught, you may have great trouble ever getting an insurance quote again - the insurance companies regard this offence nearly as seriously as drink-driving on your record, so don't do it!

Tricks 'n' tips
When ringing for quotes, watch your language. Arguing with the bloke/girl on the other end will always get you a higher quote, even if it makes you feel better. Also, don't say anything if you get put on hold. Some companies will put you on speaker - if you're trying to pull a fast one and they then catch you giggling or bragging to your mates, it's game over.

The way the insurance companies work out premiums and assess risks is a mystery to most of us. In general, the smaller the engine you have in your Nova, the less you'll pay for insurance, so hopefully, a Nova 1.2 Merit will be lots less to insure than an GTE/GSi. However, it's possible that, if one company has had a lot of claims on Novas in the past, the GTE/GSi factor might 'unfairly' influence the premiums of lesser Novas, too (this is why it's important to shop around). An 'insurance-friendly' SR should be a good bet for a sensible premium, but remember that insurance companies aren't stupid - if you turn your Merit into a GTE-lookalike, they may well 'load' the premium to nearly GTE level (and that's a big jump), because the potential car-thief might not spot it's not a real one.

If your annual premium seems like the national debt of a small African country (and whose isn't!), always ring as many brokers and get as many quotes as you possibly can. Yes, there's loads better ways to spend an evening/afternoon than answering the same twenty questions over and over again, but you never know what the next quote will be. A few extra minutes spent on the phone (or on the 'net) once a year may result in an extra few hundred quid in your back pocket. Well, you live in hope don't you!

With modified cars, insurance becomes even more of a problem. By putting on all the alloys, trick body kits, nice interiors, big ICE, you're making the car much more of a target for thieves (yes, ok, we know you know this). The point is, the insurance companies know this too, and they don't want to be paying out for the car, plus all the money you've spent on it, should it go missing. There is a temptation 'not to tell the insurance' about the mods you've made. Let's deal with this right now. Our experience has been that, while it can be painful, honesty is best. Generally, the insurance company line is: '…thanks for telling us - we won't put the car 'up a group' (ie charge you more), but we also won't cover the extra cost of your alloy wheels/body kit/tasty seats in the event of any claim…'. This is fair enough - in other words, if your car goes missing, you get paid out, based on a standard car, minus all the goodies. If you particularly want all the extras covered, you might have a long hard search - most companies (if they'll offer you cover at all) will only offer 'modified for standard' policies. There are specialist insurers who are more friendly towards fully-loaded cars, but even they won't actually cover the cost of replacement goodies.

What type of cover, Sir?

For most of us, cost means there's only one option - TPF&T (third party, fire and theft). Fully-comp insurance is an unattainable dream for most people until they reach the 'magic' age of 25, but what's the real story?

Third Party only

The most basic cover you can get. Basically covers you for damage to other people's cars or property, and for personal injury claims. Virtually no cover for your own stuff, beyond what you get if you take the optional 'legal protection' cover.

Third Party, Fire and Theft

As above, with cover for fire and theft, of course! Better, but not much better. This is really only cover in the event of a 'total loss', if your car goes missing or goes up in smoke. Still no cover for your car if you stack it into a tree, or if someone breaks in and pinches your stereo (check your policy small-print).

Fully-comprehensive

In theory at least, covers you for any loss or damage. Will cover the cost of repairing or replacing your car, often with discounted windscreen cover and other benefits. If you lose control of the car on an icy road (arguably, not your fault) you get paid. If someone pinches your wheels and drops the car on the floor, you get paid - at least for the damage done to the underside, and for standard wheels and tyres. Most policies include provision of a hire car after a shunt, which is pretty useful. Some offer cheap breakdown cover packages in with the main policy. With a fully-comp policy, you can 'protect' your no-claims bonus for a small fee so you don't automatically lose all those hard-earned years' worth of discount if you prang it (generally, you can only do this on fully-comp).

All this extra cover costs, obviously, but how much? You might be surprised what the actual difference is (if they'll quote you). Think about it, anyway - it's got to be worth a couple of hundred quid more to go fully-comp, if your car's worth into four figures, surely?

Valuing your car

When your insurance pays out in the event of a total loss or write-off, they base their offer on the current market value of an identical standard model to yours (less your excess). The only way you'll get more than the average amount is to prove your Nova is in above-average nick (with photos?) or that the mileage was especially low for the year.

With this in mind, don't bother over-valuing your Nova in the hope you'll get more in the event of a claim - you won't! The only way to do this is to seek out an 'agreed-value' deal, which you can usually only get on classic-car policies (with these, the car's value is agreed in advance between you, not worked out later by the company with you having no say in it). By over-valuing your Nova, you could be increasing your premium without gaining any benefit - sound smart to you?

Equally though, don't under-value, in the hope you'll get a reduction in premium. You won't, and if there's a total loss claim, you won't get any more than your under-valued amount, no matter how loudly you complain.

Work on what you paid for the car, backed up with the sort of prices you see for similar cars in the ads (or use a secondhand car price guide). Add no more than 10% for the sake of optimism, and that's it.

Your car? Or your Dad's?

Insurance really costs when you're the wrong side of 25. Ever been tempted to tell your insurance that your full-on sorted Nova belongs to your Dad (old insurance-friendly person), then get him to insure it, with you as a named driver? Oh dear. This idea (known as 'fronting') is so old, it's grown a long white beard. And it sucks, too. First of all, insurance companies aren't stupid. They know your Dad (or your Mum, or old Uncle Bert) isn't likely to be running around in a kid's pocket-rocket, and they treat any 'named driver' application with great suspicion. Even if they do take your money, don't imagine they've been suckered. In the event of a claim, they'll look into everything very carefully, and will ask lots of awkward questions. If you get caught out in the lie, they've taken your money, and you've got no insurance - who's been suckered now?

This dubious practice also does you no favours in future years. All the time you're living the lie, you're not building up any no-claims bonus of your own - you're just delaying the pain 'til later, and without having real cover in the meantime.

"Legit" ways to limit your premium

If you do enough ringing around for quotes, you'll soon learn what the 'right answers' to some of the questions are - even if you can't actually give them (but don't tell lies to your insurance company). Mind you, with a little thought, you can start to play their game and win - try these:

Limit your mileage. Most companies offer a small discount if you only cover a small annual mileage. To get any meaningful reduction, the mileage has to be a lot less than 10,000 per year. Few companies, though, ever ask what the car's current mileage is - so how are they gonna know if you've gone over your self-imposed limit?

Volunteer to increase your excess. The 'excess' is put there to stop people claiming for piddling little amounts - when they pay out, it's always the repair/replacement cost minus whatever the 'excess' is. So, for instance, if you've got a £200 theft excess, it means you'll automatically get £200 less than the agreed value of your car, should it be stolen. Most policies have 'compulsory' excess amounts, which you can do nothing about. By increasing excesses voluntarily, you're limiting the amount you'll get still further. Insurance companies like this, and should reduce your premium in return - but this only goes so far, so ask what the effect of different voluntary excesses will be. Don't increase your excess too far, or you'll get paid nowt if you claim!

Make yourself the only driver. Pretty self-explanatory. The more people who drive your car, the greater the risk to the company, and a car's owner will always drive more carefully (it's their money that bought it) than any named driver. If you've built up 2 years' worth of no-claims, but your partner hasn't, putting them on your insurance will bump it up, due to their relative inexperience

Get a garage - and use it. Where you park can have a big effect on your premium. Parking it on the street is the worst. Park off the road (on a driveway) when you're at home. The best thing is to have a garage of your own (don't pretend you use your Dad's garage) - see if you can rent one locally, even if it means walking a few hundred yards. If you're a student living away from home, tell your company where the car will be parked during term-time - if you're at Uni in London, this is a bigger risk than living at home 'in the country'.

Fit an approved alarm or immobiliser. See if you can get a list from your company of all their approved security devices, and fit whatever you can afford. Not all companies approve the same kit, so it might even be worth contacting more than one company for advice. Any device with a Thatcham or Sold Secure rating should be recognised. In some cases, the discounts offered are not that great any more - but an alarm is still a nice way to get peace of mind.

Build up your no-claims bonus. You'll only do this by owning and insuring a car in your own name, and then not making any claims. Simple really. One rather immoral (but not actually illegal) dodge is to buy an old banger, insure it cheap, then never drive it. You'll need to keep it fully road-legal (with tax, MOT) if you park it on the road. For every year you do this, you'll build up another year of NCB.

Hang onto your no-claims bonus. Obviously, the less you claim, the less your insurance will cost. If something happens to your car, don't be in too big a hurry to make a claim before you've thought it all through. How much will it cost to fix? How much is your excess? How much will your renewal premium be, next year? If you have a big enough accident which you're sure isn't your fault, ring your company, but make it quite clear you're NOT claiming yet - just informing them of the accident. It should be down to the other driver's insurance to pay. You don't always lose all your no-claims, either, even if it was your fault - depends how many years you've built up. Once you've got a few years, ask whether you can 'protect' your no-claims.

Avoid speed cameras and The Law. Yes, okay, easier said than done! But anything less than a clean licence is not good from the insurance perspective. One SP30 won't hurt much, but the second strike will, so take it easy. Don't get caught on traffic-light cameras, either - just one is a major no-no.

Insurance-friendly mods?

Insurers don't like any changes from standard, but some things you'll do are worse from their viewpoint than others. The guidelines below are just that - for guidance. No two companies will have the same outlook, and your own circumstances will play a big part too.

Golden Rule Number One: Before you spend huge money modifying the car, ring your insurance, and ask them how it will affect things.

Golden Rule Number Two: If in doubt, declare everything. Insurance companies are legally entitled to dispute any claim if the car is found to be non-standard in any way.

Body mods - Even a tiny rear spoiler could be classed as a 'bodykit' (yes, it's daft, but that's how it is). Anything which alters the exterior appearance should be declared. As long as the mods don't include a radical full-on bodykit, the jump in premium should be fairly small. Any Vauxhall add-ons (GSi bumpers) might not cost at all - bonus.

Brakes - The companies view brake mods as tampering with safety-related kit, and modifying the brakes implies that you drive fast and hard. You might get away with standard-sized grooved/drilled discs and pads, but fitting bigger discs and replacement calipers will prove expensive.

Engine mods - 'Mild' mods, such as induction kits and exhausts don't give much more power, so don't generally hurt. But 'chipping' your Nova will lead to drastic rises in premiums, or a complete refusal of cover. With complete engine transplants, you'll be required to give an engineer's report, and to get your wad out.

Interior mods - Don't assume that tarting up the inside won't interest the insurance company. By making any part of the car more attractive, you're also attracting the crims. Cars get trashed for parts, as often as not - and your racing seats and sexy steering wheel could be worth major money. Still, the effect on premiums shouldn't be too great, especially if you've got an alarm/immobiliser.

Lights - Change the car's appearance, and are safety-related. You'll probably get asked for lots of details, but as long as you've kept it sensible (and legal, as far as possible), the effect on your wallet shouldn't be too harsh.

Security - Make sure you mention all security stuff - alarms, immobilisers (including mechanical devices), locking wheel nuts, large Alsatian in the back seat... But - don't over-sell the car. Tell the truth, in other words. If you've got a steering wheel lock, do you always fit it? If you didn't when your car went missing, you're in trouble. Don't say you've got a Cat 1 alarm if it really came from Argos, and don't tell them you garage the car at night if it's stuck out in the road.

Suspension - Changes the car's appearance, and is safety-related. Some enlightened companies once took the view that modded suspension helps the car corner better, so it's safer. Drops of only 30 to 40 mm shouldn't mean bigger premiums.

Wheels - Very appearance-altering, and very nickable. At least show some responsibility by fitting some locking nuts/bolts and an approved alarm/immobiliser. Quite likely to attract a low-to-moderate rise in premium, which still won't cover your wheels properly - you could arrange separate cover for your wheels, then at least you'll get paid. Some companies ask for a photo of the car with the wheels on.

And finally - a new nightmare

Not telling the insurance the whole truth gets a little tricky when you make a claim. If the insurance assessor comes to check your bent/burnt/stolen-and-recovered 'standard' Nova, and finds he's looking at a vehicle fitted with trick alloys/bodykit/radical interior, he's not going to turn a blind eye. Has the car got an MOT? Oh, and did you declare those points on your licence? No? You're then very much at the mercy of your insurer, especially if they can prove any mods contributed to the claim. At best, you'll have a long-drawn-out battle with your insurer to get a part-payout, and at worst they'll just refuse to get involved at all.

One more thing - *be careful what you hit*. If your insurance is declared void, they won't pay out for the repairs to the other car you smacked into, or for the lamp-post you knock down (several hundred quid, actually). And then there's the personal injury claims - if your insurance company disowns you, it'll be you who has to foot the bill. Even sprains and bruises can warrant claims, and more serious injuries can result in claims running into lots of zeroes! Without insurance cover, **you'll** have to pay. Probably for a long, long time. Think about it, and we won't see you in court.

Security

Lock me or lose me

It's a sad fact, but making your car attractive to the opposite sex also tends to attract attention of a less-welcome kind, from less-than-human pond life.

Avoiding trouble

Now come on - you're modifying your car to look cool and to be seen in. Not a problem - but be careful where you choose to show your car off, and who to. Be especially discreet, the nearer you get to home - *turn your system down* before you turn into your road, for instance, or you'll draw unwelcome attention to where that car with the loud stereo's parked at night.

Without being too paranoid, watch for anyone following you home. At night, if the car behind switches its lights off, be worried. If you suspect this is happening, do not drive home - choose well-lit public places until they give up. Believe us - it happens.

If you're going out, think about where you're parking - well-lit and well-populated is good.

Thieves hate light being on them, so don't make it easy by parking somewhere dark - think about this if you park up in daylight, knowing you won't be back 'til late.

Hands up, who doesn't lock their car when they get petrol? Your insurance company has a term for this, and it's 'contributory negligence'. In English, this means you won't get a penny if your car goes missing when you haven't locked it.

If you're lucky enough to have a garage, use it. On up-and-over garage doors, fit extra security like a padlock and ground anchor.

A clever thief will watch your movements and habits over several days before trying your car. Has it got an alarm, and do you always set it? Do you only fit your steering wheel lock when you feel like it? Do you always park in the same place, and is the car hidden from the house or from the road? Don't make his life easier. Ask yourself how YOU'D nick your car…

A word about your stereo

From the moment you bolt on those nice alloys, it's taken as read that you've also got stereo gear that's worth nicking - and the thieves know it. All the discreet installation in the world isn't going to deter them from finding out what's inside that nice motor.

Please don't advertise your love of ICE around your car. Your nice stereo gear will fit other cars too, and can be ripped out in nothing flat. You may be very proud of your ICE install, but nothing is more of an 'invite' than a huge ICE sticker or sunstrip. If you've fitted one just to look cool, replace it now with something less provocative - seriously. Your set might not actually be very expensive, but you could still lose a side window for advertising something better.

You'll have got a CD player, obviously, but don't leave discs or empty CD cases lying around inside the car. A nice pair of 6x9s in full view on the back shelf is an invite to having your rear window smashed - stealth shelf, anyone? When you're fitting your system, give some thought to the clues you could accidentally leave in plain view. Oxygen-free speaker cable is great stuff, but it's also a bit bright against dark carpets, and is all the clue necessary that you're serious about your speakers. Hide amps and CD changers under your front seats.

Most modern sets are face-off or MASK, so if they've got security features like this, use them - take your faceplate off when you leave the car, and take it with you rather than leaving it in the door pocket or glovebox (the first places a thief will look).

Things that go beep in the night

Unless your insurance company demands it up front, fitting an alarm is something generally done as an after-thought. We know alarms aren't exactly sexy, but don't skimp - an alarm may never be put to the test, but if it is, you'll be glad you spent wisely...

The simplest first step to car security is to fake it. Tacky *'This car is fitted with an alarm'* stickers won't fool anyone, but if you want cheap, just fit a flashing LED. We know it's not the real thing, but everyone else will think you've got a posh alarm. An LED is cheap to buy and easy to fit, and can be rigged to a discreet switch inside the car.

Don't overlook the value of so-called 'manual' immobilisers, such as steering wheel locking bars and gear-to-handbrake lever locks. These can be a worthwhile deterrent - a thief not specifically after your car may move on to an easier target. Some of the items offered may be 'Sold Secure' or Thatcham Cat 3, accolades well worth checking out, since it means they've withstood a full-on brute force attack for a useful length of time.

The only way to combat the more determined thief is to go for a well-specified and intelligently-installed alarm. Immobilisers alone have their place, but sadly, even a pro-fitted immobiliser on its own won't stop someone pinching your wheels, or having it away with the stereo gear. Neither, incidentally, will a cheap alarm - you have to know how the thieves operate to stand any chance defeating them. Any alarm you fit yourself probably won't gain you any insurance discount, but it will give you peace of mind, and DIY means you can do a real trick installation, to make it very hard work for the gyppos.

Finally, one other scam which you might fall victim to. If you find your alarm is suddenly going off a lot at night, when previously it had been well-behaved, don't ignore the problem. It's an old trick for a thief to deliberately set off your alarm several times, each time hiding round the corner when you come out to investigate, then to wait until the fifth or sixth time when you don't reset it (in disgust), leaving him a clear run. If your alarm does keep false-alarming

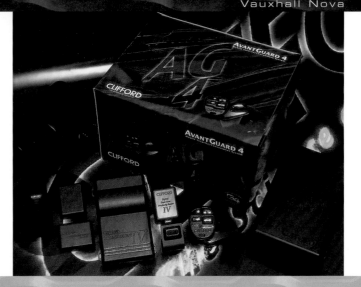

without outside assistance, find out the cause quickly, or your neighbours will quickly become 'deaf' to it.

Thatcham categories and meanings:

1 Cat 1. For alarms and electronic immobilisers.

2 Cat 2. For electronic immobilisers only.

3 Cat 2-1. Electronic immobilisers which can be upgraded to Cat 1 alarms later.

4 Cat 3. Mechanical immobilisers, eg snap-off steering wheels, locking wheel bolts, window film, steering wheel locks/covers.

5 Q-class. Tracking devices.

Other alarm features

Two-stage anti-shock - means that the alarm shouldn't go off, just because the neighbour's cat jumps on your car roof, or because Little Johnny punts his football into your car. Alarm will only sound after a major shock, or after repeated shocks are detected.

Anti-tilt - detects any attempt to lift or jack up the car, preventing any attempt to pinch alloys. Very unpopular with thieves, as it makes the alarm very sensitive (much more so than anti-shock). Alarm may sound if car is parked outside in stormy conditions (but not if your suspension's rock-hard!).

Anti-hijack - immobiliser with built-in delay. If your motor gets hijacked, the neanderthals responsible will only get so far down the road before the engine cuts out.

Rolling code - reduces the chance of your alarm remote control signal from being 'grabbed' by special electronic equipment.

Total closure - module which connects to electric windows/sunroof and central locking, which closes all items when alarm is set. Alarms like this often have other nifty features such as remote boot opening.

Pager control - yes, really - your alarm can be set to send a message to your pager (why not your mobile?) if your car gets tampered with.

Current-sensing disable - very useful feature on some cars which have a cooling fan which can cut in after the ignition is switched off. Without this feature, your alarm will be triggered every time you leave it parked after a long run - very annoying.

Volumetric-sensing disable - allows you to manually disable the interior ultrasonics, leaving the rest of the alarm features active. Useful if you want to leave the sunroof open in hot weather - if a fly gets in the car, the alarm would otherwise be going off constantly.

Talking alarms - no, please, please no. Very annoying, and all that'll happen is you'll attract crowds of kids daring each other to set it off again. Unfortunately, these are becoming more popular, with some offering the facility to record your own message!

The knowledge

What people often fail to realise (at least, until it happens to them) is the level of violence and destruction which thieves will employ to get your stuff - this goes way beyond breaking a window.

It comes as a major shock to most people when they discover the serious kinds of tools (weapons) at many professional thieves' disposal, and how brutally your lovingly-polished car will be attacked. Many people think, for instance, that it's their whole car they're after, whereas it's really only the parts they want, and they don't care how they get them (this means that these parts are still attractive, even when fitted to a basic car which has yet to be fully modded). Obviously, taking the whole car then gives the option of hiding it to strip at leisure, but it won't always be the option chosen, and you could wake up one morning to a well-mangled wreck outside.

Attack 1 The first option to any thief is to smash glass - typically, the toughened-glass side windows, which will shatter, unlike the windscreen. Unfortunately for the thief, this makes a loud noise (not good), but is a quick and easy way in. The reason for taking this approach is that a basic car alarm will only go off if the doors are opened (voltage-drop alarm) - provided the doors aren't opened, the alarm won't go off.

Response 1 A more sophisticated alarm will feature shock sensing (which will be set off by the impact on the glass), and better still, ultrasonic sensing, which will be triggered by the brick coming in through the broken window.

Response 2 This kind of attack can also be stopped by applying security film to the inside of the glass, which holds it all together and prevents easy entry.

Attack 2 An alternative to smashing the glass is to pry open the door using a crowbar - this attack involves literally folding open the door's window frame by prising from the top corner. The glass will still shatter, but as long as the door stays shut, a voltage-drop alarm won't be triggered.

Response This method might not be defeated by a shock-sensing alarm, but an ultrasonic unit would pick it up.

Incidentally, another bonus with ultrasonic alarms is that the sensors are visible from outside - and act as a deterrent.

Attack 3 The next line of attack is to disable the alarm. The commonest way to kill the alarm is either to cut the wiring to the alarm itself, or to disconnect the battery, 'safely' hidden away under the bonnet. And just how strong is a bonnet? Not strong enough to resist being crowbarred open, which is exactly what happens.

Response 1 If your alarm has extra pin-switches, be sure to fit one to the bonnet, and fit it in the bonnet channel next to the battery, so that it'll set off the alarm if the bonnet is prised up. Also make sure that the wire to the pin-switch cannot be cut easily though a partly-open bonnet.

Response 2 Make sure that the alarm module is well-hidden, and cannot be got at from underneath the car.

Response 3 Make the alarm power supply connection somewhere less obvious than directly at the battery terminal - any thief who knows his stuff will immediately cut any 'spare' red wires at the battery. Try taking power from the fusebox, or if you must source it under the bonnet, trace the large red battery lead to the starter motor connections, and tap into the power there.

Response 4 Always disguise the new alarm wiring, by using black insulating tape to wrap it to the existing wiring loom. Tidying up in this way also helps to ensure the wires can't get trapped, cut, melted, or accidentally ripped out - any of which could leave you with an alarm siren which won't switch off, or an immobiliser you can't disable.

Response 5 An alarm which has a 'battery back-up' facility is a real kiss of death to the average thief's chances. Even if he's successfully crowbarred your bonnet and snipped the battery connections, the alarm will still go off, powered by a separate battery of its own. A Cat 1 alarm has to have battery back-up.

Fitting
a basic
LED

All you need for this is a permanent live feed, an earth, a switch if you want to be able to turn it on/off, and the flashing LED itself (very cheap, from any car accessory shop).

An LED draws very little current, so you'll be quite safe tapping into almost any live feed you fancy. If you've wired in your ICE, take a live feed from the permanent (radio memory supply) wire at the back of your head unit, or have a delve into the back of the fusebox with your test light (as featured in the full alarm fitting procedure, further on). An earth can easily be tapped again from your head unit, or you can make one almost anywhere on the metal body of the car, by drilling a small hole, fitting a self-tapping screw, then wrapping the bared end of wire around and tightening it.

The best and easiest place to mount an LED is into one of the many blank switches the makers seem to love fitting. The blank switch is easily pried out, and a hole can then be drilled to take the LED (which usually comes in a separate little holder). Feed the LED wiring down behind the dashboard to where you've tapped your live and earth, taking care not to trap it anywhere, nor to accidentally wrap it around any moving parts.

Connect your live to the LED red wire, then rig your earth to one side of the switch, and connect the LED black wire to the other switch terminal. You should now have a switchable LED! Tidy up the wiring, and mount the switch somewhere discreet, but where you can still get at it. Switch on when you leave the car, and it looks as if you've got some sort of alarm - better than nothing!

Wiring basics

With your wires identified, how to tap into them? Before we even get that far, is that wire you're planning on playing with live?

Switch off the ignition at least - and ideally disconnect the battery before you do anything else. On cars with airbags, don't go tapping into any of the airbag wiring, which is usually bright yellow. With that cleared up, how were you planning on joining the old and new wires together?

Here's our advice:

Soldering - avoids cutting through your chosen wire - strip away a short section of insulation, wrap your new wire around the bared section, then apply solder to secure it. If you're a bit new to soldering, practice on a few offcuts of wire first - it ain't rocket science! Re-insulate the soldered connection afterwards, with tape or heatshrink tube.

Bullet connectors - cut and strip the end of your chosen wire, wrap your new one to it, push both into one half of the bullet. Connect the other end of your victim wire to the other bullet, and connect together. Always use the 'female' half on any live feed - it'll be safer if you disconnect it than a male bullet, which could touch bare metal and send your motor up in smoke.

Block connectors - so easy to use. Just remember that the wires can come adrift if the screws aren't really tight, and don't get too ambitious about how many wires you can stuff in one hole (block connectors, like bullets, are available in several sizes). Steer clear of connectors like the one below - they're convenient, but they can give rise to problems.

With any of these options, always insulate around your connection - especially when soldering, or you'll be leaving bare metal exposed. Remember that you'll probably be shoving all the wires up into the dark recesses of the under-dash area - by the time the wires are nice and kinked/squashed together, that tiny bit of protruding wire might just touch that bit of metal bodywork, and that'll be a fire...

Fitting an auxiliary fusebox

You'll need plenty of fused live feeds from the battery during the modifying process, for stereo gear, neons, starter buttons - and alarms, and it's always a pain working out where to tap into one. If you make up your own little fusebox, mounted somewhere easy to get at, you'll never have this problem again - and it's easy enough to do.

The first job is to run a main supply cable from the battery positive terminal, to inside the car - but don't connect the wire up to the battery terminal just yet. Make sure that the main cable is man enough for all the loads you're likely to put on it - starting with eight-gauge wire (available from all good ICE suppliers) will mean you're never short of current.

Make a note of which fuse is for which circuit, and carry the paper around in the glovebox (along with some spare fuses). If a fuse ever blows, you won't end up with your head stuck under the dash, trying to remember where you tapped in, and where the fuse is. You'll just pull the cover off, and replace the fuse. Who would've thought electrical safety could be so cool?

01 Inside the car, we decided our fusebox would go in the driver's kick panel, in the footwell. To improve access, we first removed the driver's side oddments shelf above the pedals (two screws - one each end).

02 Peel back the door weatherstrip . . .

07 Now the box is taken care of, we need some volts inside the car, from the battery. Having done a little 'research' up behind the dash, we return to the engine compartment, and drill a hole through next to the battery. A strip of masking tape stops the drill bit skating about.

08 Feeding our thick new wire through. The most important detail to notice here is the rubber grommet we fitted to the newly-drilled hole - an essential fitment. Any live wire in contact with a sharp metal edge is a fire waiting to happen - be safe.

09 Make a neat job of fitting the main live feed to your battery terminal, too. This is the proper way, with a ring terminal.

10 We could just have joined the single live feed to the six wires from our fusebox, using a large bullet connector, or a terminal block. Both these are a bit 'bodgy'. We bought a junction box from the same place as the fusebox - this simply gives you two nut-and-bolt connection terminals, and is a much neater solution.

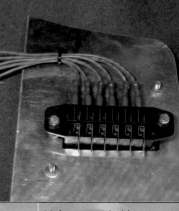

03 . . . remove a screw or two from the front of the sill trim panel . . .

04 . . . then push through the pin securing the side panel . . .

05 . . . and slide the side panel out from the footwell. Removing this panel also gives you access to run wires through into the doors (central locking and ICE). For now, we're going to make up an alloy panel, to take our new fusebox.

06 Make up a suitable panel by trimming up a card template first (or use the old side panel as a guide to the right shape). This is the back of our fusebox (we bought ours from our local Lucas branch), with all six live 'in' feed wires attached. To get a live feed, fit your new wire to the other side of the 'box, and plug in a fuse.

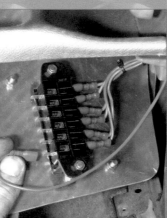

11 With all the connections made for now, the fusebox's alloy panel can be mounted to the car. Don't make too good a job of this - you'll want to get that panel off again, to connect your new feeds as you need them.

12 Here's our first customer - we needed a live feed for our interior neons. All we do is fit a feed wire (off to the neon tubes) to one of our new fusebox terminals . . .

13 . . . plug in a suitable fuse (10A in this case) . . .

14 . . . and clip on the fusebox cover. See how easy it is, to get at the new fuses if they should blow in future? A very well-engineered solution, and far better than tapping into the wiring at random.

Achtung!
Disconnect the battery negative (earth) lead before starting work, and only reconnect it when all live leads and terminals have been securely connected.

Alarm fitting

The alarm we've chosen to fit is a MicroScan, which, whilst it isn't a Clifford, still offers a decent level of protection, and a useful array of features for a sensible price. When it goes off, it actually sounds like a Clifford - result!

As with everything else in this book, remember that we're showing you just how this *particular* alarm is fitted. All the same, whatever alarm you fit, it'll still be useful to pick out the fitting principles and tips. Always refer to the instructions which come with your alarm, and don't go joining the red wire to the yellow wire, just because WE say so...

01 Disconnect the battery negative lead, and move the lead away from the battery, or you'll be blowing fuses and your new alarm will go mental the minute it's rigged up.

06 Well, that was the easy bit - now there's wires to play with. Most of them should go thorough into the car, but not all - check your alarm's instructions. We've got a bonnet pin switch and an earth wire which can stay in the engine bay. The rest? Get out the electrical tape, and wrap that bunch of wires into a neat loom, to go inside.

07 Next to the battery is a fair place to drill through into the car - this grommet was there already on our Nova. Drill a hole in the centre of that, and feed your loom through. If you make a hole of your own, dismantle some dash first, and feel inside for any obstructions. Don't forget the rubber grommet on any sharp-edged hole with a wire passing through.

08 That earth wire's the easiest to deal with - first give it a ring terminal. Now you want a bolt fitted tightly to the car body as an earth point. Well, how about the alarm bracket bolts we just drilled? And this is hard?

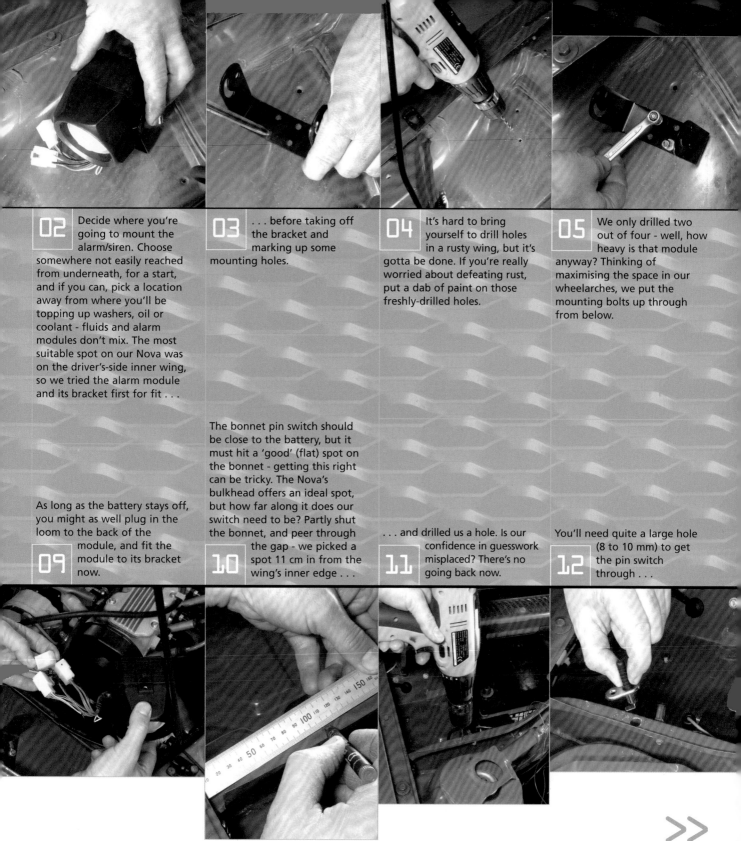

02 Decide where you're going to mount the alarm/siren. Choose somewhere not easily reached from underneath, for a start, and if you can, pick a location away from where you'll be topping up washers, oil or coolant - fluids and alarm modules don't mix. The most suitable spot on our Nova was on the driver's-side inner wing, so we tried the alarm module and its bracket first for fit . . .

03 . . . before taking off the bracket and marking up some mounting holes.

04 It's hard to bring yourself to drill holes in a rusty wing, but it's gotta be done. If you're really worried about defeating rust, put a dab of paint on those freshly-drilled holes.

05 We only drilled two out of four - well, how heavy is that module anyway? Thinking of maximising the space in our wheelarches, we put the mounting bolts up through from below.

As long as the battery stays off, you might as well plug in the loom to the back of the module, and fit the module to its bracket now.

09

The bonnet pin switch should be close to the battery, but it must hit a 'good' (flat) spot on the bonnet - getting this right can be tricky. The Nova's bulkhead offers an ideal spot, but how far along it does our switch need to be? Partly shut the bonnet, and peer through the gap - we picked a spot 11 cm in from the wing's inner edge . . .

10

. . . and drilled us a hole. Is our confidence in guesswork misplaced? There's no going back now.

11

You'll need quite a large hole (8 to 10 mm) to get the pin switch through . . .

12

Testing's a lot easier with a posh multi-meter, set to read continuity (resistance), and with an audible signal. Connect one terminal to the pin switch spade, and the other to a good earth. Shut the bonnet, and when the beep stops is the point your alarm would go off. You can duplicate this test with a simple test light, but instead of a good earth, connect one test light wire to the battery positive (+) terminal.

15

13 . . . and another, smaller, one to fit the self-tapping screw that secures it (and gives the earth connection).

14 Fit a spade terminal to your pin switch wire (brown in our case), and plug it onto the switch.

Tricks 'n' tips

Don't assume you'll automatically be able to close the bonnet fully, when you first fit your pin switch - the plunger might be too long, and you'll bust the switch if you force the bonnet shut. Also, check that the switch plunger can be pushed fully down, without catching on any other vital components. If the bonnet opens much before the switch works, you'll be giving access which the crims can exploit. Just trim off some of the plastic switch plunger until all's well - trimming the pin switch down will make it 'go off' sooner, but only take off a little plastic at a time, then re-test. If you go too far when trimming down a pin switch, you can sometimes rescue the situation by screwing a little self-tapping screw into the top of the plunger. You can then 'adjust' the length of the plunger at will. The proper answer, though, is to buy a new switch.

Next on our wire target list - the indicators. The easiest way to get at the indicator wiring is by removing the indicator stalk. This was easy for us, with the steering wheel off - but you only need remove the column shrouds (see fitting a new wheel). The stalk is only held by two clips - press in top and bottom to release . . .

20

21 . . . then unplug the wiring.

You should find a black/white and a black/green wire among the indicator wiring - these are the feeds for the left and right indicators. Again, strip off a little insulation, wrap on the two alarm grey wires, solder, and insulate with tape.

22

Our man's never happy unless he's drilling something. This time it's a hole in the oddments tray for mounting our alarm's LED holder (typically, it's an 8 mm hole you want). To act as a deterrent (and as an indicator of the alarm's status), the LED must be somewhere highly visible.

23

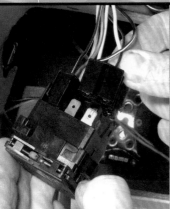

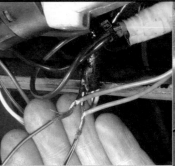

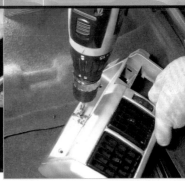

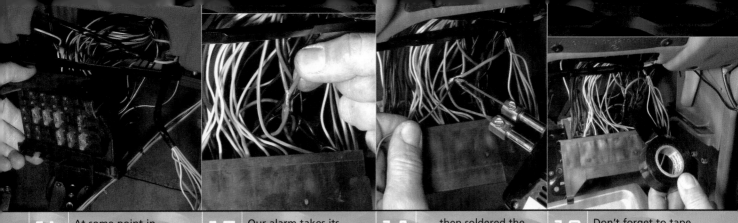

16 At some point in fitting almost any alarm, you'll want to get to the fusebox - the car's central nervous system. With a little persuasion, this just unclips from the dash - remove the driver's-side shelf first (two screws).

17 Our alarm takes its power supply from the fuse for the interior light. From the Haynes manual (and the symbols on the fusebox lid), we knew we wanted fuse 16, and a red wire. This red wire, in fact - which we stripped, then wrapped the alarm red wire round it . . .

18 . . . then soldered the joint to make it permanent (all with the battery off, of course).

19 Don't forget to tape up soldered joints. Even if you use bullet connectors, a little tape is never a bad idea.

On our Nova, we needed another hole in the rear part of the dash, to feed the LED through . . .

24

. . . before it finally emerged where we wanted it. The LED's a push fit into its holder, then the holder itself should be a tight push fit into the dash. Looking good - what's left? If your alarm has ultrasonics, the sensors need to be fed into place and fitted. If you want the alarm to work the door locks, wire in a central locking interface (or fit central locking first, as described in the body & exterior section).

25

So come on - does it work? Most alarms require you to 'programme in' the remotes before they'll work. Test all the alarm features in turn, remembering to allow enough time for the alarm to arm itself (usually about 30 seconds). When you test it for the first time, don't forget to either shut the bonnet completely, or do like us, and hold the bonnet pin switch down. Our way, you can pull out the alarm fuses and shut it up, if something goes wrong!

26

Set the anti-shock sensitivity with a thought to where you live and park - will it be set off every night by the neighbour's cat, or by kids playing football? Finally, and most important of all - next time you park up, remember to set it!

27

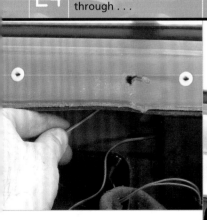

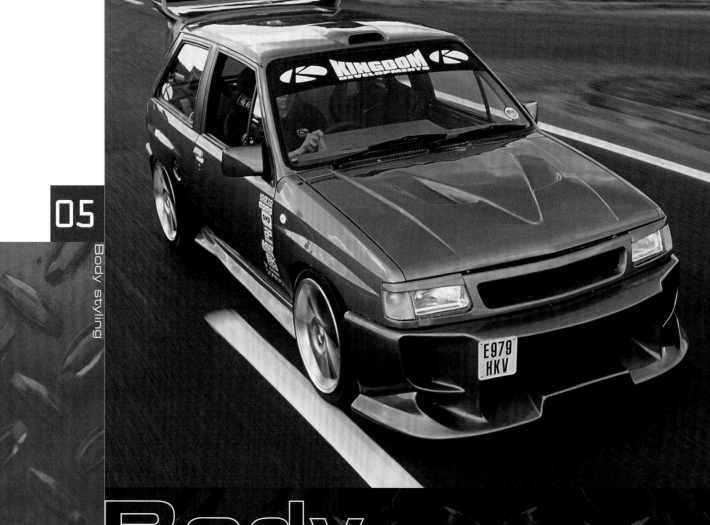

Body styling

If you're planning a major body job, you've probably already got some good ideas about how you want your Nova to look, from a Nova website, one of the modding mags, or maybe from a friend's car. While it can be good to have a target car to aim for, if you're just starting out on the road towards a fully-loaded car, you probably don't want (or can't quite afford) to go 'all the way' all at once.

If you're new to the world of modifying, it's a good idea to start with smaller jobs, and work up to the full body kit gradually, as your skills increase; spending loads on a body kit is a pretty lame idea if you then make a mess of fitting it! There's plenty of small ways to improve the look of your Nova, which don't cost much, and which are simple enough to fit; start with some of these before you go too mad!

One golden rule with any body mods is to plan what you're going to do, and don't rush it. It's better that the car looks a bit stupid for a week (because you couldn't get something finished) than to rush a job and have the car look stupid forever. Do half the job properly instead of messing up all of it. Try and think the jobs through - plan each stage. Have you got all the tools, screws or whatever before you start, or will you have to break off halfway through? If you get stuck, is there someone you can get to help, or have they gone off for the weekend? Above all, if something goes wrong - don't panic - a calm approach will prove to be a huge bonus (that job doesn't have to be done today, does it?).

If a piece of trim won't come off, don't force it. If something feels like it's going to break, it probably will - stop and consider whether to go on and break it, or try another approach. Especially on an older car, things either never come off as easily as you think, or else have already been off so many times that they either break or won't fit back on properly. While we'd all like to do a perfect job every time, working on an older car will, sooner or later, teach you the fine art of 'bodging' (finding valid alternative ways of fixing things!). Don't assume that you'll have to bodge something back on, every time - if a trim clip breaks when you take something off, it might be easier and cheaper than you think to simply go to your Vauxhall dealer, and buy a new clip (remember, even Vauxhall mechanics break things from time to time, so they will keep these things in stock!).

Mirror, mirror

Mirrors are another simple to fit, must-have accessory. The DTM or M3-style door mirrors are well established on the modified car circuit, but there are lots of variations of mirror styles and finishes, so finding some you like won't be hard.

If you want to be just a little different, try some 'California' mirrors. The trouble with being different is it's always more work - California mirrors are 'universal fit', meaning you have to make them fit your car. You bought a Nova 'cause it's a popular car, so why make life difficult? Buy some Nova mirrors (or at least some Nova mirror bases), and your new M3 or Cup mirrors can be fitted in minutes.

Fitting Cup mirrors

01 Removing the old mirrors also takes just minutes - even less, if those mirrors are going for scrap (and as you'll soon see, our Nova mirrors were fit for nothing else). First, the adjuster knob's got to go - one tug and it's away.

02 Next, the trim panel inside the mirror just prises off, with a little help from your friend, the small screwdriver.

03 Three cross-head screws later, and . . .

04 . . . oh, dear. Look at the state of that. That's one shot mirror. Why we're being so careful not to drop it on the floor is a mystery.

05 Even unpainted, these new universal Cup mirrors look way better than the ones we've just scrapped. The mirrors are a standard size and shape, but you buy bases which are shaped and drilled to mate up with your Nova.

06 Three screws hold the mirror to its Nova base . . .

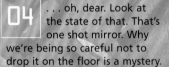

. . . then three more secure the assembly to the Nova door. You could now just clip that trim panel back on inside, and that's the job done (apart from spraying them). But - you can see the inside of the mirror base through the door glass, which looks a bit poor, and there's a hole in that trim plate, where the adjuster knob poked **07** through. Just going to leave it?

08 A small strip of alloy plate, and a little hot glue, and we've sorted the hole in the trim panel.

Some more alloy offcuts, and we're making a metal strip to fit on the inside rear edge of the new mirror base. **09** Mark it up, trim it with some snips . . .

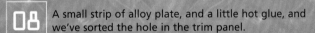

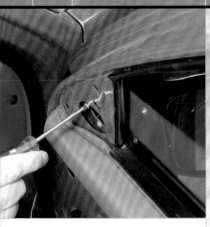

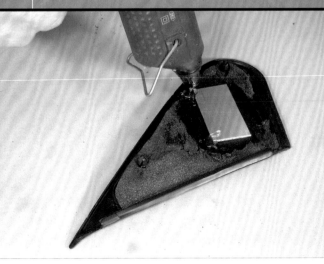

10 . . . and glue it on. If you haven't woken up to the power of a hot glue gun, it's time you did. Dead cheap to buy, and the glue's good enough for all sorts of modding stuff.

11 Now the view of our mirror from the inside's nearly as good as it is from outside. Don't just follow the herd - innovate. You know it's stuff like this that'll impress your mates, and for just a few minutes' extra work.

Fitting a racing
filler cap

Ah, the humble fuel filler cap - what you decide to do here really is a matter of taste. The Nova item's large and chunky, in unsexy black plastic, so doing nothing isn't an option. So - do you make it a feature, by fitting an alloy race cap, or take the stock item off and colour-code it?

Colour-coding's easiest, cheapest, and quite effective. The trick is not to get paint down the key slot - otherwise, prep it the same as you would any other plastic panel, inside or out.

For those who really want to impress, it's got to be a complete racing conversion, which does away with the dull black filler cap, in favour of a fully-functional alloy item to grace the Nova flanks. Trouble is, they're often difficult to fit - so what's the answer? Novatech claim their race cap can be fitted without the need for bodyshop assistance - are they right?

Well, the first stage in fitting should be pretty obvious - take off the old cap. Our 'locking' Vauxhall original was so knackered, locking it made no difference - long overdue for an upgrade, then.

01

And here's the new cap, complete with key. As you can see, we're having some difficulty with this - those tabs on the back of the cap only just line up with the filler neck, and . . .

02

. . . there it is, fitted. Just kidding, weren't we? Anyone who can't fit one of these very fine caps should sell their Nova now, and forget all about modifying.

03

Smoothly does it

If you've bought a basic Nova, it's understandable that you might not want to declare this fact loudly from the rear end of your car. Badges also clutter up the otherwise clean lines, and besides, you're trying to make your Nova look different, so why give them obvious clues like a badge?

Most Novas also come with admittedly-useful but actually quite ugly side rubbing strips of some sort - lose these, or at least colour-code, if you're at all serious about raising your game.

General bodywork smoothing (including de-seaming) takes time and skill, and is probably best done on a car which is then getting the full bodykit and wicked respray treatment. There's no doubt, however, that it really looks the business to have a fully-flushed tailgate, or even to have those ugly roof gutters trimmed off (but the gutters conceal the spot-welds holding the roof panel on, so just trimming them off would be a quick way to a one-off Nova Cabrio!). Probably best to put the pros at a bodyshop to work on this. De-badging and de-stripping you can definitely do at home, so get to it.

De-badging

01 The tailgate badges are easy to dispose of, and leave no holes behind afterwards - bonus! First, soften the glue with a heatgun, remembering you're not trying to melt the badges - okay? Any wide-bladed tool will do to prise the badge off, but it might be wise to wrap the blade with some tape, to avoid wrecking your paint.

02 Scrape the remains of the sticky foam tape with the same 'protected' scraper . . .

03 . . . and a touch of meths later, you're one step nearer a smoothed tailgate.

04 You might be a devoted Vauxhall fan, but there's really no excuse for leaving the huge Vauxhall griffin behind. Get it gone. Heating the badge softens the glue underneath . . .

05 . . . but there's a problem, in the shape of two tiny holes left behind - just so someone could stick the badge on straight at the factory. Brilliant.

De-stripping

01 Side rubbing strips. Good - they save your paint if Mr Numpty opens his rusty Metro door into your car. Bad - they look hideous. If looks are important, removal is easy. Warm the strip thoroughly (without melting it) using a heatgun or hairdryer, then carefully peel it off.

02 The more heat you use, the softer the glue will be, and the less cleaning-up you'll have to do later. A pinstripe removal tool like this (made of rubber, available from bodyshops) is one way of dealing with excess glue . . .

03 . . . then there's the old favourites like meths or white spirit.

04 Even on a metallic finish, the paint behind the strip might be a different shade. But with metallic paint, it's not so easy to do something about. Being red, this won't have been the first time our Nova had seen T-Cut.

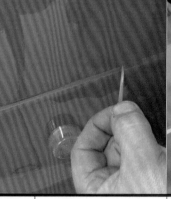

05 Modern cars just don't have pinstripes any more - but the Nova's not really a modern car. Luckily, removing a pinstripe needn't be hard - warm it up . . .

06 . . . and if you're lucky, you might even peel it off by hand, in one go . . .

07 . . . but if not, there's always the pinstripe removing tool we mentioned earlier. Mounts in a drill, doesn't take the paint off, and is cheap - what more do you want? Your Nova is now one step less 'sensible' than it was before. Speaking of sensible, you haven't still got mudflaps on, have you?

Filling holes - a cunning plan

When it comes to car bodywork, every hole is not a goal. At least small holes can be filled without stretching your talent envelope too far. First, cover the area around your chosen hole (two holes, in this case) with masking tape - make sure you get a decent working area around the hole.

01

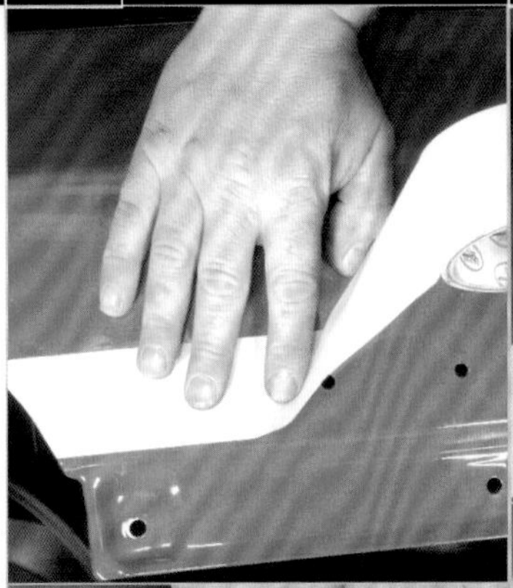

Now neatly cut out your holes in the tape.

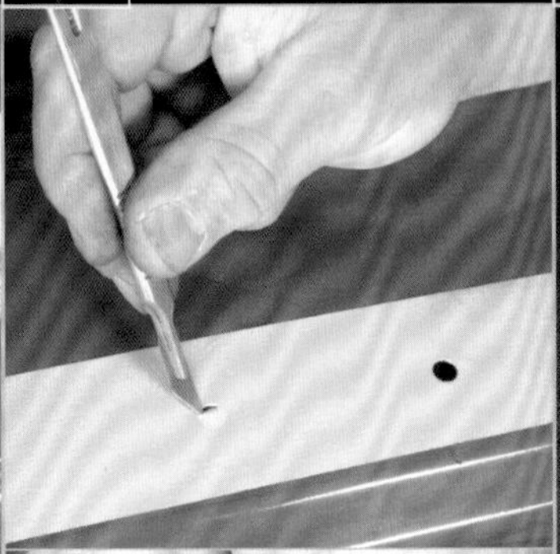

02

Here's where we start to see the true cunning of this plan - mix up some Araldite (or similar glue for bonding metals), and apply a blob of it to a washer large enough to cover the hole, on the inside. Rich types among you may prefer to use a coin.

03

Stick the washer or coin on from inside, then stand around looking stupid, holding it in place while the glue dries.

04

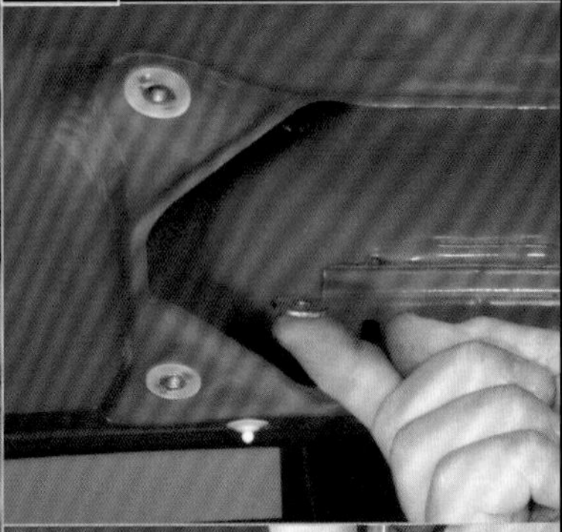

05 Mix up some filler, and apply to your hole - the masking tape prevents any getting on the paintwork. Apply more than one layer, and build the filler up evenly.

06 We found that the filler could be trimmed flat using a sharp Stanley blade, used at a very shallow angle. The filler doesn't really 'take' to the masking tape, making it easier to trim away the excess.

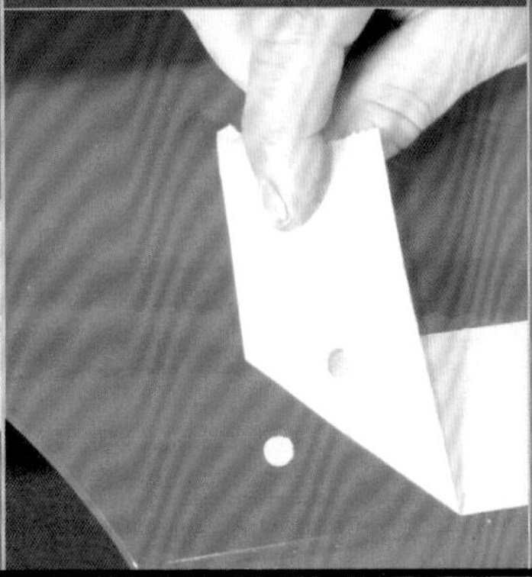

07 Peel away the masking tape, and your hole is filled - all it needs is paint.

08 If you haven't done such a great job, remember that you can improve things by applying layer after layer of paint (wait for each one to dry). When you've built the paint up proud of the hole, T-Cut it back smooth.

Beesting
aerial

Novas are old cars. Sorry, but it's true. One of the best pieces of evidence is the very sad standard telescopic aerial, poking up from the front wing. It looks hideous, and unlike modern cars with a roof aerial, you can't even unscrew the standard mast and fit a stumpy anodised replacement. But - if you're brave enough to drill a hole in your roof (and can also deal with the hole you leave in the wing), you can treat your Nova to a styling touch first seen on that other classic modified motor, the Mk 2 Golf. We're talking about a beesting aerial.

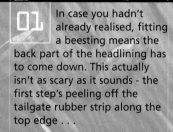

01 In case you hadn't already realised, fitting a beesting means the back part of the headlining has to come down. This actually isn't as scary as it sounds - the first step's peeling off the tailgate rubber strip along the top edge . . .

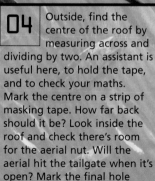

02 . . . which reveals the folded-over and glued-on edge of the headlining. This has to be carefully peeled off - on a really old Nova, this might have deteriorated way too much to put back later.

03 To really get some movement in the headlining, the wire support strips must be unclipped from the roof - peer inside with a torch to see what's what.

04 Outside, find the centre of the roof by measuring across and dividing by two. An assistant is useful here, to hold the tape, and to check your maths. Mark the centre on a strip of masking tape. How far back should it be? Look inside the roof and check there's room for the aerial nut. Will the aerial hit the tailgate when it's open? Mark the final hole position . . .

05 . . . ready for drilling. There's no going back now.

06 When the hole's big enough to take the aerial mounting stud, give it a clean-up with a file, then get some touch-up paint on the bare metal - encouraging rust is something you don't need to do.

07 To get a decent earth connection, the inside of the roof must now be cleaned up. We found stuck-on insulation which had to be scraped off . . .

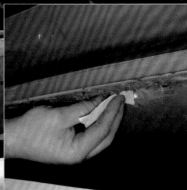

08 . . . before we could get in seriously with the sandpaper, and take off the thin layer of paint. Remember - we'd quite like our aerial to work, as well as look cool.

09 Now pop the aerial into its hole . . .

10 . . . then feed the wires down through, and fit the nut and shakeproof washer. Do the nut up tight to ensure a good earth. Our beesting (supplied by ABC Design) is an amplified type, which explains the extra red wire (this gets connected to a 12V supply, to improve reception).

11 To get the aerial lead started on its journey to the front of the car, we taped it to a length of stiff welding wire, and poked it forwards inside the headlining (this is okay as long as you don't stick it straight through the headlining). Having released the seal around the driver's door, we retrieved the lead, and fed it on down the windscreen pillar to the back of the headset.

12 With the beesting in place, we now appear to have an overdose of aerials. It's time to adios the old one. Vauxhall thoughtfully provide a small access panel at the back of the offside wheel arch (even if you can see it, you might have fun undoing the two screws).

>>

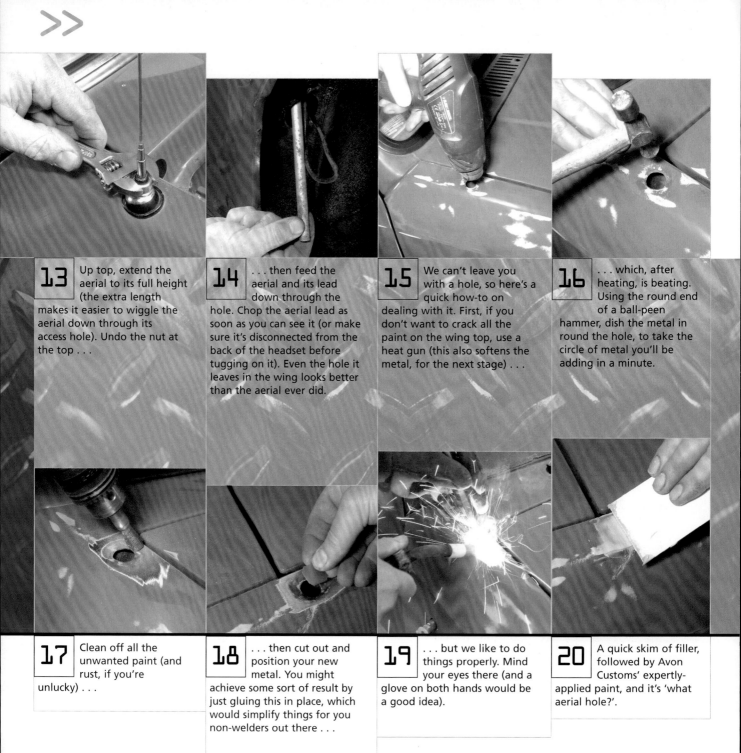

13 Up top, extend the aerial to its full height (the extra length makes it easier to wiggle the aerial down through its access hole). Undo the nut at the top . . .

14 . . . then feed the aerial and its lead down through the hole. Chop the aerial lead as soon as you can see it (or make sure it's disconnected from the back of the headset before tugging on it). Even the hole it leaves in the wing looks better than the aerial ever did.

15 We can't leave you with a hole, so here's a quick how-to on dealing with it. First, if you don't want to crack all the paint on the wing top, use a heat gun (this also softens the metal, for the next stage) . . .

16 . . . which, after heating, is beating. Using the round end of a ball-peen hammer, dish the metal in round the hole, to take the circle of metal you'll be adding in a minute.

17 Clean off all the unwanted paint (and rust, if you're unlucky) . . .

18 . . . then cut out and position your new metal. You might achieve some sort of result by just gluing this in place, which would simplify things for you non-welders out there . . .

19 . . . but we like to do things properly. Mind your eyes there (and a glove on both hands would be a good idea).

20 A quick skim of filler, followed by Avon Customs' expertly-applied paint, and it's 'what aerial hole?'.

Travelling incognito

If you is a gangsta wiv da Staines massive, blacking those windows is a must. Window tinting is also one of the best ways to disguise a naff standard interior, or a good way to hide a sorted interior (or ICE install) from thieving eyes...

Tints look right with almost any car colour (limo-tint on a black Nova is virtually essential, while mirror film looks trick on a silver car), and with 'reflex film' available in various rainbow colours, there's something for everyone. Only downside is - not all tints are legal to be run on the road, and you'll be chancing it buying any advertised as 'for show cars only'. Tints don't suit everybody - if you're doing your car to pose around in (and why not?) it's hard enough to see you in there anyway, without blacking-out the windows!

Because window tinting involves sticking a layer of film to the inside of the glass, fitting tints might help to prevent a break-in, since your side windows won't shatter when hit. Car security firm Toad market an adhesive film specifically designed to prevent break-ins in this way, and even humble window-tinting kits are claimed to offer the same effect.

Generally, window tint comes on a roll, but you can sometimes buy pre-cut kits for popular cars. Buying a kit (if you can) sounds a better deal, but if you muck up fitting one section, you'll be buying another complete kit. With a roll of film, check how many windows you'll be able to do with it - one roll usually isn't enough for the whole car.

At this point, we'd better 'fess up and tell you that tinting will severely try your patience. If you're not a patient sort of person, this is one job which may well wind you up - you have been warned. Saying that, if you're calm and careful, and you follow the instructions to the letter, you could surprise yourself - our mechanic did, when we tried it for the first time and got a near-perfect result!

In brief, the process for tinting is to lay the film on the outside of the glass first, and cut it exactly to size. The protective layer is peeled off to expose the adhesive side, the film is transferred to the inside of the car (tricky) and then squeegeed into place (also tricky). All this must be done with scrupulous cleanliness, as any muck or stray bits of trimmed-off film will ruin the effect (not easy, if you're working outside). The other problem which won't surprise you is that getting rid of air bubbles and creases can take time. A long time. This is another test of patience, because if, as the instructions say, you've used plenty of spray, it will take a while to dry out and stick... just don't panic!

Legal eagle

The law on window tinting currently is that there must be no more than a 25% reduction in light transmission through windscreens, and a limit of 30% reduction on all other glass. Yes, yes, all very well, but how the heck do you measure light reduction? Also, consider that many cars come with tinted glass as standard - so can you fit a tinting kit on top and still be legal? Hard to know what line to take, if you're stopped by Plod - try and choose a tinting kit which is EC-approved (ask before you buy, and if you think it could be a serious issue, get a letter from the company to support the legality of the kit, to use in your defence). Some forces now take this seriously enough to have portable test equipment they can use at the roadside - if your car fails, it's an on-the-spot fine.

Tinting windows

It's worth picking your day, and your working area, pretty carefully - on a windy day, there'll be more dust in the air, and it'll be a nightmare trying to stop the film flapping and folding onto itself while you're working.

Applying window tint is best done on a warm day (or in a warm garage - if there is such a thing), because the adhesive will begin to dry sooner. For fairly obvious reasons, don't try tinting when it's starting to get dark! It's a good idea to have a mate to help out with this job, but you might get fed up hearing 'you've missed another bubble' or 'you can still see that crease, y'know'.

01 Get the window being tinted clean - really clean - inside and out. Don't use glass cleaners (or any other product) containing ammonia or vinegar, since both will react with the film or its adhesive, and muck it up. Also clean the area around the window - it's too easy for stray dirt to attach itself to the film - and by the time you've noticed it, it could be too late. On door windows, wind them down slightly, to clean all of the top edge, then close them tight to fit the film.

02 Before you even unroll the film, take note - handle it carefully. If you crease it, you won't get the creases out - ever. First work out which way up the film is, by applying a small bit of really sticky tape to the front and back side - use the tape to pull the films apart, just at one corner.

03 Lay the film onto the glass, with the clear side facing you. Unroll the film, and cut it roughly to the size of the window (on a door window, leave plenty at the bottom edge for now). Some kits have a logo on the film, which seems daft - tinting's difficult enough, without having to get a logo straight! The only benefit of a logo is to establish which layer is the tint. Make life easier - lose the logo.

04 Spray the outside of the window with a weak soapy water solution (Folia Tec supply a small bottle of Joy fluid in their kit, but you could use a few drops of ordinary washing-up liquid). Get one of those plant sprayers you can buy cheap in any DIY store, if your kit doesn't contain a sprayer.

05 Lay the roughly-cut sheet of tint back onto the glass, and spray the outside of the film with soapy water . . .

06 . . . then use a squeegee to get out the air bubbles, sticking the film to the outside of the glass.

07 On a door window, trim the bottom edge to leave some excess to tuck down inside the door - this stops the film peeling off on the bottom rubber when you roll the window down!

08 Using a sharp knife (and taking care not to damage your paint or the window rubber), trim round the outside of the window. An unimportant piece of plastic (like an expired video club card) is brilliant for tucking the film into the edges to get the shape right, but don't trim the film right to the absolute edge - leave a small, even gap of just a few mill all round (this helps to get rid of excess water when you squeegee it on the inside - you'll see).

09 Now go inside, and prepare for receiving the tint. On fixed glass, waterproof the side trim panels in anticipation of the soapy water which will be used, by taping on some plastic sheet (otherwise, you'll have some very soggy panels. And seats. And carpets). Spray the inside of the glass with the soapy solution.

10 Back outside, it's time to separate the films. Use two pieces of sticky tape to pull the films slightly apart at one corner. As the films come apart, spray more solution onto the tinted piece underneath, to help it separate cleanly. Try not to lift the tint film too much off the glass when separating, as this increases the risk of creasing.

11 Have your willing helper on standby, to assist with transferring the film to the inside (a prime time for messing it all up). Peel the tint film off the glass, keeping it as flat as you can. Without letting it fold onto itself, move it inside the car and place it fairly accurately on the inside of the glass. The surface which was outside should now be on the inside of the glass (now that you've cut it, it will only fit one way!). Carefully slide the film into the corners, keeping it flat.

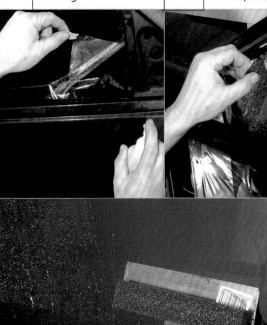

12 On a door window, use your unimportant plastic to tuck the film into the door - try to stick it to the glass by wedging-in a wad of paper cloth too.

13 Spray the film with the soapy water . . .

14 . . . then carefully start to squeegee it into place, working from top to bottom. We found that, to get into the corners, it was easier to unscrew the blade from the squeegee, and use that on its own for some of it.

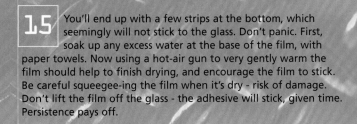

15 You'll end up with a few strips at the bottom, which seemingly will not stick to the glass. Don't panic. First, soak up any excess water at the base of the film, with paper towels. Now using a hot-air gun to very gently warm the film should help to finish drying, and encourage the film to stick. Be careful squeegee-ing the film when it's dry - risk of damage. Don't lift the film off the glass - the adhesive will stick, given time. Persistence pays off.

Fitting a
sunstrip

The modern sunstrip, first seen as a lovely green shadeband on Cortinas and Capris back in the 70s, usually bearing imaginative slogans such as 'DAVE AND SHARON'. Just goes to show that some things improve with age.

There are two options to make your car look (and maybe even feel) cooler:

a The sunvisor, a screen tint band inside the screen, which is usually a graduated-tint strip. As this fits inside, there's a problem straight away - the interior mirror. The Nova mirror is bonded to the screen, and it seriously gets in the way when trying to fit a wet and sticky (nice!) strip of plastic around it. Go for a sunstrip instead.

b The sunstrip, which is opaque vinyl, colour-matched to the car, fits to the outside of the screen. Much more Sir.

A really wide sunstrip imitates the 'roof chop' look seen on American hot rods, and colour-coded, they can look very effective from the front - plus, of course, you can use the space to advertise your preferred brand of ICE (no, no, NO! Not a good idea!). As it's fitted to the outside of the screen, the sunstrip has a good chance of seriously interfering with your wipers (or wiper, if you've been converted). If this happens to the point where the wipers can't clean the screen, Mr MOT might have a point if he fails your car... The wiper blades may need replacing more often, and the sunstrip itself might start peeling off - still want one? Well, you've got to, really.

01 This is only stuck to the outside, so only the outside of the screen needs cleaning - excellent! Do a good job of cleaning, though - any dirt stuck under the strip will ruin the effect.

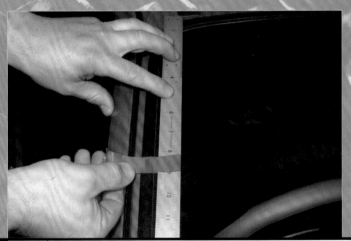

02 With the help of an assistant (if you have one handy), lay the strip onto the car, and decide how far down the screen you're going to go. Legally-speaking, you shouldn't be lower than the wiper swept area - so how much of a 'badboy' are you? If you measure and mark the bottom of the strip with tape, you'll be sure to get it level, even if it's not legal.

Legal eagle

The rule for tinting or otherwise modifying the windscreen is that there must be no more than a 25% light reduction from standard. In theory, this means you can have a sunstrip which covers up to 25% of the screen area, but some MOT testers may see it differently. A sunstrip's got to come down the screen a fair way, to look any sense (otherwise, why bother?). You could argue that accurately measuring and calculating the windscreen area isn't actually that easy, if you get stopped, and anyway, a sunstrip also cuts out harmful glare! If you go so far down the screen that you can't see out, though - well, that's just stupid.

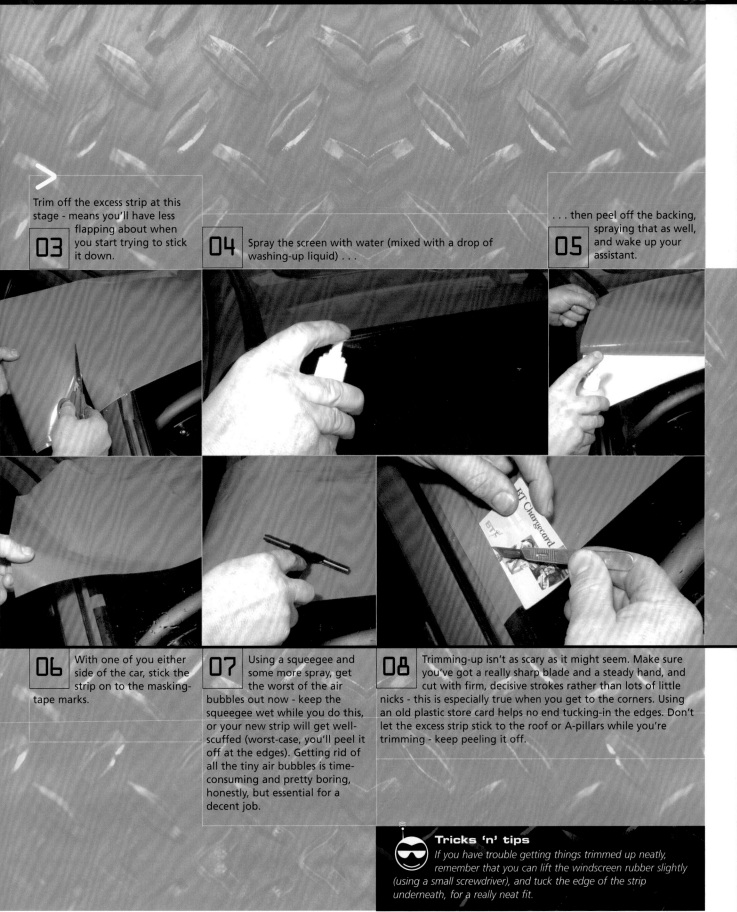

> Trim off the excess strip at this stage - means you'll have less flapping about when you start trying to stick it down.

03

04 Spray the screen with water (mixed with a drop of washing-up liquid) . . .

05 . . . then peel off the backing, spraying that as well, and wake up your assistant.

06 With one of you either side of the car, stick the strip on to the masking-tape marks.

07 Using a squeegee and some more spray, get the worst of the air bubbles out now - keep the squeegee wet while you do this, or your new strip will get well-scuffed (worst-case, you'll peel it off at the edges). Getting rid of all the tiny air bubbles is time-consuming and pretty boring, honestly, but essential for a decent job.

08 Trimming-up isn't as scary as it might seem. Make sure you've got a really sharp blade and a steady hand, and cut with firm, decisive strokes rather than lots of little nicks - this is especially true when you get to the corners. Using an old plastic store card helps no end tucking-in the edges. Don't let the excess strip stick to the roof or A-pillars while you're trimming - keep peeling it off.

Tricks 'n' tips
If you have trouble getting things trimmed up neatly, remember that you can lift the windscreen rubber slightly (using a small screwdriver), and tuck the edge of the strip underneath, for a really neat fit.

Single wiper conversion

Another saloon-car racing-inspired item, the single wiper conversion is a really smart way to make your Nova stand out from the crowd. Presumably, the saloon racers fit single wipers to enhance the view forward (one less wiper arm obscuring the view could make all the difference), improve the aerodynamics, and maybe even to save weight! Many Nova owners want the single wiper because it helps to remove clutter - put two Novas side by side, and the one with one less wiper looks way better. It's a fairly 'neutral' mod, too - unlike some, it works as well on a 'sport-Nova' as on a 'luxury-Nova'. Our Mono Style kit came from Demon Tweeks.

01 Unsurprisingly, the first job is to remove your old wiper arms. Make sure that the wipers are in their 'parked' position, if necessary by flicking the wipers on, then quickly off. Flip up the cap at the base of each arm, unscrew the nut, and pull the arms off their splined fittings. Hopefully, yours will come off as easy as ours.

This has to be one of the easiest standard linkages to remove. One (much smaller) spanner is now required, to remove the wiper motor arm nut. The only tricky bit is - you can't see it very well, tucked inside the bulkhead . . .

03

Next, one large spanner's needed to remove the large plastic nut which holds each wiper spindle to the windscreen scuttle panel - at least it can't rust on.

02

. . . but if yours looks like this, you'll know you've undone the right nut - pull the wiper motor arm off . . .

04

05 . . . then release the wiper spindles from the scuttle panel by pulling them down and forwards, and the old linkage is removed. Easy, wasn't it?

06 Never a thing of beauty, the Nova wiper linkage is only made worse by a healthy dose of rust. But before we can get to the shiny new linkage, we need to salvage some old bits. To help with dismantling, a squirt of WD-40's a good start.

07 First, prise off the top circlip, and collect the washer underneath. Below that sits the plastic spindle collar.

08 We only need one good plastic collar, which was lucky on our car, as the driver's side one had worn itself oval. This is the perfect one from the passenger's spindle. We also need the wave washer and O-ring from the base of one old spindle.

09 Enough of the depressing rusty linkage - let's see the new one. Fit the wave washer . . .

10 . . . then dig out the grease, and lube that spindle . . .

11 . . . we don't want our old plastic collar wearing any more, after all.

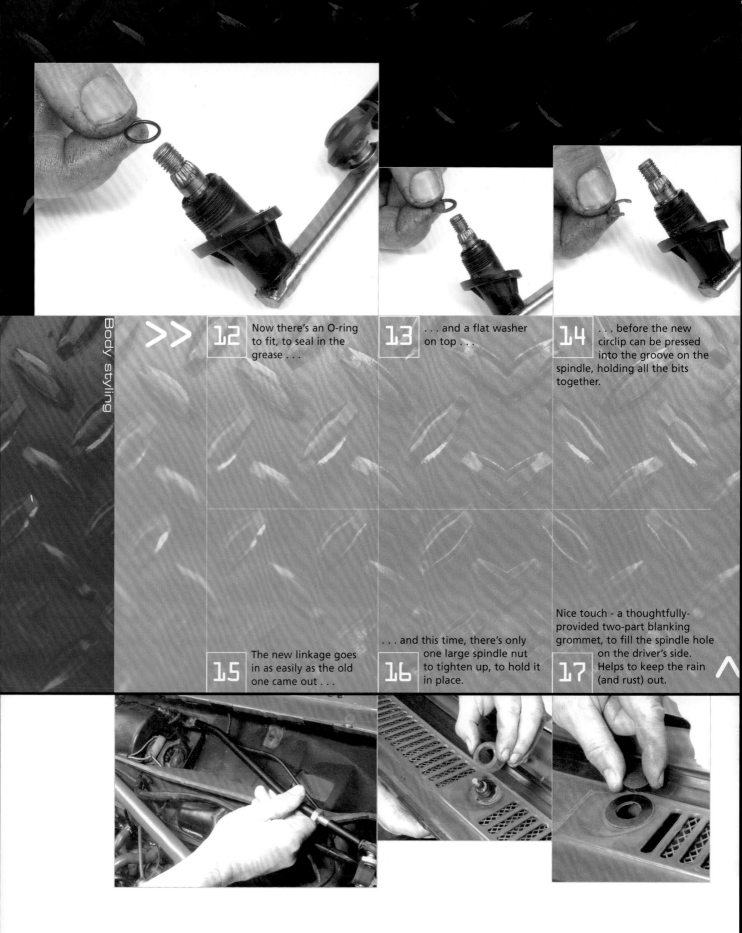

>>

12 Now there's an O-ring to fit, to seal in the grease . . .

13 . . . and a flat washer on top . . .

14 . . . before the new circlip can be pressed into the groove on the spindle, holding all the bits together.

15 The new linkage goes in as easily as the old one came out . . .

16 . . . and this time, there's only one large spindle nut to tighten up, to hold it in place.

17 Nice touch - a thoughtfully-provided two-part blanking grommet, to fill the spindle hole on the driver's side. Helps to keep the rain (and rust) out.

18 At the other end of the new linkage, fit the wiper motor arm to the motor. For now, the arm should be fitted roughly in line with the linkage . . .

19 . . . tighten the motor arm nut enough to hold it in place - further adjustments may be needed.

20 What's this man doing with his hand? He's feeling in under the new spindle, to see how close the end of the linkage is to the bulkhead. Close is fine, but if it hits the bulkhead, the linkage could be damaged.

Mono Style say that their linkage should be supplied set in virtually the exact position, so don't be too quick to adjust it. But - if it's hitting the bulkhead, you've got no choice. Loosen **21** the locknut and turn the rods until all's well, then tighten it back up.

With our wiper motor arm and linkage set as it is, the instructions say the wiper blade will park on the passenger's side. So we fitted our new wiper arm/blade over on the passenger's side, and switched the wipers on for a test. Guess **22** what? They weren't lying, and the wiper swept the screen fully.

If you want a centre-parking blade (potentially an MOT fail), loosen the motor arm nut (making sure the motor doesn't move from the park position), then prise the motor arm off. Turn the **23** arm so it points downwards, moving the wiper arm/blade at the same time, then re-tighten the motor arm nut. Time for a beer.

Glow **for it**

Ever since 'The Fast and the Furious' first glued us to our screens, every cruise-goer wants a cool neon glow under their car. Wanting's one thing - make it a reality, and you'll have to explain it to the Law. Under-car neons are totally illegal on the road, and rather an obvious 'come-and-nick-me' to Plod (who will then have a field day with any other semi-legal features on your Nova). So - you have been warned. But we know you still want them, anyway…

01 First, the car's got to get airborne - look in 'Wheels & tyres' for info on jacking the car up, and supporting it safely. Offer the first tube in place, and see where it fits best. It mustn't interfere with the jacking points on the sills (but you're probably using these already). Those tubes are fragile (no - really?), so don't drop 'em…

02 The Folia Tec neons we used came with these plastic mounting clips, which you just slip onto the tubes (use three on the longer tubes). With the tubes fitted inside the sill flange, we marked through the clips for the mounting holes.

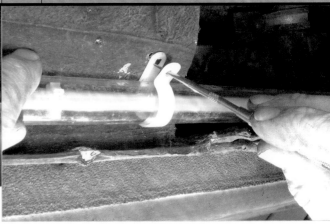

03 Yes, we're drilling holes in the floor. Are we bothered about making our Nova rust even more? Well, maybe we should be - before subjecting your hole-y Nova to the British weather, get some silicone or underseal on round those clips (without plastering it on your tubes, of course).

04 Inside the car, take the door sill plastic trims off (only a few screws), and lift the edges of carpet, to find where your holes ended up. Poke a bolt down through, then go underneath and fit the tube and its clip to the bolt. Tightening the nut and bolt is one time when an assistant comes in pretty handy.

05 As a last check, we've taken the Nova's jack out of the boot, and we're making sure there's still room to get it on the jacking point. We're so paranoid - but in a good way.

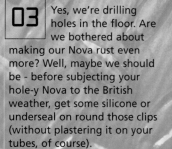

06 The neon across the front of the car's about the easiest to fit. First, make up a small bracket (we used some cut-down brackets from our local DIY store) to fit to the plastic clamp, with one small nut and bolt . . .

07 . . . then offer the tube and clamps under the front crossmember, and you should find you can attach the bracket to the front suspension tie-rod bracket bolt, by screwing on an extra nut.

08 At the back, the exhaust and rear bumper cause problems fitting our last tube. We trimmed away part of the plastic bumper, and fitted two more of our DIY-store brackets . . .

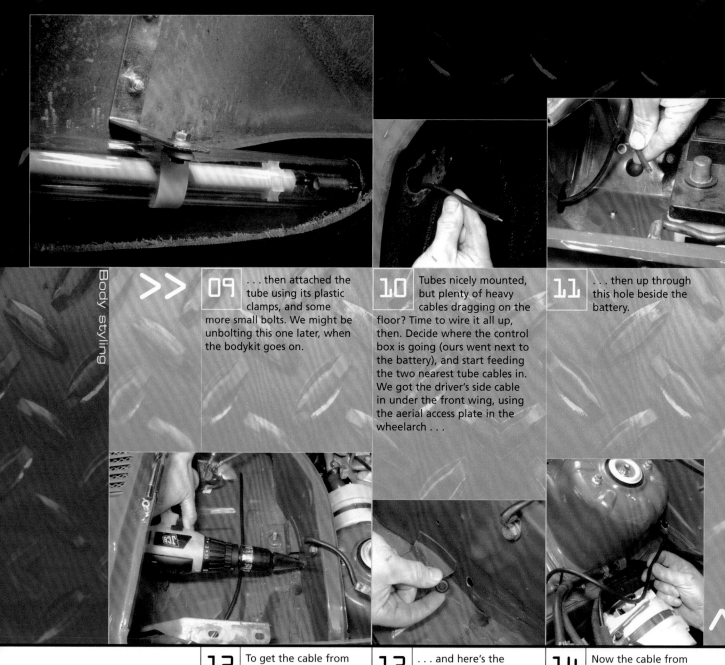

>>

09 . . . then attached the tube using its plastic clamps, and some more small bolts. We might be unbolting this one later, when the bodykit goes on.

10 Tubes nicely mounted, but plenty of heavy cables dragging on the floor? Time to wire it all up, then. Decide where the control box is going (ours went next to the battery), and start feeding the two nearest tube cables in. We got the driver's side cable in under the front wing, using the aerial access plate in the wheelarch . . .

11 . . . then up through this hole beside the battery.

12 To get the cable from the front neon into the battery area, we needed a new hole - fortunately, our cordless drill just fitted . . .

13 . . . and here's the most important bit - fitting a grommet to the new hole. If you study the neon's control box, you'll see it mentions something about 6000 volts. If one of those cables rubs through on a sharp-edged hole - we'll leave the rest to your imagination.

14 Now the cable from the front neon can be fed along the inner wing, and into the battery area through our hole in the bulkhead. Try and use the clips provided by Vauxhall to secure the wiring - we don't want a 6000-volt wire flapping about.

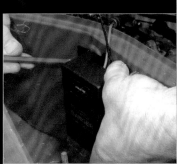

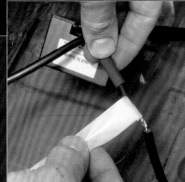

15 Mounting the control box somewhere near the battery seems a good move - lots of lives and earths close to hand. However, if you've removed the battery (like we did) to give yourself more room, check before finally fitting the box that the battery will go back in. That's what we call a Homer moment.

16 Joining these neon cables together requires a special technique - and not one we're used to recommending. What you do is - strip about an inch off the thick insulation of each wire you want to join . . .

17 . . . and twist the bared ends together as best you can. Do not use solder. Do not use bullets, terminal blocks, or any other joiners. Do not pass Go. Apparently, any method other than the wires-twisted-together one might cause the tubes to malfunction. So there.

18 You are allowed to tape up the joint - which is just as well, with all those volts going through it. Don't be shy with the tape.

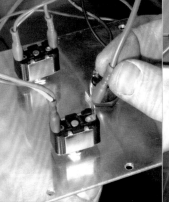

19 Better than tape, slip on some heatshrink tubing (before you twist the wires together) and, er… shrink it. With heat. Use this method to join all the tubes together, around the car, to form a complete circuit.

20 Two more wires to go now, at the control box - a red live, and a black earth. We've got the battery earth lead right in front of us - shame not to use it. Unbolt it from the car, and fit the black wire to the earth lead mounting bolt, using a ring terminal.

21 You must be able to control under-car neons - a switch is essential. Run the red wire from the control box into the car, and feed it to one side of your new switch (our red wire became a blue wire by the time it reached the switch). Here, we're joining on another red wire, which is going to be our live feed. We fitted our switch in the centre console, on a new alloy plate.

22 To get a live feed, you have several options. You can poke about behind the fusebox with a test light and your Haynes wiring diagrams for an existing wire to join onto (tricky), or you can run one into the car from the battery (easy). For a really cool solution, make an auxiliary fusebox of your own, like us (refer to the security section).

Painting by numbers

This is not the section where we tell you how to respray your entire Nova in a weekend, using only spray cans, okay? Mission Impossible, we ain't. This bit's all about how to spray up your various plasticky bits before final fitting - bits such as door mirrors, light brows, spoilers, splitters - hell, even bumpers if you like. As we've no doubt said before, with anything new, fit your unpainted bits first. Make sure everything fits properly (shape and tidy up all parts as necessary), that all holes have been drilled, and all screws etc are doing their job. Then, and only when you're totally, completely happy with the fit - take them off, and get busy with the spray cans.

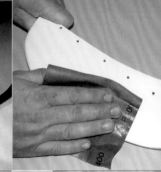

01 The first job is to mask off any areas you don't want painted. Do this right at the start, or you could be sorry; on these door mirrors, we decided to mask off just at the lip before the glass, to leave a black unpainted edge - if we hadn't masked it as the very first job, we would've roughed up all the shiny black plastic next, and wrecked the edge finish.

02 Remove any unwanted 'seams' in the plastic, using fine sandpaper or wet-and-dry. Some of these seams look pretty cool, others don't - you decide. Also worth tidying up any other areas you're not happy with, fit-wise, while you're at it.

Especially with 'shiny' plastic, you must rough-up the surface before spray will 'bite' to it, or - it'll flippin' flake off. Just take off the shine, no more. You can use fine wet-and-dry for this (used dry), but we prefer Scotchbrite. This stuff, which looks much like a scouring pad, is available from motor factors and bodyshops, in several grades - we used ultra-fine, which is grey. One advantage of Scotchbrite is that **03** it's a bit easier to work into awkward corners than paper.

Once the surface has been nicely 'roughened', clean up the surface using a suitable degreaser ('suitable' means a type which won't dissolve plastic!). Generally, it's ok to use methylated spirit or cellulose thinners (just don't inhale!), but **04** test it on a not-so-visible bit first, so you don't have a disaster.

Before you start spraying (if it's something smaller than a bumper) it's a good idea to try a work a screw into one of the mounting holes, to use as a **05** 'handle', so you can turn the item to spray all sides.

Another good trick is to use the screw to hang the item up on a piece of string or wire - then **06** you can spin the item round to get the spray into awkward areas.

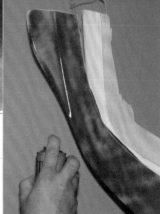

07 If you like a bit of wildlife in your paint, you can't beat the great outdoors. If it's at all windy, you'll end up with a really awful finish and overspray on everything (which can be a real nightmare to get off). Even indoors, if it's damp weather, you'll have real problems trying to get a shine - some kind of heater is essential if it's cold and wet (but not one with a fan - stirring up the dust is the last thing you want).

08 If you're a bit new at spraying, or if you simply don't want to muck it up, practise your technique first (steady!). Working left-right, then right-left, press the nozzle so you start spraying just before you pass the item, and follow through just past it the other side. Keep the nozzle a constant distance from the item - not in a curved arc. Don't blast the paint on too thick, or you'll have a nasty case of the runs - hold the can about 6 inches away - you're not trying to paint the whole thing in one sweep.

09 Once you've got a patchy 'mist coat' on (which might not even cover the whole thing) - stop, and let it dry (primer dries pretty quickly). Continue building up thin coats until you've got full coverage, then let it dry for half an hour or more.

10 Using 1000- or 1200-grade wet-and-dry paper (used wet), very lightly sand the whole primered surface, to take out any minor imperfections (blobs, where the nozzle was spitting) in the primer. Try not to go through the primer to the plastic, but this doesn't matter too much in small areas.

Rinse off thoroughly, then dry the surfaces - let it stand for a while to make sure it's *completely* dry, before starting on the top coat.

11

12 Make sure once again that the surfaces are clean, with no bits left behind from the drying operations. As with the primer, work up from an initial thin mist coat, allowing time for each pass to dry. As you spray, you'll soon learn how to build a nice shine without runs - any 'dry' (dull) patches are usually due to overspray landing on still-wet shiny paint. Don't worry if you can't eliminate all of these - a light cutting polish will sort it out once the paint's hardened (after several hours).

13 Especially with a colour like red (which is notorious for fading easily), it's a good idea to blow on a coat or two of clear lacquer over the top - this will also give you your shine, if you're stuck with a very 'dry' finish. It's best to apply lacquer before the final top coat is fully hardened. The spraying technique is identical, although pro sprayers say that lacquer should be applied pretty thick - just watch those runs! Lacquer also takes a good long while to dry - pick up your item too soon, for that unique fingerprint effect!

There's no way in

One very popular way to tidy up the Nova lines is to do away with the door locks, and even the door handles - but be careful. Flushing the rear door handles (on 4- or 5-door models) is okay, legally/MOT-speaking, but removing the front door handles will land you in trouble, come MOT time.

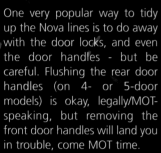

Construction & Use regs require your car to have an independent mechanical means of door opening from outside (so fire-fighters can get you out, if you stick your all-action Nova on its roof, or in a ditch…) If you must lose the front handles, find some trick mirrors which have door catches built-in, underneath.

01 As we've already said, it's not a good idea to remove and flush your handles, unless you've got a very understanding, very unobservant, or very easily-bribed, MOT tester. The only reason you'd remove your handles is to colour-code them, okay? Inside the door, there's two small nuts to undo . . .

02 . . . and another operating rod to unhook from the door lock.

03 Meanwhile, outside, the handle is removed from the door, and the other end of the rod gets unhooked from it. Simple.

04 Colour-coding the handles shouldn't tax anyone's skills - even if you've not done much spraying before, you'd have to try hard to muck this up. Most important is the need to get rid of any silicone residue (from polish or cockpit sprays), so rough-up the surface with fine emery paper or Scotchbrite.

05 Before you start to spray, give the surface a final wipe over with meths or paint thinners, and try to handle it as little as possible from then on.

06 Using a plastic primer is essential if you want the paint to stick - you should only need a light coat.

07 The top coat is obviously the most important. Don't try to spray this on in one hit, or you'll get runs - better to build up several coats, allowing a minute or so for each one to dry. We're using genuine Vauxhall paint, for (hopefully) the best guarantee of a good colour match.

Removing **door lock barrels**

Those now-absent lock barrels leave behind holes which are way too big for filler alone. The best solution is to weld a metal plate behind, then a skim of filler and paint will finish the job nicely.

04 First, clean off around the hole . . .

01 First, the door trim panel has to come off - but you knew that already. Look in 'Interiors' for door trim panel removal - the plastic membrane has to come off too (don't just rip it). Removing the barrels is laughably easy - pull this horseshoe clip out to the side . . .

02 . . . then unhook the stumpy operating rod from the door lock (at the back edge of the door) . . .

03 . . . and remove the barrel and rod from outside. That was the easy bit - getting rid of the hole (and providing a new means of working the door locks) will be tougher. But we won't leave you out in the cold.

. . . then cut a piece of metal just larger than the hole, and get a brave assistant to hold it on inside the door

05 (using an insulated tool of some kind, of course).

Now it's time to put your welding skills (or those of a competent mate) to work - just a few dabs will hold

06 that little plate in place.

07 The end result, ready for a skim of filler . . .

. . . and here's our man Kevin, giving it just that. Hardly a challenge, for a man of his abilities. Next time you see this,

08 it'll be painted - and no-one will suspect a hole ever lived there.

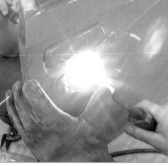

Remote **locking**

So you can lock and unlock your freshly de-locked doors, you'll need to buy and fit a remote central locking kit. If your Nova already has central locking, you're in luck - buy yourself a cheap car alarm, and a central locking interface (see 'Security' for how we fitted ours).

Tricks 'n' tips

If your battery goes flat, you'll be locked out. We ran two thin wires from the battery terminals (with a 10-amp fuse in the live, and the ends insulated), and tucked them away for access from below in an emergency. By connecting a slave battery to these wires (do not try jump-starting), you'll put enough juice into the system to operate the locks, saving you a red face. Think it over.

Central locking **kit**

If your Nova doesn't have central locking as standard, don't despair, there's several kits out there to help you towards your goal - our Microscan kit came from Demon Tweeks.

Take one of the four-wire solenoids, and hook on one of the 'bike spokes' in the kit. This is the solenoid's new operating rod, which you'll be joining to the door lock button operating rod at the top of the door, later on - for now, just make sure the new rod will reach that far.

01

The solenoid must be mounted vertically - its rod has to move vertically, the same as the door lock button's does. When the solenoid's plunger extends, it will push the door lock button upwards, and unlock the door. Try it in place, and see where it can be mounted.

02

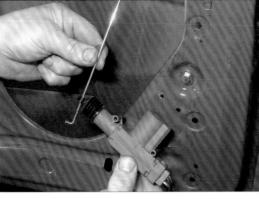
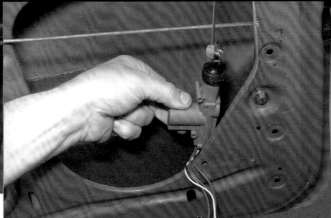

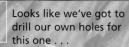 **03** Looks like we've got to drill our own holes for this one . . .

04 . . . then, once the first hole's drilled, measure the distance between the solenoid's two mounting holes, and you can work out where the second hole has to be. Simple, really.

05 If you've done it right, that solenoid will slip into place like it grew there. Notice we've slipped on one of the rod clamps? Now we'll join the old and new rods together.

06 Slide the clamp up the new rod to the top of the door, and slip the other side of the clamp onto the door button's rod (back the screw off first). With the solenoid plunger down, the door button should also be down - it's important they're in the same positions when you tighten the clamp screws. Do them tight, too - any slippage might see you locked out.

07 That's the 'mechanical' side done - all that's left to do now is the wiring. The kit came with a full loom (a lot of which you won't need, on a 3-door Nova). For now, join the loom up inside the door - blue to blue, green to green. Just like being five years old again.

08 On a Nova with no door electrics, there's the small problem of how you get wiring into the vital area. You can just drill a hole in the door, another in the door pillar, but it's tricky, and the wires have a rough time with all the door opening and shutting going on. Better to remove the doors completely - first, tap out the check strap roll pin . . .

09 . . . then tap out the hinge roll pins. Use lots of WD-40 beforehand, and get a parallel pin punch which just fits inside the hinge. Access to the hinge pins isn't easy, and don't damage the roll pins during removal, or they'll jam and never come free. Best solution is to buy a door pin removal kit - Draper do one for just over a tenner.

10 See how much easier drilling holes in your door is, when the thing's off the car?

11 Now we've gone this far, we don't want to skimp the job by just poking bare wires through the holes we'll be making. Check the scrapyards for rubber gaiters, commonly used on front doors and tailgates. Our rubber tubes came from a scrap Sierra tailgate, and they're made for the job.

Inside the car, all that wiring ends up at a major relay, which we'll be tucking up behind the dash any time soon. Once the main wiring plug's gone on, there's just a little earth lead to connect . . . **15**

. . . and an earth point to find, to connect it to. There's an ideal earth point, just behind the bonnet pull - fit a ring terminal to the (black) earth wire, and add it to the brown that's already there. **16**

Of course, the coolest way to have your central locking wired-in is linked to your alarm - for this, you'll need an alarm/locking interface box (Microscan make these as well). Ho-hum - more wiring. You'll need at least one live feed (this is where our auxiliary fusebox comes in handy) . . . **17**

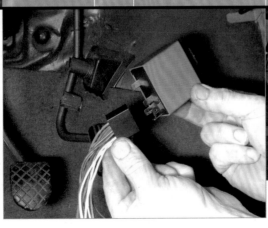
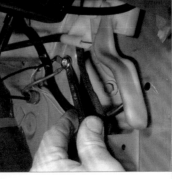
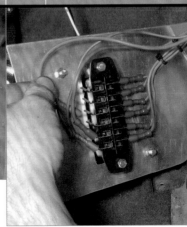

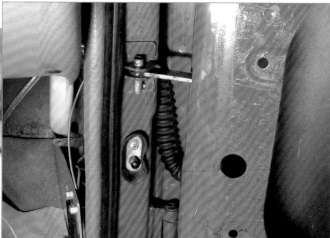

12 Drilling the door pillar is made harder by the often-thick metal. On our car, the ideal drilling spot was marked by a small dimple, virtually in line with the check strap locating bracket.

13 Feed the central locking wiring out from the car, into the rubber gaiter . . .

14 . . . then, with the door back on, admire the professional job you've made of the door wiring. If you don't do the rubber gaiter, feed the wiring through at two different heights like this (reduces strain on the wires as the door moves), and seal up the holes with silicone.

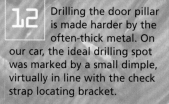

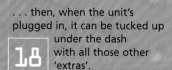

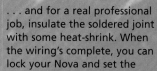

. . . then, when the unit's plugged in, it can be tucked up under the dash with all those other 'extras'.

18

Your alarm will almost certainly have a 'trigger' wire, designed to 'fire' the central locking, electric windows, etc. Join the trigger wire to the correct one from the locking interface (time to read those instructions). You can use bullets, but we like soldering stuff . . .

19

. . . and for a real professional job, insulate the soldered joint with some heat-shrink. When the wiring's complete, you can lock your Nova and set the alarm with one very cool press on the remote. Sweet.

20

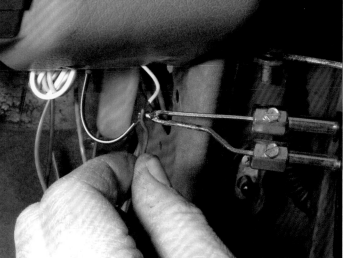

Don't mesh with me, boy

Meshing a Mk 2 grille

A meshed grille or bumper is just one way to demonstrate who's the daddy of the cruise, and it does a great job of dicing any small insects or rodents foolish enough to wander into the path of your motor. So if you're sick of scrubbing off insect entrails from your paint, and fancy getting even, read on…

Which style of mesh to choose? Classic diamond-shape, or round-hole? In our humble opinion, the round-hole mesh works best on modern roundy-shaped cars (like say, a Corsa) - for everything else, we'll settle for the original and best. But wait - the choice doesn't end with what shape you want. Mesh can now be had in various anodised colours too, to match or contrast with the rest of your chosen paint scheme.

01 First, we need the grille off - preferably in one piece. There's a clip each side, next to the headlight - use a screwdriver to help press down the spring clip.

02 At the base of the grille, there's several clips - one each end, fitted to the base of the headlight . . .

Having carefully removed the grille, it's now time to get a bit brutal with it. Unlike some cars, the Nova's plastic grille wasn't designed to be easily unclipped and removed, so a hacksaw's the only answer. Trim through the grille vertical sections as close to the hole edges as possible, without scratching the grille surround paint.

05 Here's one we did earlier - looks better already.

03 . . . and four more, fitted downwards into the bumper (just tip the grille back to free these, but remember they're there when you come to refit the grille).

04

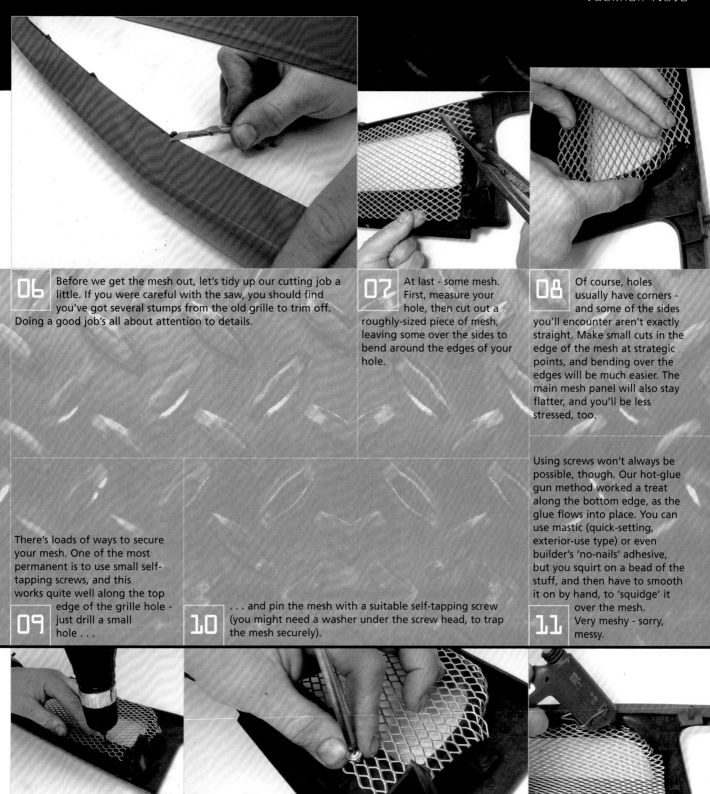

06 Before we get the mesh out, let's tidy up our cutting job a little. If you were careful with the saw, you should find you've got several stumps from the old grille to trim off. Doing a good job's all about attention to details.

07 At last - some mesh. First, measure your hole, then cut out a roughly-sized piece of mesh, leaving some over the sides to bend around the edges of your hole.

08 Of course, holes usually have corners - and some of the sides you'll encounter aren't exactly straight. Make small cuts in the edge of the mesh at strategic points, and bending over the edges will be much easier. The main mesh panel will also stay flatter, and you'll be less stressed, too.

Using screws won't always be possible, though. Our hot-glue gun method worked a treat along the bottom edge, as the glue flows into place. You can use mastic (quick-setting, exterior-use type) or even builder's 'no-nails' adhesive, but you squirt on a bead of the stuff, and then have to smooth it on by hand, to 'squidge' it over the mesh.

There's loads of ways to secure your mesh. One of the most permanent is to use small self-tapping screws, and this works quite well along the top edge of the grille hole - **09** just drill a small hole . . .

10 . . . and pin the mesh with a suitable self-tapping screw (you might need a washer under the screw head, to trap the mesh securely).

11 Very meshy - sorry, messy.

Bumpers 'n' bodykits

If you can't find a kit you like for a Nova, you're not trying!

Even though the car must be coming to the end of its life, there's still companies bringing out fresh stuff for it. We can't name-check all the kits out there, but Novadose, Evolution, Magnum, Abyss and Kingdom are among the most popular. Equally popular in the bumper stakes is fitting the standard GSi front bumper (easy DIY job), especially when you also treat it to a SEAT or Renault Laguna splitter underneath. One alternative supplier to these well-established names is BAT Motorsport - we chose a full BATsport 2 kit for our Nova, so let's see what it's like to fit.

Front bumper

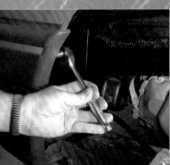

01 The radiator grille's gotta come off first on Mk 2 models (see the section on meshing) - on Mk 1 models, undo the three screws at the top of the grille. With the front wheels off (not essential), and a ridiculously-clean wheelarch, the two bumper mounting bolt heads are easy to see. Are they easy to undo? Try soaking with WD-40 (two more in the other wheelarch).

02 Two further bolts hold the back edges of the bumper to the wheelarch (again, these might be suffering exposure to the elements) . . .

03 . . . then hopefully, the bumper can be unclipped from the arches, and slid forwards to remove the mounting rails from the chassis legs. There - removing the old bumper is easy (and a lot simpler than fitting the new one, as we'll see).

04 Here we see the reason why you must try a bumper for fit as early as poss. Look at that gap - you could nearly get your fist in there! And we're not exaggerating.

05 You expect a little trimming on even the best kit, but modifying like this is unusual. To make up the gaps either end, our lads at Avon Customs had to add strips of glassfibre. To do this properly, you first attach a shaped piece of metal, as a 'former' to lay up the matting on, which gives it the right shape. Like your own mini-mould.

06 With the former in place, the additional matting can be cut and placed in, to be secured using the resin. Once this layer's gone solid, the former is taken off, and another layer of matting gets attached to the 'outside'. This had to be done for the bumper ends, and the tops where it meets the front wing.

07 Seen from this angle, it's not hard to spot where we had to add material. Only now we've added too much, and we need to trim it to the shape of the original arch. Marking this one up for cutting is best done from underneath the car.

08 Trimming glassfibre's so much easier when you've got an air hacksaw, and no decent bodyshop could exist for long without one.

09 We're re-fitting our Mk 2 grille, which has pegs at the base, to locate in the original bumper. You guessed it - the next job is to make some cut-outs in the new bumper, or the grille won't fit properly. Drop the grille in place, and mark the peg positions onto the bumper . . .

10 . . . then use a suitable tool to create the cut-outs at the right spots in the bumper edge. Incidentally, the strip of masking tape with the line on is the exact centre of the bumper. It's important to have reference marks like this, to keep it all in line.

11 The bumper brackets supplied with the kit didn't inspire us with confidence. Rather than risk having the bumper fall off, we made our own brackets.

12 For some reason there weren't any mounting holes provided for fixing the bumper ends to the arches, so again, we made our own.

Rear bumper

01 Taking off the back bumper's virtually the same deal as the front - there's two nuts inside each arch securing the bumper ends, then a nut each side, inside the back edge of the boot.

02 Before getting carried away and pulling the bumper off, don't forget the number plate light, which you prise out . . .

03 . . . and disconnect the wiring from. We'll be recycling the light later on - your new bumper's illegal without some form of number plate lighting. Now the bumper can be unclipped from the arches, and pulled away. Shan't be wanting that again.

04 Here we go then, and the most important first job - try the bumper for size. Not a bad fit.

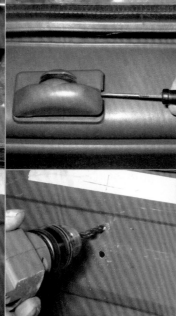

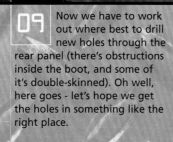

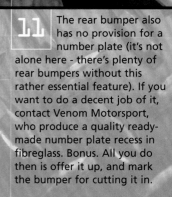

08 This is the mounting bracket supplied with our kit. Yes, really - that's it. We had to offer the bumper up, and guess the best locations for the brackets (no instructions provided).

09 Now we have to work out where best to drill new holes through the rear panel (there's obstructions inside the boot, and some of it's double-skinned). Oh well, here goes - let's hope we get the holes in something like the right place.

10 The brackets themselves also have to be drilled, before fitting to the rear panel.

11 The rear bumper also has no provision for a number plate (it's not alone here - there's plenty of rear bumpers without this rather essential feature). If you want to do a decent job of it, contact Venom Motorsport, who produce a quality ready-made number plate recess in fibreglass. Bonus. All you do then is offer it up, and mark the bumper for cutting it in.

05 The bumper ends wouldn't pull into place, leaving a gap between the rear wing and the sides of the bumper. Also, left like this, the rear wheel would've hit the bumper end, so some surgery was needed.

06 After some careful trimming, we found that just removing this small notch out of the bumper end made a huge difference to the fit.

07 A little further shaping of the bumper sides, and the bumper was declared fit.

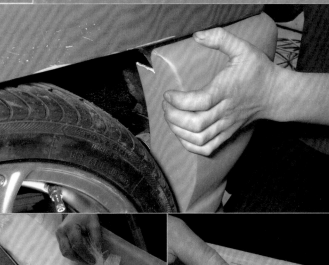

12 Obviously, a recess originally intended for a Mk 2 Golf bumper will probably need a little trimming to get the best fit, but after not very much work, our bodyshop had it fitting very nicely. Like it grew there.

13 Here's the recess, seen from behind, and the first stage of sticking it in place. With something like this, lay on a few strips of glassfibre matting at strategic points, then 'paint' on the resin to secure it (this was also the method we used to stick our bumper mounting brackets to the inside of the bumper).

14 Now we've got a number plate recess, it'd be a waste if we don't light the rear plate as well. There's enough room to refit the original number plate light, upside-down - just mark and cut a suitable hole (measure the hole in the old bumper). Plenty of other lights waiting in scrapyards, if a Nova one won't fit your new bumper.

15 As with the front bumper, the final stage in fitting was to offer the bumper in place, and drill through two holes each side where it will attach to the arches.

So what's the deal with side skirts, then?

Well, they're an 'artificial' way of visually lowering the car, making it seem lower to the ground than it really is, and they also help to 'tie together' the front and rear sections of a full bodykit. This much we know from our magazines. But where did skirts really come from?

As with so much else in modifying, it's a racing-inspired thing. In the late 70s, the Lotus 'ground-effect' F1 cars ran very, very low (for the time) and had side skirts made of rubber (or bristles), to give a flexible seal against the track. With a clear downforce advantage, Lotus blew the opposition away.

So will fitting skirts to your Nova give you race-car levels of downforce, greatly increasing your overtaking chances at the next roundabout? You already know the answer, I'm afraid…

Side skirts

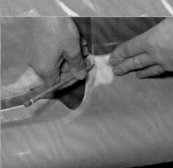

01 Based on our experiences so far, we weren't over-optimistic when we tried the Batsport side skirts in place for the first time. But we needn't have worried - apart from a slight case of catching on the door, things looked good. It's important to check every aspect of fit early on - discovering the doors won't shut too late to fix it, isn't our idea of fun.

02 Working out which bits to trim off takes time, but it's time well spent if you want to get it right.

03 When you're happy with the fit, it's time to go make some holes in your sills. As in drilled holes, for fitting the skirts. Make sure the skirt's in exactly the right position (tape it in place temporarily), then drill through. The screws don't all have to stay - once the mastic's gone off, most of them could be taken out, and the holes filled.

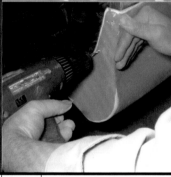

04 It's usually better to leave the screws fitted, at the front and rear arch attachment points. The trick in drilling these is guessing where the original arch actually is (and how rusty is that arch, exactly?).

05 Give the sill and rear wing a wipe with meths or panel wipe, then do the same for the edges of the skirt - it's mastic-time, and we want it to stick. Bathtub sealant is not an option - get some proper mastic designed for the job (try a bodyshop or car paint suppliers). Wear gloves when using the good stuff, as it's hell to get off hands.

06 Try to line the skirt up accurately when it first goes back on - this will reduce the mess from the mastic. Press it firmly on . . .

07 . . . then get the screws in to hold it. For the perfect finishing touch, apply another thin bead of mastic along the body joints, and smooth it off. When it's set firm, most of the screws could be removed (you might need to, if they interfere with the door shutting) and the holes fillered.

Spoil your Nova rotten

If you've 'only' got a base Nova, you might kill to have an SR/GSi rear window spoiler on your car. And why not? It's better than nothing, even if it is a standard item. Not the easiest item to fit, as there's no pre-drilled factory holes to help you, and you need to go through two layers of tailgate.

All you can do is offer the thing in place roughly, mark the hole positions as best you can, then be prepared to enlarge them to get it sitting right. You might do well to take off the tailgate completely, so you don't drill through the rubber seal, etc - and make sure you seal those mounting holes with mastic before final fitting.

Our rear spoiler came from Batsport, and was ridiculously easy to fit - but it can't be that easy, surely? Will it stay on properly?

01 Fitting a rear spoiler is much easier with the tailgate off, but this one's so easy, it's hardly necessary to go to all that trouble. Offer it on, and see how it fits . . .

02 . . . and the answer is - not too badly. This spoiler, though, offers no chance of attaching it to the tailgate except using mastic (gluing it on, in other words), which means getting it to hug the tailgate's contours is vital . . .

03 . . . so careful and accurate trimming is what we're talking here.

04 As with fitting the side skirts, you must get proper mastic for this, or your new spoiler will quickly give in to the effects of gravity. Check also that the tailgate's fully clean, if you want it to stick.

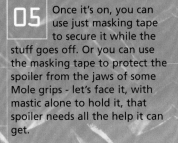

05 Once it's on, you can use just masking tape to secure it while the stuff goes off. Or you can use the masking tape to protect the spoiler from the jaws of some Mole grips - let's face it, with mastic alone to hold it, that spoiler needs all the help it can get.

06 When it's gone off, any excess mastic can be trimmed off with a blade.

07 As a belt-and-braces measure, it's not a bad idea to run a thin bead of mastic along the edges of the spoiler. Might help it stick, and also smoothes the joint between it and the tailgate.

Tailgate smoothing

Achieving the complete 'smooth-tailgate' look isn't too involved a procedure, providing you know someone who can weld, and are handy with filler and spray.

Completely smoothing the tailgate is a logical extension of de-badging - the first thing to go is the rear wiper. Rear wipers are undoubtedly useful, and were put there for a good reason, but hey - that's just boring. Remove the rear wiper and the lock button, and fill over the holes - easy, eh?. Well, yes, except that most of the holes are too big to just filler over, and will probably need glassfibre matting or welding.

If you're going to de-lock the tailgate, some means of opening the thing afterwards would be handy, if only so your mates can admire your ICE install. Which means you'll need a boot solenoid kit, wired up to a convenient switch.

And where's the number plate going, and how will it be lit up at night? And you thought dealing with holes in your tailgate was hard. Well, don't worry - your friends at Haynes are on the case for you now…

Tailgate wiper

01 A rear wiper has no place on a racing Nova, sort-of useful though it admittedly is. First, undo the nut and prise off the wiper arm (if it's badly rusted-on, serious force might be needed to shift it, but don't wreck the tailgate in the process).

02 Now there's this plastic cover to persuade off . . .

03 . . . before undoing the wiper spindle nut underneath.

04 Inside, prise out the plastic clips around the trim panel . . .

05 . . . and take it down, for your first look at the wiper motor in all its non-glory.

06 To the left of the motor itself is the wiper wiring plug. Separate the wiring plug halves, but don't do them any further damage for now - that wiring will come in handy for our tailgate solenoid, later on.

07 Remove the screw securing the brown earth wire, then it's just two mounting bolts before . . .

08 . . . the tailgate wiper motor is just a bad memory - leaving behind a gaping hole, complete with rubber grommet. More work for your tame bodyshop?

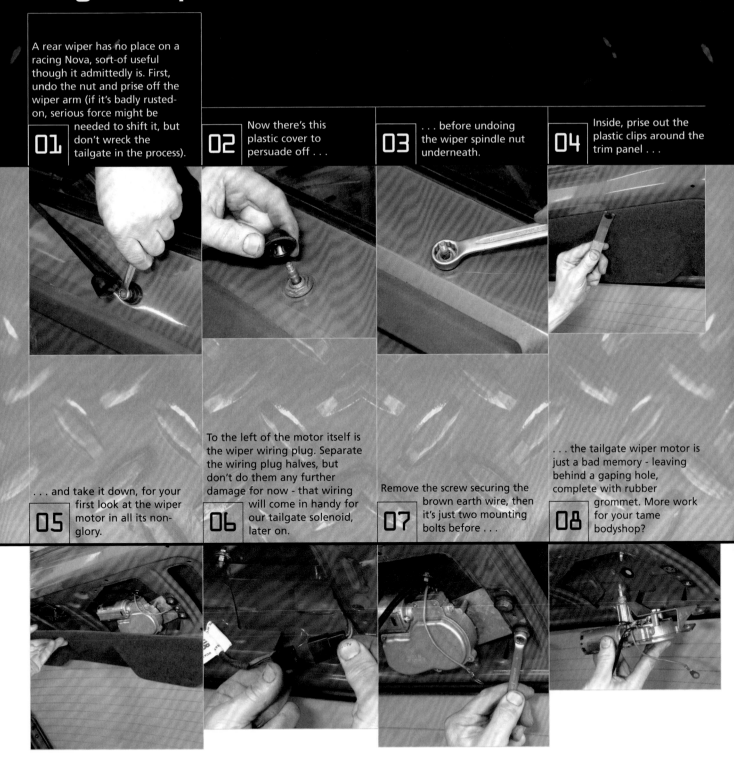

Tailgate washer

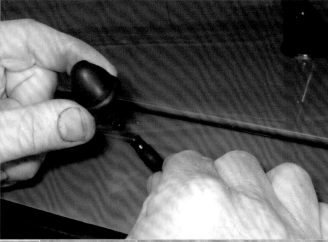

01 This is an easy one - the jet just pulls out of the tailgate.

02 Disconnecting the washer tube without inflicting severe damage on it is trickier - it just doesn't want to come off. You now have the choice of either blocking the tube at the washer end, or clamping it at the front of the car. Alternatively, you'll have to remember not to use the tailgate washer, from now on (or risk soaking your ICE in the boot).

Tailgate lock

A word of warning - if you choose to de-lock your Nova tailgate, you sure do leave yourself lots of holes to fill in. Inside the trim panel once more, and we first find **01** two nuts holding the lock assembly in place . . .

02 . . . then unhook the operating rod (which we'll need later, for the boot solenoid), and off it comes.

03 Now there's two more nuts (one either end) to remove . . .

04 . . . before the lock button trim comes away. Was that really necessary, Mr Vauxhall? One useless piece of plastic, and now we've got four holes. Great.

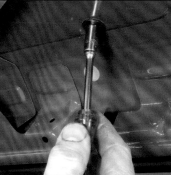

Boot lock **solenoid kit**

A pretty essential early fitment after you've de-locked your Nova tailgate, a boot solenoid's a lot easier to fit than you might think. First, chop the wiggly end off the lock operating rod you unhooked earlier, leaving plenty to play with.

01

Now take one of the new rods supplied in the kit (which look a lot like bicycle spokes), and chop it down to size. These hook into the eye at the top of the new solenoid unit. To join the old rod to the new one, you also get a set of screw clamps - fit one to the new rod . . .

02

. . . then offer up the solenoid, and do a trial fitting. Slide the end of the old rod into the other hole in the clamp, and tighten the screw.

03

Now you need some means of mounting the solenoid. You do get plenty of Meccano-like metal strips in the kit, but we chose to make an alloy plate, to bridge the members inside the tailgate.

04

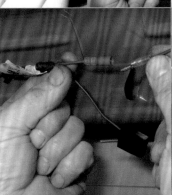

05 Having drilled our holes, we used pop-rivets to secure the plate (you could use self-tappers). The solenoid must be mounted vertically, or the push/pull plunger won't be able to operate properly.

06 Deciding where to drill the holes through our new plate for the solenoid required some inspired guesswork (or do I mean 'careful measuring' ?), but we go them close enough.

07 Now to wire it up, which is the easiest bit of all, thanks to that tailgate wiper we removed earlier. Testing with a multimeter revealed that the black wire was permanent live, and the blue was intermittent-live (for the intermittent rear wipe function). We cut the blue wire, then added a bullet and joined it to the green wire from our solenoid.

08 The blue wire from the solenoid got a ring terminal attached to it, and we earthed it using our plate and one of the solenoid mounting screws (or you could re-use the old earth point for the brown wire from the wiper motor). Working the rear wiper stalk (briefly) now opens the boot! Depending on your kit, you might need to swap the solenoid connections before you achieve success.

Tailgate **smoothing**

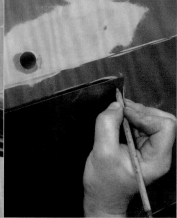

01 Don't imagine you can flush your Nova tailgate using just filler - you can try, but that amount of filler's bound to crack or fall out. The professional approach is to weld on a metal plate to fill the recess - here's one we trimmed up earlier, being offered in for the first time.

02 To make up the gap at the base of the tailgate, the new metal needs to have a folded-over edge, which will also need trimming to fit . . .

03 . . . and those top corners aren't completely square, so more careful marking and trimming is required. Remember, the idea of fitting metal is to use as little filler as poss, and the better the metal fits, the fewer skims will be needed.

04 A few little tack-welds are all that's really needed to secure the new metalwork - running a bead of weld round also runs the risk of warping the tailgate.

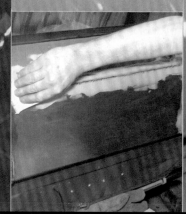

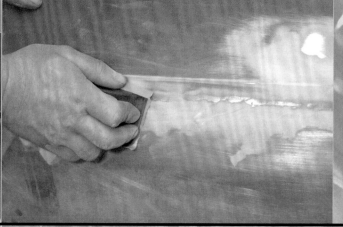

05 All that should be needed now is a light skim of filler around the edges . . .

06 . . . not forgetting the base (which will be very visible when the tailgate's open, remember, so do a good job) . . .

07 . . . and after a quick rub-down, the back end's ready for paint.

Bonnet **vents**

Once you've got your bodykit on, it's only natural you'll want a bonnet vent, isn't it? Respect. But this is one scary job to tackle yourself, unless you're really that good, or that brave. Plenty of options - you can get little louvres stamped in as well, to complement your Evo, Impreza, Integrale or F50 main vent. A more recent trend is the Focus WRC vent, and there's even been a feature car with a bonnet scoop from a (sensible) Kia Sedona people carrier! Truly, anything goes.

If you want to stay true to the Nova's roots, try fitting some Astra GSi bonnet vents, which really suit the Nova's angular lines (available cheap from Vauxhall dealers, oddly enough). These offer the dubious advantage of making you cut two small-ish holes in your bonnet, instead of one huuuge one. Hmmm.

Wheelarch mods

The law states that your wide rubber shouldn't be so wide that it sticks out from your arches, and the MOT crew will not be impressed if your new rubber's rubbing, either. This presents something of a problem, if you're determined to get 17s on, especially if the car's also having a radical drop job (like our Nova, on coilovers). If you've exhausted all possibilities with spacers (or wheels with a more friendly offset - see *'Wheels & tyres'*), further work will be needed.

Sometimes, all you need to stop those nasty grinding noises is a small amount of violence. Any non-vital protrusions into the under-arch area can be trimmed off or flattened with a hammer.

Serious wheelarch mods are best done at a bodyshop. Nova rear arches are very restricting (especially on Mk 1 cars), and most will have rust in by now, making modifying even trickier for the home DIYer. Usually, the best approach with problem arch lips is to trim off the offending metal, but on the rear arches, you'll seriously weaken your bodyshell if you just chop the lips off (the lips are spot-welded), as well as encouraging rust. Having the arches professionally rolled, using the proper tool, should only cost about £50 per arch (assuming they haven't also got rust or filler to deal with as well).

The best answer to arches which just aren't roomy enough is, of course, a wide-arch bodykit. And bank loans are so cheap these days.

01 For those of you who've never seen one before, this is the arch-rolling tool. Lots of ironmongery, adjustable bits and bobs, and a large nylon (plastic) wheel to do the actual rolling. The whole lot bolts to your wheel hub.

02 So the bodyshop doesn't end up cracking your expensive paint, before any bending of metal takes place, the whole arch lip is heated with a hot-air gun. This also makes the metal softer, and more 'persuadable'.

03 With the right kit (and the know-how to use it), rolling round arches is easy. Apply more pressure on the roller as you go, and the arch lip gets folded neatly up.

04 Nova arches are not completely round, however, so older methods are needed. Fortunately, Avon Customs are also experts on the old-fashioned way of doing things, like the hammer-and-dolly approach. The dolly is a shaped metal block, used to keep the outer skin of the arch flat while the inner lip is given 'the treatment' with a hammer. Skilful stuff.

05 That's the front arch dealt with, but most of you will want to sort the rear arches. The method's just the same, but arches crumbling with rust and filler won't roll, they'll disintegrate - check carefully. Heat first, to avoid wrecking the paint . . .

06 . . . then expertly tap up the arch lip, using at least a wooden block (if not a metal one) to stop the wing from being badly dented. If you don't think you're expert enough, practice on something else first - find a car in a quiet corner of a scrapyard, perhaps?

Respraying

Not happy with your Nova's 'hearing-aid beige' paint? Fancy something just a tad more head-turning than stomach-churning? There's really only one answer - and it's time to call in the pros. DIY is what we're all about, but we're not going to pretend this is something we'd undertake lightly ourselves - there's no such thing as a simple respray (not one that'll look good afterwards, at any rate). We just thought you'd like to see some of the stages involved.

01 Doing a full respray means getting all those door shuts and other areas of painted metal inside, but not the dash, seats, and carpets (unless you're going to completely gut the entire dash and interior afterwards). You can never do too much masking, and the lads at Avon Customs know this better than anyone.

02 Hang on, are you sure that's still our Nova under there? For a full respray, it's often better to remove fixed glass completely, rather than spend time masking it all up. That means windscreen, tailgate, and all the side glass. Still fancy having a go yourself?

Once the primer's on, a good bodyshop will apply a very thin coat of paint, called a 'guide coat'. This can be any colour, providing it contrasts the primer. As it's rubbed down, the guide coat shows any lumps in the primer, and highlights any mis-shaped panels (it also shows whether any bits haven't been rubbed down!).

07

With the main car ready for the top coat, we turn our attention to the bumpers, which deserve the same prep work as the body. Most of the screw-ups in any spray job can be traced directly back to poor preparation. Any plastics demand a special primer, to ensure the new paint will 'bite'.

08

On a two-tone car, you choose where to split the two colours, and a natural choice is the 'swage line' (crease) down the side of the car. But we don't want to give you that. We wanted our paint job to have graphic side-effects (geddit?), so here's our man Kevin masking up our 'claws' design.

09

03 Or how about now? You must get the bonnet shuts, but the only way to do it is masking the entire engine bay. This is the level of masking required for a successful respray (or have they just got shares in a brown paper company?).

04 Besides the filler needed to blend in the bodykit, our 12-year-old Nova had collected plenty of small dings in its life, along with the inevitable rust damage. All this filler has to be flatted down, washed, panel-wiped, and finally cleaned prior to spraying using tack-rags (net-like material, impregnated with resin - very sticky, picks up any bits).

05 On a red car which had seen so much (amateur) minor repair work in its history, a careful bodyshop won't just primer the shell - they seal it first. Never mind that it's the most hideous shade known to man - if you don't want the new paint to react, this is an essential step.

06 Rub the sealer coat down if necessary, then it's time for the primer. Several primer coats may be needed. If there's still any doubt about the bodywork, a bodyshop can choose to use a 'high-build' primer, which 'fills' any small imperfections in the paint below.

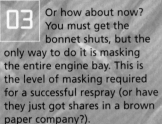

Making sure the paint surface is clean between steps is another often-overlooked essential item. Avon Customs use a water-based wash, as solvent-based products can lift the paint (or react with the next coat).

10

What's this? Another coat of primer? We're overdoing this, surely? No, despite it being white and looking like primer, this is actually a white base coat. The base coat makes a huge difference to the shade of the final topcoat, especially when you're working with proper custom paint like ours.

11

Mixing the paint is an important, but often overlooked, stage in any spraying process. Topcoats and lacquer especially have complex mixing ratios for the thinners, hardener, activator, and any 'flex' additives for bumpers and such - get it wrong, and even the best paint won't work.

12

The bottom half of the car's been sprayed a wicked shade of blood red, now here's the upper top coat (Galaxy Grey, one of the Shimrin range) going on. After several finishing 'flow' coats of lacquer, it should look the dog's when it turns out of the spray booth... We can't wait...

13

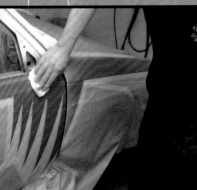

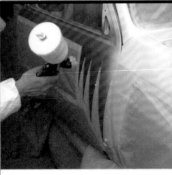

Lights & bulbs

Being scene

Lights - one of the easiest and coolest ways to trick up your Nova. Several options here, so we'll start at the front, and work back.

Headlights

Almost nothing influences the look of your Nova more than the front end, so the headlights play a crucial role.

What's available?

The popular cheap option is stick-on headlight 'brows', which do admittedly give the rather bland Nova front end a tougher look. The brows are best sprayed to match the car, before fitting - most are fitted using stick-on Velcro pads. Street-cred on the cheap, and (if you choose the Fox-style brows) a cheap alternative to a proper 'badboy' bonnet.

Another cheap option is again stick-on - this time, it's stick-on covers which give the twin-headlight look. This is basically a sheet of vinyl (shaped to the headlights, and colour-matched to your car) with two holes cut in it. Dead easy to fit, but dare we say, a bit tacky? Just our opinion. A cheap and simple way to get close to the Morette look.

If you want tinted headlights, you could try spray-tinting them, but go easy on the spray. Turning your headlights from clear glass to non-see-through is plain daft, even if it's done in the name of style. A light tint is quite effective, and gives you the chance to colour-match to your Nova. With tinted headlights, you'd be wise to tint those clear front indicators too, of course.

If you've got a Mk 1 Nova with orange indicator lenses, the clear ones became standard-fit from late 1990 onwards - a cheap upgrade, if you find some in a scrapyard.

Pub trivia

The popular twin-headlight look was derived from a cunning tweak first employed in the Touring Cars, years ago. Some teams homologated a twin-headlight unit, but for racing, turned one pair of the 'headlights' into air inlets, to direct air from the front of the car to brake ducts or into the engine air intakes, as required. Think about it - why else would the touring cars bother with headlight mods? Until recently, there were no night races!

Another 'headlight' option often featured on Novas actually belongs in the bodywork section - it's the 'badboy' bonnet. By cunningly welding-in a couple of triangular plates to your standard Nova bonnet, a bodyshop (or handy DIY-er) can create a really mean look, using just the standard lights. Excellent. A cheap alternative to a badboy bonnet is something first seen on Mk 2 Golfs - the badboy bonnet spoiler.

About this point, we'd normally start telling you about Morette twin headlights - very popular, and available for loads of top modded motors. But not, surprisingly, for Novas. Twin headlights for Novas are therefore rare, and when you look around, it's actually not that common to see any Novas with headlight mods *(Stop Press: Quad Conversions have just announced twin-headlight conversion kits for all Nova models)*. So what do you do if you really want your Nova to stand out? Try fitting standard headlights from another car altogether, or at least lose the front indicators. Definitely one for the bodyshop, but you won't beat it for effect.

Headlight
brows

01 This is the cheap 'n' cheerful approach, and it really doesn't get much simpler than this. This is even a mod you can 'undo' easily, if your MOT guy objects. So what do you get? Two bits of triangular plastic, and two strips of Velcro.

02 It's worth doing a quick trial fitting first, to make sure you've been sent the right ones, but unless you like black brows, the first job's painting. Which means preparation - don't assume those fresh-from-the-packet bits of plastic will take paint straight away. A little roughing-up with fine emery paper or Scotchbrite, then a wipe with meths or thinners, and we're off.

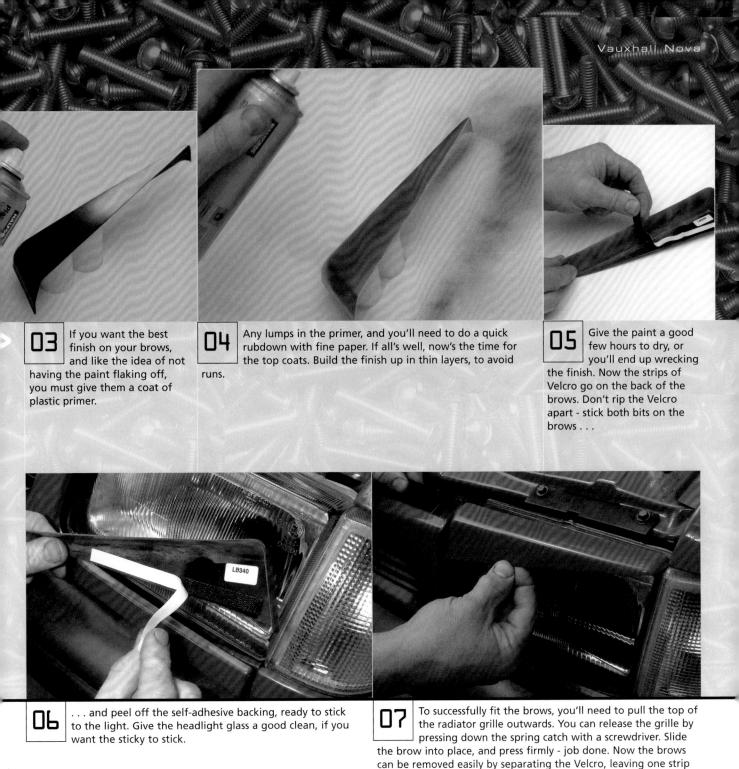

03 If you want the best finish on your brows, and like the idea of not having the paint flaking off, you must give them a coat of plastic primer.

04 Any lumps in the primer, and you'll need to do a quick rubdown with fine paper. If all's well, now's the time for the top coats. Build the finish up in thin layers, to avoid runs.

05 Give the paint a good few hours to dry, or you'll end up wrecking the finish. Now the strips of Velcro go on the back of the brows. Don't rip the Velcro apart - stick both bits on the brows . . .

06 . . . and peel off the self-adhesive backing, ready to stick to the light. Give the headlight glass a good clean, if you want the sticky to stick.

07 To successfully fit the brows, you'll need to pull the top of the radiator grille outwards. You can release the grille by pressing down the spring catch with a screwdriver. Slide the brow into place, and press firmly - job done. Now the brows can be removed easily by separating the Velcro, leaving one strip still on the light for refitting.

Front indicators

Removal

This isn't where we tell you how to remove your front indicators - you've got an ordinary Haynes manual for that. We're telling you here how to deal with the hole left after you've taken them out. First, wrap a piece of card around the hole, and mark the shape required inside . . .

01

. . . transfer the card shape to metal, then after some rolling and folding around suitable curved objects . . .

02

. . . we get this - a metal shape which fits the indicator recess a treat.

03

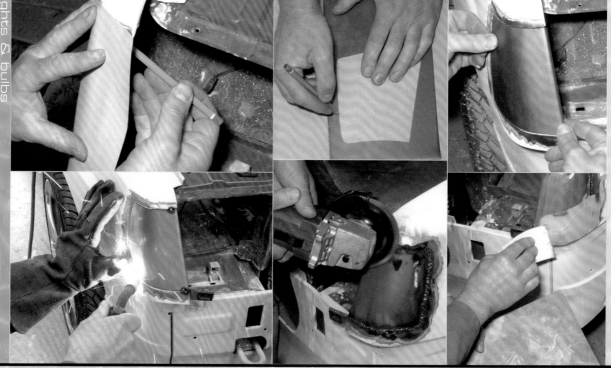

04 Weld that plate into place. Of course, if you've got a tame bodyshop at your disposal, you could get them to create any front-end look you desire. In theory, the only limit is your imagination.

05 Grind down the welds . . .

06 . . . then blend the new metal into the wing with a skim of filler. Quite a subtle mod, but as we all know, modding's all about getting the details right.

Refitting

Having no indicators is a top way to invite a pull. So we're fitting some new indicators into the new front bumper. But where, exactly? Well, they can't be too low, too close together, or too close to other lights (see the ABC Design tech tips page on their website). Measure and mark the light centres . . .

01

. . . then place the new light on, and mark its outline for drilling. No, these are not side repeaters - if they were, they'd be illegal to use as indicators, because side reps only have 5-watt bulbs in. These are motorbike fairing indicators, which look the same, but have 23-watt bulbs (available from MPS).

02

Time to be brave, and make some no-going-back holes in your expensive new fibreglass. Just for the record, our bumper's upside-down in this shot - we are fitting these indicators near the top, not the bottom.

03

In it goes, secured in place by a large plastic nut which threads on from behind. Looking good - but having them working is what really counts - time for some wiring-up.

04

05 No reason to be shy, wiring these things up - you can't go wrong. The new indicators have a red and a black wire sticking out the back, which you just join onto some new flex, and feed up behind the headlights.

06 Time for a little surgery on the old indicator wiring plug . . .

07 . . . then we join the new flex to the old wires. If you want to do it right, the red wire from the new light goes to the black/white wire from the car (but it should work, either way round).

Headlight
bulbs

Make your Nova look like an Audi or a Beemer, the easy way. Bad-weather and 'blue' headlight bulbs are an excellent way to boost headlight performance, and are perfect with other blue LED accessories like washer jets and number plate screws. The blue bulbs you buy in most accessory shops will be legal, 60W/55 bulbs, and are no problem. Don't be tempted to buy the mega-powerful bulbs you can get from rallying suppliers (any over 60W/55 are in fact illegal for use in this country) - as with all other non-standard lights, the boys in blue will love pulling you over for a word about this, so ask before you buy.

Even if you're not bothered about the legality of over-powerful bulbs (and you might well argue that being more powerful is the whole point of fitting), there's other problems with monster bulbs. First, they give off masses of heat, and loads of people have melted their headlights before they found this out. Don't believe us? Try fitting some 100W/90s and put your hand in front of the light, close to the glass. Hot, isn't it? The excess heat these bulbs generate will damage the headlights eventually, either by warping the lens, burning off the reflective coating, or melting the bulbholders. Maybe all three.

The increased current required to work big bulbs has also been known to melt wiring (this could lead to a fire) and will almost certainly burn out your light switch. There's no headlight relay fitted as standard, so the wiring and switch were designed to cope only with the current drawn by standard-wattage bulbs; if you're going for high power, a relay must be fitted (much as you'd have to, to fit foglights or spots).

Front fog/spotlights

Extra lights are a must on the Nova, if only to give some features to the rather bland front end. Most bodykits (and all GSi bumpers) have the facility for one or more pairs of lights, so it's gotta be done, really.

If you're fitting fogs, they must be wired in to work on dipped-beam only, so they must go off on main beam. The opposite is true for spotlights. Pop out the main light switch (or pull down the fusebox) and check for a wire which is live only when the dipped beams are on. The Haynes wiring diagrams will help here - on our Nova, it was a white wire we needed, fed by fuse number 2 (pull the fuse to check you've got the right wire).

Once you've traced your wire, this is used as the live (+ve) feed for your foglight relay. Did we mention you'll need a relay? You'll need a relay. A four-pin one will do nicely. Splice a new wire onto the feed you've found, and feed it through to the engine (there's a huge bulkhead grommet inside the passenger footwell). Decide where you'll mount the relay (next to the battery seems obvious) and connect the new wire onto terminal 86.

For your other relay connections, you'll need an earth to terminal 85 (plenty of good earth spots around the battery). You

also need a fused live supply (buy a single fuseholder, and a 15 or 20 amp fuse should be enough) and take a new feed straight off the battery positive connection - this goes to terminal 30 on your relay.

Terminal 87 on your relay is the live output to the fogs - split this into two wires, and feed it out to where the lights will go. Each foglight will also need an earth - either pick a point on the body next to each light, or run a pair of wires back to the earth point you used earlier for your relay. Simple, innit?

With the wiring sorted, now you'd best fit the lights. Over to you. Most decent foglights come with some form of mounting brackets. To look their best, hopefully your new lights can slot into pre-cut holes in your new front bumper/bodykit.

To connect the wiring to the lights, you'll probably need to splice on your wires from terminal 87 to the new wiring plugs which came with the lights - not too difficult. Plug it all together, and test - you should now have some rather funky fogs!

Side repeaters

There's a range of 'standard' colours that side reps come in, but most people go for clear or smoked, to colour-code with their rear clusters. Clear lenses can be coloured using special paint, but the paint must be applied lightly and evenly to the lens, or this will invite an easily-avoided MOT failure. Bodyshops can colour clear lenses to the exact shade of your car, by mixing a little paint with loads of lacquer - very trick.

Side repeaters must still show an orange light, and must be sufficiently bright (not easy to judge, and no two coppers have the same eyesight!). The stock bulbs are clear, so make sure you get orange bulbs too. You can actually get orange bulbs that look clear, to avoid the 'fried egg' effect. Alternatively, get LED side repeaters, like we did on our Fiesta project car.

Besides the various colour effects, side repeaters are available in many different shapes. Any shape other than standard goes, really - one popular choice for now are the Focus-style triangular lights, but the standard Nova items are so dull, even oval repeaters are an improvement.

Or how about ditching the repeaters altogether, and get some tasty Merc-style mirrors, with side reps built-in? You could smooth your front wings, then...

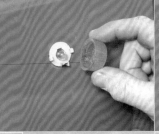

01 Fitting new side repeaters isn't actually that easy on Novas, so pay attention. Getting rid of the old orange lens is about the simplest part - it just twists off.

02 Now you have to release the bulbholder from the wing, and it's not keen on coming out. We're not-re-using the old bulbholder, so some damage is acceptable here (as long as it's not to the paintwork). We used a small screwdriver to release the tag at the base of the light (push upwards), and then broke the top lug getting the rest out. Oh well.

The old bulbholder wiring now gets chopped, and the new one connected on. But wait - if you cut both wires at once, they drop back inside the wing, and make life very difficult. Our advice? Chop one wire at a **03** time, and connect it straight onto the new light.

It doesn't matter which wire goes where, but a good connection is important - these lights are stuck on, and un-sticking them won't **04** be easy, so do a good job.

Check that the new orange bulb is fitted before you stick the light in place, or you'll feel particularly stupid. Most lenses just twist **05** off.

Before sticking the light in place, check that it actually works. Oh, and cleaning the paint around the hole might not be a bad idea, if you want the light to stay stuck. When all's well, peel off the backing and stick the light in position. Press it home without **06** cracking the plastic lens.

Rear lights

Oh dear - not much choice here, and what there is - often isn't legal (no rear fogs or reflectors). Mr. Plod is well-informed on this point, and those sexy rear lights are way too big a come-on for him to ignore.

You can buy stick-on reflectors, but these are about as sexy as NHS specs (you'd have to be pretty unlucky to get pulled just for having no rear reflectors, but don't say we didn't warn you). And what happens if your car gets crunched, parked at night with no reflectors fitted? Will your insurance try and refuse to pay out? You betcha.

The rear foglight problem could perhaps be solved by spraying the clear bulb itself red (you can also buy ready-made red bulbs), but it won't fool every MOT man. Other ideas? Cut a hole in your new rear bumper, and find a cool-looking rear fog to mount inside (the Peugeot 206 unit's pretty sweet). If you don't mind a bit extra work, source an exhaust tailpipe trim roughly the same size as your existing pipe, mount it on the right-hand side of the car, and fit a round foglight inside the end.

The best solution? Only buy UK-legal lights (if you can find some) or lightly spray-tint your standard units. Any questions on light legality? Why not check out the ABC Design website tech tips page, at www.abcdesignltd.com - if you've any questions after that, you can E-mail them. We're so good to you.

Spray-tinting lights

01 Spraying your rear lights is a top idea if funds are too tight for replacements, or if you simply don't fancy paying loadsamoney for illegal lights which also don't fit very well. The first job before spraying is to get the old lights clean - we used meths, which works well enough to get off all the old silicone products and polish residue.

02 As with most spray-painting, the trick is to get the stuff on evenly, which means applying light coats. Blasting it on too thick will give you the runs, which is never pleasant.

03 How thick is too thick? Well, this is what one of our standard Nova lights looked like, after a couple of light coats. This might be too subtle a look for you, but don't go too mad if you want to avoid attention from the Law.

Smoked rear lights

01 First, those gakky old rear lights have to go. Open the boot, and unclip this cover . . .

02 . . . for access to the bulbholder, which detaches by pressing the side lugs inwards, top and bottom.

03 Now there's two bolts to remove (one top and bottom) . . .

04 . . . before the light parts company from the car. It might be 'stuck' on, if it's been there a while. Persuade it.

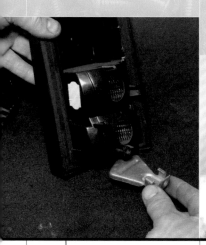

05 If you were wondering whether these funny metal brackets are important or not - trust us, they are. If yours didn't actually fall off your old lights, unclip them now and transfer them to your new lights.

06 Refitting your new lights is much the same as removing the old ones - a reversal of removal, in fact. Now where have I read that before? Not all aftermarket lights are this good a fit (no matter how much you paid), so check they're waterproof, and apply a little silicone sealant where necessary.

07 And finally - a picture showing fitting the rear reflectors supplied in the box. We know you probably won't, but they don't look that hideous, especially on a red car like ours.

Tricks 'n' tips
If you drop the rear light mounting bolts down inside the back of the car, it won't make your day. Kit yourself out with a telescopic magnetic pick-up tool, available for a couple of quid from any cheap-jack shop, car boot sale or market stall, and be prepared.

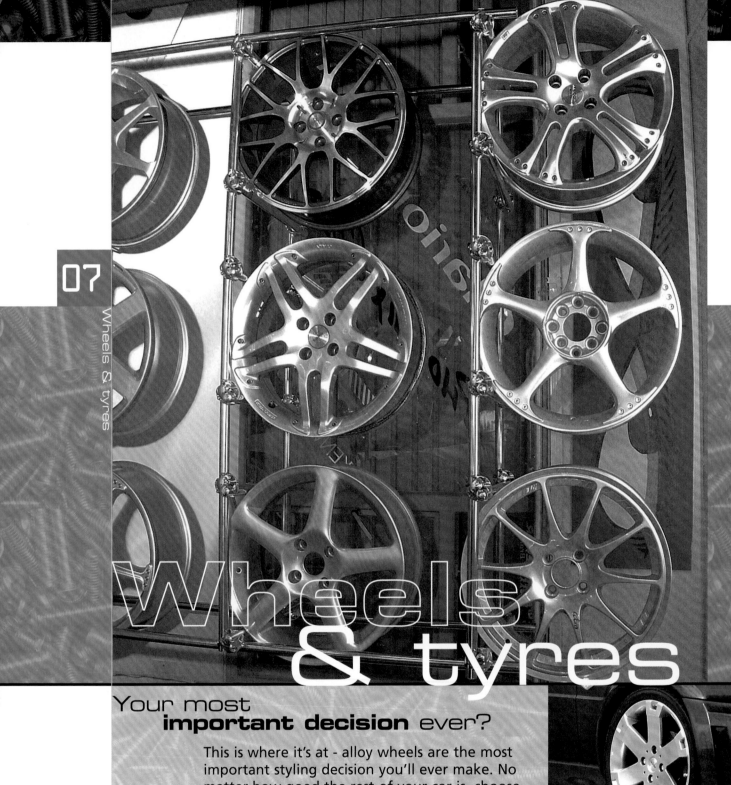

Wheels & tyres

Your most important decision ever?

This is where it's at - alloy wheels are the most important styling decision you'll ever make. No matter how good the rest of your car is, choose the wrong rims and your car will never look right. Choose a good set and you're already well on the way to creating a sorted motor. Take your time and pick wisely - wheel fashions change like the weather, and you don't want to spend shedloads on a set of uncool alloys.

None of the standard alloys cut it, and should very quickly be dumped. Advice on which particular wheels to buy would be a waste of space, since the choice is so huge, and everyone will have their own favourites. For what it's worth, though, the likes of Speedline Alessio, Mille Miglia Spider, 100+ Phantom and Wolfrace Voodoo all look sweet on a Nova, but go for something a little more original by all means. We chose the new Wolfrace Urban Racer wheel for our project car, and in a 17, it looks huge. Beyond those words of dubious wisdom, you're on your own - car colour and your own chosen other mods will dictate what will look right on your car.

One 'problem' with the Nova, and with many other Vauxhalls, is the wheel offset. Most normal cars fall somewhere in the mid-30s to early 40s, but the Nova has a peculiar offset of 49. This can limit your choice of wheels somewhat, so make sure you mention they're for a Nova at an early stage in negotiations (if the person you speak to sounds a bit thick, 'remind' them of the offset problem). Many wheel manufacturers don't actually recognise the 49 offset, and insist on supplying Nova wheels in something like a 45 or 46. Don't go any lower than a 45 offset, as this makes the wheel 'stick out' more, and your arches won't just have to be 'trimmed' - they'll be butchered! Fitting wheels with the wrong offset may also do unpleasant things to the handling.

Lead us not into
temptation

Before we go any further into which wheels are right for you, a word about insurance and security. Fitting tasty alloys to your Nova is one of the first and best ways to make it look cool. It follows, therefore, that someone with dubious morals might very well want to unbolt them from your car while you're not around, and make their own car look cool instead (or simply sell them, to buy spot cream and drugs).

Since fitting a set of top alloys is one of the easiest bolt-on ways to trick up any car, it's no surprise that the market in stolen alloys is as alive and kicking as it currently is - your wheels will also look very nice on any number of other cars, and the owners of those cars would love to own them at a fraction of the price you paid... It's not unknown for a set of wheels to go missing just for the tyres - if you've just splashed out on a set of fat Yokohamas, your wheels look even more tempting, especially if you've got a common-size tyre.

Tell your insurance company what you're fitting. What will probably happen is that they'll ask for the exact details, and possibly a photo of the car with the wheels on. Provided you're happy to then accept that they won't cover the extra cost of the wheels if they get nicked (or if the whole car goes), you may find you're not charged a penny more, especially if you've responsibly fitted some locking wheel bolts. Not all companies are the same, though - some charge an admin fee, and yes, some will start loading your premium. If you want the rims covered, it's best to talk to a company specialising in modified cars, or you could be asked to pay out the wheel cost again in premiums. The daftest thing you can do is say nothing, and hope they don't find out - we don't want to go on about this, but there are plenty of documented cases where insurance companies have refused to pay out altogether, purely on the basis of undeclared alloy wheels.

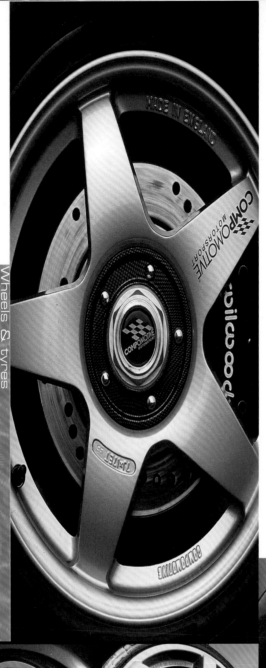

How **cheap** are you?

Hopefully, you'll be deciding which wheels to go for based on how they look, not how much they cost, but inevitably (for most ordinary people at least), price does become a factor. Surely buying a cheaper wheel must have its pitfalls? Well, yes - and some of them may not be so obvious.

Inevitably, cheaper wheels = lower quality, but how does this manifest itself? Cheap wheels are often made from alloys which are more 'porous' (a bit like a sponge, they contain microscopic holes and pockets of air). Being porous has two main disadvantages for a wheel, the main one being that it won't be able to retain air in the tyres. The days of tyres with inner tubes are long gone (and it's illegal to fit tubes to low-profile tyres), so the only thing keeping the air in are the three 'walls' of the tyre, with the fourth 'wall' being the inside of the wheel itself. If you like keeping fit by pumping up your tyres every morning, go ahead - the rest of us will rightly regard this as a pain, and potentially dangerous (running tyres at low pressure will also scrub them out very effectively - what was that about saving money?).

Porous wheels also have difficulty in retaining their paint or lacquer finish, with flaking a known problem, sometimes after only a few months. This problem is made worse by the fact that porous wheels are much harder to clean (brake dust seems to get ingrained into the wheels more easily) - and the more you scrub, the more the lacquer comes off.

The final nail in the coffin for cheap wheels is that they tend to corrode (or 'fizz') more. This not only looks crap if visible from outside, but if you get corrosion between the wheel and the hub, you won't even be able to take the damn things off! Yes seriously, grown men with all the specialist tools in the world at their disposal will be scratching their heads when faced with wheels which simply **will not** come off.

Tricks 'n' tips
Whenever you have your wheels off, clean off any hub corrosion with wet-and-dry paper, then coat the hub mating surfaces with copper (brake) grease. There's no way you'll suffer stuck-on wheels again. 'Proper' alloys come with a plastic collar which fits inside the wheel - an essential item, it centres the wheel properly and reduces wheel-to-hub corrosion. Do not chuck out.

Buying an established, popular make of wheel has another hidden benefit, too. Choosing a popular wheel will mean more suppliers will stock it, and the manufacturers themselves will make plenty of them. And if you're unlucky enough to have an accident (maybe a slide on a frosty road) which results in non-repairable damage to one wheel, you're going to need a replacement. If you've chosen the rarest wheels on the planet, you could be faced with having to replace a complete set of four, to get them all matching... A popular wheel, even if it's a few years old, might be easier to source, even second-hand.

The Sunday morning ritual
It's a small point maybe, but you'll obviously want your wheels to look as smart as possible, as often as possible - so how easy are they going to be to clean?

The real multi-spokers and BBS-style 'wires' are hell to clean - a fiddly toothbrush job - do you really want that much aggro every week? The simpler the design, the easier time you'll have. For those who like nothing better than counting their spokes, though, there are several really good products out there to make your life less of a cleaning nightmare.

Tricks 'n' tips
It's worth applying a bit of car polish to the wheels - provided it's good stuff, and you can be sure of getting the residue out of the corners and edges, a polished wheel will always be easier to clean off than an unpolished one. You can also buy waxes which are tailor-made for the job.

Bolt from the blues
Don't forget about locking wheel bolts (see *'Hold on to your wheels'* further on) - bargain these into a wheel/tyre package if you're buying new.

A word of warning about re-using your existing wheel bolts, should you be upgrading from steel wheels. Most steel-wheel bolts are not suitable for use with alloy wheels (and vice-versa, incidentally). Make sure you ask about this when buying new wheels, and if necessary, bargain a set of bolts into the price. Most bolts for use with alloys will have a washer fitted, for two very good reasons - 1) the bolt will pull through the wheel hole without it, and 2) to protect the wheel finish.

Another point to watch for is that the new wheel bolts are the correct length for your fitment, taking into account whether you've fitted spacers or not. Bolts that are too short are obviously dangerous, and ones that are too long can foul on drum brakes, and generally get in the way of any turning activities. If in doubt ask the retailer for advice. Always check that the wheels turn freely once they've been put on, and investigate any strange noises before you go off for a pose.

Tricks 'n' tips
If you're keeping a steel wheel as your spare (or even if you're keeping an original alloy), keep a set of your original wheel bolts in a bag inside the spare wheel. Locking bolts especially might be too long when fitted to a thin steel wheel, and might jam up your brakes!

Other options
If you're on a really tight budget, and perhaps own a real 'basic' model Nova, don't overlook the possibility of fitting a discarded set of standard alloys, possibly from another Vauxhall entirely (Tigra wheels are a good bet) - check that the stud pattern's the same, obviously (Calibra/ Cavalier Turbo and Vectra rims are five-stud).

If the Vauxhall range of wheels is too limiting, don't be too quick buying (for instance) alloys suitable for other makes altogether. For instance, some Honda, Renault and VW alloys have the same stud pattern (4x100), so they'll go on alright, but the offset is more than a bit different (like, 38 for VeeDub rims, where it should be at least 45 for a Vauxhall - have fun). In the case of some alloys (Ford, for example), the stud pattern may be only fractionally different (4x108), but if you put these on, the strain on the bolts is too great, and they can fracture or work themselves loose...

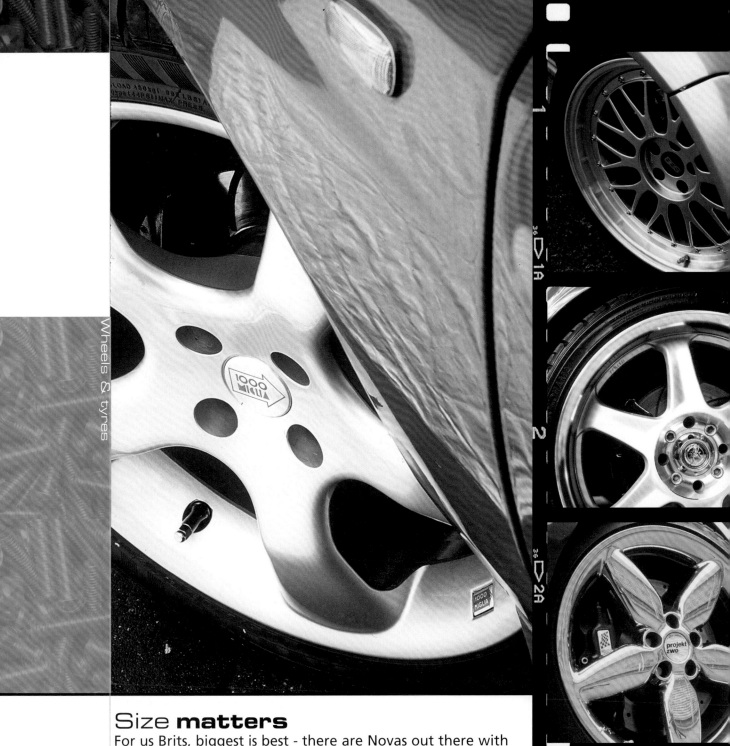

Size **matters**

For us Brits, biggest is best - there are Novas out there with 18s and up. And yes, the mags all say you can't be seen with anything less than 17-inchers. In Europe, meanwhile, they're mad for the small-wheel look, still with seriously dropped suspension of course.

On many small cars (the Nova included), 15-inch rims are the biggest you can sensibly fit before you really have to start looking at sorting the arches, but they'll still improve the handling (unlike 17s, which often have the exact opposite effect!). Keep the wheel width to 6.5J as well, if you can - 7J rims will lead to headaches. Going bigger than 15s, we wouldn't rule out the possibility of some arch massaging even on 16s, especially if they're 7Jx16s on a Mk 1 Nova, and you're determined to slam the car down. Don't get too suckered into the whole 17-inch rims thing - if you slam the car down, modern 15s and 16s look nearly as good, and are much less work.

The only standard Novas that'll take 17s easily are the Mk 2 models (late 1990 onwards), thanks to their 5 mm wider rear arches. We're going for 17s on our Mk 2 Nova because we're brave, and we've got a decent bodyshop on the case if it all goes Pete Tong.

Novas will only really have problems on the rear, running 17s. It's vital that your rims are as close to the ideal 49 offset as possible - much less than this figure, and there'll be major rear arch work required. Though you won't find many rims with an offset higher than 49, bear in mind that a higher offset will pull the wheels inwards, where they'll rub on your suspension. Sorting the rear arches means having them rolled at a bodyshop - trying this yourself will probably result in distorting the rear wings and/or cracking the paint, which will also result in a trip to see the pros. If your rear arches have already suffered rust and filler (most have, by now), DIY arch-rolling will be a disaster from the start. Trimming the excess rear arch lip isn't an option either, as you'll be cutting off vital spot welds which give strength to the rear of the car, and giving rust an easy chance to take hold.

We like a challenge

To be honest, successfully fitting big wheels in combination with lowered suspension is one of life's major challenges.

As much as anything, tyre width is what ultimately leads to problems, not so much the increased wheel diameter.

If the tyres are simply too wide (or with wheels the wrong offset), they will first of all rub on the suspension strut (ie on the inside edge of the tyre). Also, the inside edges may rub on the arches on full steering lock - check left and right. Rubbing on the inside edges can be cured by fitting offsets or spacers between the wheel and hub, which effectively pull the wheel outwards, 'spacing' it away from its normal position (this also has the effect of widening the car's track, which may improve the on-limit handling - or not). Fitting large offsets must be done using special longer wheel studs, as the standard ones may only engage the bolts by a few threads, which is highly dangerous.

Rubbing on the outside edges is a simple case of wheelarch lip fouling, which must be cured by rolling up (or trimming off) the wheelarch return edge, and other mods. If you've gone for REALLY wide tyres, or have already had to fit offsets, the outer edge of the tyre will probably be visible outside the wheelarch, and this is a no-no (it's illegal, and you must cover it up!).

The other trick with fitting big alloys is of course to avoid the 'Nova 4x4 off-road' look, which you will achieve remarkably easily just by popping on a set of 17s with standard suspension. The massive increase in ground clearance is fine for Farmer Palmer, but your 'fistable' arches won't win much admiration at cruises. Overcoming this problem by lowering can be a matter almost of inspired guesswork, as much as anything (see 'Suspension').

Speedo error? Or not?

One side-effect of fitting large wheels is that your car will go slower. Yes, really - or at least - it will appear to go slower, due to the effects of the mechanically-driven speedometer.

As the wheel diameter increases, so does its circumference (distance around the outside) - this means that, to travel say one mile, a large wheel will turn less than a smaller wheel. Because the speedometer is driven from the gearbox final drive, the apparent vehicle speed is actually based on the number of complete revolutions of the wheel. Therefore, for a given actual speed, since a larger-diameter wheel will be turning at a slower rate than a smaller wheel, and the method for

measuring speed is the rate of wheel rotation, a car with larger wheels will produce a lower speedo reading than one with smaller wheels - but it's NOT actually going any slower in reality. So don't worry if you think you've reduced your Nova's performance somehow with the monster rims, 'cos you 'aven't.

With the ever-increasing number of those lovely grey/yellow roadside boxes with a nasty surprise inside, spare a thought to what this speedo error could mean in the real world. If (like most people) you tend to drive a wee bit over the posted 30s and 40s, your real speed on 17s could be a bit more than the bit more you thought you were doing already, and you could get an unexpected flash to ruin your day. What we're saying is, don't drive any faster, to compensate for the lower speedo reading. Actually, the speedo error effect on 17s really is tiny at around-town speeds, and only becomes a factor over 70. But then, Officer, you couldn't possibly have been going over 70, could you? Officer?

Jargon explained

Rolling Radius - You may have come across the term 'rolling radius', which is the distance from the wheel centre to the outer edge of the tyre, or effectively, half the overall diameter. The rolling radius obviously increases with wheel size, but up to a point, the effects are masked by fitting low-profile tyres, with 'shorter' sidewalls. Above 16-inch rims, however, even low-profiles can't compensate, and the rolling radius keeps going up.

PCD - this isn't a banned substance, it's your Pitch Circle Diameter, which relates to the spacing of your wheel holes, or 'stud pattern'. It is expressed by the diameter of a notional circle which passes through the centre of your wheel studs, and the number of studs/bolts. Unlike the offset, the PCD often isn't stamped onto the wheels, so assessing it is really a matter of eyeing-up and trying them on the studs - the wheel should go on easily, without binding, if the stud pattern is correct. On a Nova, the PCD is 100 mm with four studs, which is given as 100/4, or 4 x 100.

Offset - this is determined by the distance from the wheel mounting face in relation to its centre-line. The offset figure is denoted by ET (no, I mustn't), which stands for einpress tiefe in German, or pressed-in depth (now I KNOW you're asleep). The lower the offset, the more the wheels will stick out. Fitting wheels with the wrong offset might bring the wheel into too-close contact with the brake and suspension bits, or with the arches. Very specialised area - seek advice from the wheel manufacturers if you're going for a very radical size (or even if you're not). The correct offset for Novas of all sizes is ET 49.

Hold on to your wheels

The minute you bang on your wicked alloys, your car becomes a target. People see the big wheels, and automatically assume you've also got a major stereo, seats and other goodies - all very tempting, but that involves breaking in, and you could have an alarm. Pinching the wheels themselves, now that's a doddle - a few tools, some bricks or a couple of well-built mates to lift the car, and it's easy money.

The trouble with fitting big wheels is that they're only screwed on, and are just as easily screwed off, if you don't make life difficult for 'em. If you're unlucky enough to have to park outside at night (ie no garage), you could wake up one morning to a car that's *literally* been slammed on the deck! Add to this the fact that your car isn't going anywhere without wheels, plus the damage which will be done to exhaust, fuel and brake pipes from dropping on its belly, and it's suddenly a lot worse than losing a grand's worth of wheels and tyres...

The market and demand for stolen alloys is huge, but since most people don't bother having them security-marked in any way, once a set of wheels disappears, they're almost impossible to trace. Thieves avoid security-marked (or 'tattooed') wheels (or at least it's a pretty good

deterrent) - and it needn't look hideous!

When choosing that car alarm, try and get one with an 'anti-jacking' feature, because thieves hate it. This is sometimes now called 'anti-tilt', to avoid confusion with anti-hijacking. Imagine a metal saucer, with a metal ball sitting on a small magnet in the centre. If the saucer tilts in any direction, the ball rolls off the magnet, and sets off the alarm. Highly sensitive, and death to anyone trying to lift your car up for the purpose of removing the wheels - as we said, the crims are not fond of this feature at all. Simply having an alarm with anti-shock is probably not good enough, because a careful villain will probably be able to work so as not to create a strong enough vibration to trigger it - mind you, it's a whole lot better than nothing, especially if set to maximum sensitivity.

Locking nuts/bolts

Locking wheel bolts will be effective as a deterrent to the inexpert thief (kids, in other words), but will probably only slow down the pro.

Thieves want to work quickly, and will use large amounts of cunning and violence to deprive you of your stuff. If you fit a cheap set of locking bolts, they'll use a hammer and thin chisel to crack off the locking bolt heads. Some bolts can easily be defeated by hammering a socket onto the bolt head, and undoing the locking bolt as normal, while some of the key-operated bolts are so pathetic they can be beaten using a small screwdriver. So - choose the best bolts you can, but don't assume they'll prevent your wheels from disappearing. Insurance companies seem to like 'em - perhaps it shows a responsible attitude, or something…

There seems to be some debate as to whether it's okay to fit more than one set of locking bolts to a car - some people we know value their wheels so highly that they've fitted four sets of bolts - in other words, they've completely replaced all the standard bolts! The feeling against doing this is that the replacement locking bolts may not be made to the same standard as factory originals, and while it's okay to fit one set on security grounds, fitting more than that is dangerous on safety grounds (bolt could fail, wheel falls off, car in ditch, owner in hospital…).

Obviously, you must carry the special key or tool which came with your bolts with you at all times, in case of a puncture, or if you're having any other work done, such as new brakes or tyres. The best thing to do is rig this onto your keyring, so that it's with you, but not left in the car. The number of people who fit locking bolts and then leave the key to them cunningly 'hidden' in the glovebox or the boot… You don't leave a spare set of car keys in your glovebox as well, do you?

Jacking up

You might think you know all about this, but do you really?

Okay, so you know you need a jack and wheelbrace (or socket and ratchet), but where are the jacking points? If you want to take more than one wheel off at a time, have you got any axle stands, and where do they go? If you've only ever had wheels and tyres fitted by a garage, chances are you're actually a beginner at this. It's surprising just how much damage you can do to your car, and to yourself, if you don't know what you're doing - and the worst thing here is to think you know, when you don't…

What to use

If you don't already have one, invest in a decent hydraulic (trolley) jack. This is way more use than the standard car jack, which is really only for emergencies, and which isn't really stable enough to rely on. Lifting and lowering the car is so much easier with a trolley jack, and you'll even look professional. Trolley jacks have a valve, usually at the rear, which must be fully tightened (using the end of the jack handle) before raising the jack, and which is carefully loosened to lower the car down - if it's opened fully, the car will not so much sink as plummet!

Axle stands are placed under the car, once it's been lifted using the jack. Stands are an important accessory to a trolley jack, because once they're in place, there's no way the car can come down on you - remember that even a brand new trolley jack could creep down (if you haven't tightened the valve), or could even fail completely under load (if it's a cheap one, or knackered, or both).

Under NO circumstances use bricks, wooden blocks or anything else which you have to pile up, to support the car - this is just plain stupid. Novas are small cars, sure, but they still weigh quite enough to damage you convincingly if they land on top of you - if you don't believe us, try crawling under it when it's resting on a few poxy bricks.

Where to do it

Only ever jack the car up on a solid, level surface (ideally, a concrete or tarmac driveway, or quiet car park). If there's even a slight slope, the car's likely to move (maybe even roll away) as the wheels are lifted off the ground. Jacking up on a rough or gravelled surface is not recommended, as the jack could slip at an awkward moment - such as when you've just got underneath…

How to do it - jacking up the front

Before jacking up the front of the car, pull the handbrake on firmly (you can also chock the rear wheels, if you don't trust your handbrake).

If you're taking the wheels off, loosen the wheel bolts before you start jacking up the car. It's easily forgotten, but you'll look pretty silly trying to undo the wheel bolts with the front wheels spinning in mid-air.

We'll assume you've got a trolley jack. The next question is - where to stick it? Up front, there's a chunky-looking square-section chassis member running back along the car, inside the sill. If you use this for jacking, always put a flat offcut of wood on your jack head first, to spread the load. You can jack on the sill jacking points (which are marked by little notches on the sill edges), but it's better to leave those for your axle stands.

Once you've got the car up, pop an axle stand or two under the front sill jacking points. These points are shown by having a notch

cut in the sill flange, and this is the only part of the sill it's safe to jack under or rest the car on. With the stands in place, you can lower the jack so the car's weight rests on the stands. For maximum safety, spread the car's weight between the stands and the jack - don't lower the jack completely unless it's needed elsewhere.

I'm sure we don't need to tell you this, but don't jack up the car, or stick stands under the car, anywhere other than kosher jacking and support points. This means - not the floorpan or the sump (you'll cave it in), not the suspension bits (not stable), and not under the brake/fuel pipes (ohmigawd).

How to do it - jacking up the rear

When jacking up the rear of the car, place wooden chocks in front of the front wheels to stop it rolling forwards, and engage first gear.

If you're taking the wheels off, you don't have to loosen the wheel bolts before lifting the car, but you'll be relying on your handbrake to hold the wheels while you wrestle with the bolts. Much cooler (and safer) to loosen the rear wheel bolts on the ground too.

Jacking and supporting the Nova back-end is a little trickier. Have a good look under there before making your choice. The rear 'axle' running across the car is a possible jacking point, but it's made awkward by its triangular shape, so you will need a block of wood here, or the jack will slip.

Although Vauxhall certainly wouldn't recommend it, you can jack under the rear shock absorber mounting, on the suspension arm - just go slowly, as the arm will move and compress the suspension as the jack rises. Jacking under the suspension arm is obviously no use if you're working on the rear suspension itself.

In the end, you won't beat the sill jacking point, but you'll have to play a bit clever. Arrange the jack and axle stand as close together as possible, and use a block of wood to spread the load from the jack head. Place the axle stand head right under the notch in the sill, like we've done, and you'll be fine - leave the jack under there as well, if you can.

Remember not to put your axle stands under any pipes, the spare wheel well, or the fuel tank, and you should live to see another Christmas.

Finally…

As far as possible, don't leave the car unattended once it has been lifted, particularly if kids are playing nearby - football goes under your car, they go under to get it, knock the jack, car falls… it would almost certainly be your fault.

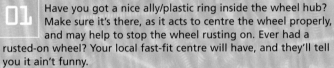

01 Have you got a nice ally/plastic ring inside the wheel hub? Make sure it's there, as it acts to centre the wheel properly, and may help to stop the wheel rusting on. Ever had a rusted-on wheel? Your local fast-fit centre will have, and they'll tell you it ain't funny.

02 Even with the plastic ring of confidence, the metal bits can still corrode on. Equip yourself with some copper brake grease, and smear some on the hub. It's not a bad idea if some of that grease finds its way onto the wheel bolts, too.

03 Pop the wheel onto the hub, then on with the nicely-greased bolts, and tighten up as far as possible by hand.

Changing wheels

04 You have got some locking bolts, haven't you? Keep your locking tool somewhere safe, but not obvious. The glovebox is convenient, but way too obvious!

05 Always tighten the wheel bolts securely (ideally, to the correct torque - 90 Nm). This can only be done properly with the wheel back on the ground. Don't over-tighten the bolts, or you'll never get them undone at the roadside, should you have a flat! D'oh!

06 If you've really blown some serious cash on your new rims, why not treat them to a special protected socket for tightening the bolts? Companies like Draper do a set of special sockets with plastic protector sleeves fitted, to stop the metal scratching your fine alloys. Makes sense to us.

Always nice to see a good brand of tyre on a decent alloy. How cool do cheap tyres look?

Tyres

To some people, tyres are just round and black - oh, and they're nearly all expensive, and don't last long enough. When you're buying a new set of wheels, most centres will quote prices with different tyres - buying a tyred-up set of rims is convenient, and usually quite good value, too.

Some people try and save money by fitting 'remould' or 're-manufactured' tyres. These aren't always the bargain they appear to be - experience says there's no such thing as a good cheap tyre, with wheel balancing problems a well-known downside, for starters.

Choosing a known brand of tyre will prove to be one of your better decisions. Tyres are the only thing keeping you on the road, as in steering, braking and helping you round corners - what's the point of trying to improve the handling by sorting the suspension if you're going to throw the gains away by fitting naff tyres? Why beef up the brakes if the tyres won't bite? The combination of stiff suspension and cheap tyres is inherently dangerous - because the front end dives less with reduced suspension travel, the front tyres are far more likely to lock and skid under heavy braking.

Cheap tyres also equals more wheelspin - might be fun to disappear in a cloud of tyre smoke, but wouldn't you rather be disappearing up the road? Another problem with really wide tyres is aquaplaning - hit a big puddle at speed, and the tyre skates over the water without gripping - it's seriously scary when your car starts

Tricks 'n' tips

When buying tyres, look out for ones which feature a rubbing strip on the sidewall - these extend over the edge of the wheel rims, and the idea is that they protect the rim edges from damage by 'kerbing'. Any decent tyre has them - discreet and very practical, and much better than a chewed-up rim.

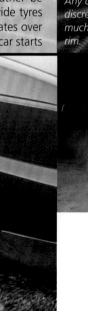

steering for you. Fitting good tyres won't prevent it, but it might increase your chances of staying in control. The sexiest modern low-profile tyres have a V-tread pattern, designed specifically to aid water dispersal, which is exactly what you need to prevent aquaplaning - try some, and feel the difference!

Finally, cheap tyres ruin your Nova's appearance - a no-name brand emblazoned in big letters on your tyre sidewalls - how's that going to look? If you're spending big dosh on wheels, you've gotta kit 'em out with some tasty V-tread tyres, or lose major points for style. Listen to friends and fellow modifiers - real-world opinions count for a lot when choosing tyres (how well do they grip, wet or dry? How many miles can you get out of them?) Just make sure, before you splash your cash on decent tyres, that you've cured all your rubbing and scrubbing issues, as nothing will rip your new tyres out faster.

Marks on your sidewalls

Tyre sizes are expressed in a strange mixture of metric and imperial specs - we'll take a typical tyre size as an example:

205/40 R 17 V

for a 7-inch wide 17-inch rim

205 width of tyre in millimetres

40 this is the "aspect ratio" (or "profile") of the tyre, or the sidewall height in relation to tyre width, expressed as a percentage, in this case 40%. So - 40% of 205 mm = 82 mm, or the height of the tyre sidewall from the edge of the locating bead to the top of the tread.

R Radial.

17 Wheel diameter in inches.

V Speed rating (in this case, suitable for use up to 150 mph).

Pressure situation

Don't forget, when you're having your new tyres fitted, to ask what the recommended pressures should be, front and rear - it's unlikely that the Vauxhall specs for this will be relevant to your new low-low profiles, but it's somewhere to start from. If the grease-monkey fitting your tyres is no help on this point, contact the tyre manufacturer - the big ones might even have a half-useful website! Running the tyres at the wrong pressures is particularly stupid (you'll wear them out much faster) and can be very dangerous (too soft - tyre rolls off the rim, too hard - tyre slides, no grip).

Speed ratings

Besides the tyre size, tyres are marked with a maximum speed rating, expressed as a letter code:

T up to 190 km/h (118 mph)

U up to 200 km/h (124 mph)

H up to 210 km/h (130 mph)

V inside tyre size markings (225/50 VR 16) over 210 km/h (130 mph)

V outside tyre size markings (185/55 R 15 V) up to 240 km/h (150 mph)

Z inside tyre size markings (255/40 ZR 17) over 240 km/h (150 mph)

If you've got marks on your sidewalls like this, you're in trouble - this has almost certainly been caused by "kerbing".

08 Suspension

If your Nova's still sitting on standard suspension, it's probably safe to say it doesn't cut it - yet. If you've decided you couldn't wait to fit your big alloys, the chances are your Nova is now doing a passable impression of a tractor. An essential fitment, then - so how low do you go, and what nasty side-effects will a lowering kit have?

The main reason for lowering is of course, to make your car look cool. Standard suspension nearly always seems to be set too soft and too high - a nicely lowered motor really stands out instantly. Lowering your car should also improve the handling. Dropping the car on its suspension brings the car's centre of gravity closer to its roll and pitch centres, which helps to pin it to the road in corners and under braking - combined with stiffer springs and shocks, this reduces body roll and increases the tyre contact patch on the road. BUT - if improving the handling is really important to you, choose your new suspension carefully. If you go the cheap route, or want extreme lowering, then you could end up with a car which don't handle at all…

As for what to buy, there are basically three main options when it comes to lowering, arranged in order of ascending cost below:

1 *Set of lowering springs.*

2 *Matched set of lowering springs and shock absorbers (suspension kit).*

3 *Set of "coilovers".*

Lowering springs

The cheapest option by far, but with the most pitfalls and some unpleasant side-effects. Lowering springs are, effectively, shorter versions of the standard items fitted to your Nova at the factory. However, not only are they shorter (lower), they are also uprated (stiffer) - if lowering springs were simply shorter than standard and the same stiffness (the same 'rate'), you'd be hitting the bump-stops over every set of catseyes. With lowering springs, you just fit the new springs and keep the original shock absorbers ('dampers'), so even if the originals aren't completely knackered, you're creating a problem caused by mis-matched components. The original dampers were carefully chosen to work with the original-rate springs - by increasing the spring rate without changing the dampers, you end up with dampers that can't control the springs properly. What this usually does before long is wreck the dampers, so you don't even save money in the end.

The mis-matched springs and dampers will have other entertaining side-effects, too. How would you like a Nova which rides like a brick, and which falls over itself at the first sign of a corner taken above walking pace? A very choppy ride and strange-feeling steering (much lighter, or much heavier, depending on your luck) are well-documented problems associated with taking the cheap option, and it doesn't even take much less time to fit, compared to a proper solution. Even if you're a hard man, who doesn't object to a hard ride if his car looks cool, think on this - how many corners do you know that are completely flat (ie without any bumps)? On dodgy lowering springs, you hit a mid-corner bump at speed, and it's anyone's guess where you'll end up.

If cost is a major consideration, and lowering springs the only option for now, at least try to buy branded items of decent quality - some cheap sets of springs will eat their way through several sets of dampers before you realise the springs themselves have lost the plot. Needless to say, if riding around on mis-matched springs and shocks is a bit iffy anyway, it's downright dangerous when they've worn out (some inside 18 months!).

Assuming you want to slam your suspension so your arches just clear the tops of your wicked new rims, there's another small problem with lowered springs - it takes some inspired guesswork (or hours of careful measuring and head-scratching) to assess the required drop accurately, and avoid that nasty rubbing sound and the smell of burning rubber. Springs are generally only available in a very few sizes, expressed by the amount of drop they'll produce - most people go for 60 mm or more, but there's usually 35 to 40 mm springs too if you're less brave (or if you've simply got massive rims). Take as many measurements as possible, and ask around your mates - suppliers and manufacturers may be your best source of help in special cases.

1A   2   2A   3   3A

Suspension **kit**

A far better choice, Sir - a matched set of springs and dampers is a genuine 'upgrade', and respect is due. There are several branded kits available, and most of the Vauxhall specialists do their own. With a properly-sorted conversion, your Nova will handle even better, and you'll still be able to negotiate a set of roadworks without the risk of dental work afterwards. Actually, you may well be amazed how well the Nova will still ride, even though the springs are clearly lower and stiffer - the secret is in the damping.

Some of the kits are billed as 'adjustable', but this only applies to the damper rates (don't mistake them as being cheap coilovers), which can often be set to your own taste by a few minutes' work. This Playstation feature can be a good fun thing to play around with, even if it is slightly less relevant to road use than for hillclimbs and sprints - but don't get carried away and set it too stiff, or you'll end up with an evil-handling car and a CD player that skips over every white line on the road!

Unfortunately, although you should end up with a fine-handling car, there are problems with suspension kits, too. If you don't have your steering geometry (camber and tracking) reset, you'll eat tyres, and once again, you're into guesswork territory when it comes to assessing your required drop for big wheels. Generally, most suspension kits are only available with a fairly modest drop (typically, 35 to 40 mm).

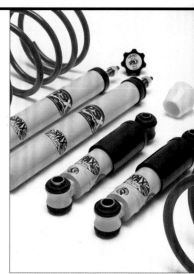

Coilovers

If you've chosen coilovers, well done again. This is the most expensive option, and it offers one vital feature that the other two can't - true adjustability of ride height, meaning that you can make the finest of tweaks to hunker down on your new rims (coilovers are an almost-essential choice if you're trying for 18s). Coilovers give you more scope to fit those big rims now, lower it down as far as poss, then wait 'til next month before you have the arches rolled, and drop it down to the deck. Coilovers are a variation on the suspension kit theme - a set of matched variable-rate springs (some have separate 'helper' springs too) and shocks, but their adjustability might not guarantee as good a ride/handling mix as a normal kit.

A coilover set replaces each spring and shock with a combined unit where the coil spring fits over the shocker (hence 'coil' 'over') - nothing too unusual in this, because so far, it's similar to a normal front strut. The difference lies in the adjustable spring lower seat, which can lower the spring (and car) to any desired height, within limits.

Unfortunately, making a car go super-low is not good for the ride or the handling. Coilover systems have very short, stiff springs, and this can lead to similar problems to those found with cheap lowering springs alone. If you go too far with coilovers, you can end up with a choppy ride, heavy steering and generally unpleasant handling. Combine a coilover-slammed car with big alloys, and while the visual effect may be stunning, the driving experience might well be very disappointing. At least a proper coilover kit will come with shock absorbers (dampers) which are matched to the springs, unlike a 'conversion' kit.

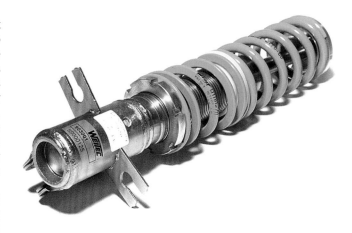

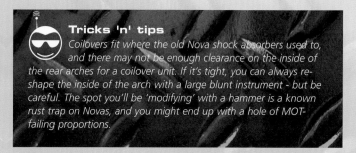

Tricks 'n' tips

Coilovers fit where the old Nova shock absorbers used to, and there may not be enough clearance on the inside of the rear arches for a coilover unit. If it's tight, you can always re-shape the inside of the arch with a large blunt instrument - but be careful. The spot you'll be 'modifying' with a hammer is a known rust trap on Novas, and you might end up with a hole of MOT-failing proportions.

Coilover conversion

A better-value option is the 'coilover conversion'. If you really must have the lowest, baddest machine out there, and don't care what the ride will be like, these could be the answer. Offering as much potential for lowering as genuine coilovers (and at far less cost), these items could be described as a cross between coilovers and lowering springs, because the standard dampers are retained (this is one reason why the ride suffers). What you get is a new spring assembly, with adjustable top and bottom mounts - the whole thing slips over your standard damper. Two problems with this solution (how important these are is up to you):

1 Your standard dampers will not be able to cope with the uprated springs, so the car will almost certainly ride (and possibly handle) like a pig if you go for a really serious drop - and okay, why else would you be doing it?

2 The standard dampers are effectively being compressed, the lower you go. There is a limit to how far they will compress before being completely solid (and this could be the limit for your lowering activities). Needless to say, even a partly-compressed damper won't be able to do much actual damping - the results of this could be... interesting...

Front Suspension

01 Loosen the wheel bolts, jack up the corner of the car you're working on, and take off the wheel. The strut is held on by two large nuts and bolts - these are not only tight, but might also be rusty, so plenty of effort may be needed to undo them. Make sure the car's very solidly supported before carrying on. See *'Wheels & tyres'* for more info on jacking up.

02 Once the base of the strut's separated from the hub, all that's holding the strut in place are two small nuts on top. As the last one's undone, hold the strut to prevent it landing on your foot . . .

03 . . . and lower the old strut out from under the wheelarch.

04 There are two clamps, each with two hooks, which sit over one of the spring coils. You may not get the hooks over the top and bottom coils, but try the next nearest. Fit the two clamps opposite each other . . .

05 . . . then tighten the big bolt up the middle of each to compress one side of the spring - this must be done evenly, one side after the other, or the un-clamped side might fly off. Respect is due here - this is scary stuff if you pratt about. Compress the spring carefully until the tension is off the strut top mounting.

06 To undo the strut inner nut, you'll need a 9 mm spanner/socket to hold the strut piston, and a 19 mm spanner to undo the nut.

07 Once the nut's removed, there's all sorts of bits to take off before you get to the spring itself . . .

08 . . . this, for instance, is the old strut bearing plate, which is just one of the old bits we'll be needing again. So don't throw anything out yet.

09 Finally, the old spring comes off. This, of course, is one bit we won't be refitting, but those clamps might come in handy for something. Like the other strut, for starters. Remember - loosen them off slowly and evenly, or you'll end up having a really bad day.

10 Ah, that's more like it. Start assembling your new strut by slipping on the shiny spring (if it's not obvious which way up it goes, be guided by the writing on it) . . .

11 . . . then slip on the new spring upper seat.

This is the first of the re-cycled old components going on - the strut bearing plate (looking

12 suspiciously like it's been cleaned, since we saw it last) . . .

13 . . . followed by this spacer . . .

14 . . . the strut upper mounting . . .

15 . . . and the support bearing stop (which is the only bit you'll see, so we gave ours a quick respray).

16 They may be small, but washers should never be overlooked. This is the last of the old bits you'll need.

17 On our kit, we had two top nuts to fit. You can never have too many nuts, I guess. Fit and tighten the first, then tighten the second onto it . . .

18 . . . using a variation on the two-spanner method used to undo the original nut. Don't fit the small spanner on the hex nut at the top (this is the damping adjuster nut) - instead use the spanner on the flats below the top nut.

19 The freshly-assembled coilover unit can now be fed into position under the arch. Hold it in position for now by loosely fitting the two top nuts.

20 Hook the base of the new strut onto the hub, and insert both of the mounting bolts, from the rear. At least clean and re-lubricate the old bolts, if you don't buy new ones . . .

21 . . . then fit the nuts and tighten to the correct torque (110 Nm, which is pretty tight). Got coilovers? While you're still underneath, set the coilover spring height, using the same method as for the rears (described later in this section).

22 Back in the engine bay, tighten the strut top mounting nuts to 30 Nm. If the old nuts have seen better days, get some replacements.

23 The damper setting for the fronts is critical to how the car drives - it affects the handling/grip, steering feel and braking efficiency. Worth a play then, but don't go too stiff to begin with (your new springs will be stiff enough as it is).

Rear Suspension

01 Loosen the rear wheel bolts, then jack the whole back end of the car, and support with axle stands under the sill rear jacking points. Have a look in *'Wheels & tyres'* for more info on jacking up. Remove the first rear wheel, then place a trolley jack directly under the suspension arm and raise the rear arms slightly, so it's supported. Phew. Make sure that jack's secure, as the shock lower mounting bolt will be tight.

02 Keep the suspension arm supported while you remove the mounting bolt, then lower the arm to make separating the base of the shock easier.

07 Assembling our new AVO coilover unit's dead easy. The new slim spring slides over the strut (try saying that after a few pints), then the upper mounting hooks on. It's ready to be poked up into its hole . . .

08 . . . after which, we add a rubber mounting and a top plate . . .

09 . . . followed by the new mounting nut, which gets tightened using the two-spanner method, same as before. According to Vauxhall, the amount of thread visible above the nut should be no more than 9 mm - how critical is this for your chosen new suspension? Read your instructions to find out.

10 With the top end sorted, it's time to introduce your coilover's lower end to the Nova suspension arm. Raise the jack under the arm until the (cleaned and re-lubed) bolt slips in. This bolt's a bit vital to your long-term health, so ideally tighten it to the correct torque (60 Nm), or next best - make sure it won't be coming undone.

03 If you now keep lowering the suspension arm, you'll find that the spring falls out. It's as easy as that.

04 Into the boot now, to finish ridding ourselves of that nasty old shock absorber. Pull off this rubber cap . . .

05 . . . and you'll need two spanners to undo the top mounting - one small (8 or 9 mm), and one large (typically, 19 mm, but we're cheating and using an adjustable here).

06 And out it comes. If your rear wheelarch looks any cleaner than ours, we'd be surprised.

11 These AVOs have adjustable damping, so don't forget to have a play with it sometime. To start with, we suggest setting it somewhere in the middle of the range, and see what it feels like. How stiff you go is up to you - but remember to set both sides the same.

12 The whole point of fitting coilovers is to slam that car as low as you can possibly get away with. And then perhaps a bit more? Use the C-spanner supplied to set the height of the lower spring seat . . .

13 . . . then lock it up - this kit uses an Allen key to pinch the spring seat in place (turn the ring so you can get at the screw), but yours might have a second locking ring, which tightens up against the seat. When you've set one side (which has to be a best-guess job, first time), measure and make a note of the height you set it to, so you can set the other side the same.

14 Before dropping the car down off the jack, spare a thought to what the winter weather's likely to do to those coilover threads. Will they corrode up, and be impossible to adjust in a few months' time? Some WD-40 (or better still, some Waxoyl) should keep things rust-free.

Nasty
side-effects

Camber angle and tracking

With any lowering 'solution', it's likely that your suspension and steering geometry will be severely affected - this will be more of a problem the lower you go. This will manifest itself in steering which either becomes lighter or (more usually) heavier, and in tyres which scrub out their inner or outer edges in very short order - not funny, if you're running expensive low-profiles! Sometimes, even the rear tyres can be affected in this way, but that's usually only after some serious slammage. Whenever you've fitted a set of springs (and this applies to ALL types), have the geometry checked ASAP afterwards.

If you've dropped the car by 60 mm or more, chances are your camber angle will need adjusting. This is one reason why you might find the edges of your fat low-profiles wearing faster than you'd like (the other is your tracking being out). The camber angle is the angle the tyre makes with the road, seen from directly in front. You'll no doubt have seen race cars with the front wheels tilted in at the top, out at the bottom - this is extreme negative camber, and it helps to give more grip and stability in extreme cornering (but if your car was set this extreme, you'd kill the front tyres VERY quickly!). Virtually all road cars have a touch of negative camber on the front, and it's important when lowering to keep as near to the factory setting as possible, to preserve the proper tyre contact patch on the road. Trouble is, there's not usually much scope for camber adjustment on standard suspension, which is why (for some cars) you can buy camber-adjustable top plates which fit to the strut tops. Setting the camber accurately is a job for a garage with experience of modified cars - so probably not your local fast-fit centre, then.

Strut brace

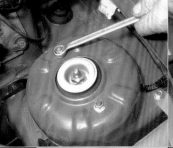

Another item which is inspired by saloon racing, the strut brace is another underbonnet accessory which you shouldn't be without. Some of them might even work…

The idea of the strut brace is that, once you've stiffened up your front suspension to the max, the car's 'flimsy' body shell (to which the front suspension struts are bolted) may not be able to cope with the 'immense' cornering forces being put through it, and will flex, messing up the handling. The strut brace (in theory) does exactly what it says on the tin, by providing support between the strut tops, taking the load off the bodyshell.

Where this falls down slightly (for road use) is that 1) no-one's going to have the car set that stiff, 2) no-one's going to drive that hard, and 3) the Nova shell isn't exactly made out of tin foil (allegedly). The strut brace might have a slight effect, but the real reason to fit one is for SHOW - and why not? They look great in a detailed engine bay, and are available in lots of designs and finishes. You're looking at parting with up to a hundred of your finest English pounds, but your mates will be impressed and the girls will love it - and you can't put a price on that!

01 The first step with any brace is to put it in its place - by doing this, you can see how much stuff it interferes with, and whether they've sent you the right one! No such worries with this decent OMP item from Demon Tweeks, so - making sure the car's on its wheels, undo the two strut top mounting nuts (don't touch the middle one) . . .

02 . . . and lay the strut brace mounting plate in position.

Remember those not-very-big nuts we're using to pin down the ends of the brace? They also hold the front struts to the car, so it would be nice if they didn't come loose unexpectedly. Ideally, do them to the correct torque (30 Nm). Time to stand back and admire your handiwork - give the brace a quick polish, so people notice it as soon as you lift the bonnet!

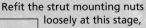

03 Refit the strut mounting nuts loosely at this stage, just to stop the plate from coming off.

With one end of the brace in position, it's time to see whether the other end will go on. If you're lucky, it'll drop straight into place - if not, some adjustment may be needed, using a spanner on the threaded section. Fit the nuts at the other end, then use the adjuster again to take out any 'slack' in the brace.

04

When the adjuster's correctly set, you'll need another large spanner to tighten up the adjuster locknuts - don't want our carefully-set-up brace coming loose on a vital corner, do we? Just joshing.

05

06

09 Brakes

Remember the middle pedal?

It's the one next to the throttle - some people don't use it much. Uprating the brakes is actually a very easy bolt-on upgrade, but there are some points to consider.

One of the strangest, given that improving the brakes should in theory also improve your chances of avoiding an accident, is that insurance companies do not like performance brakes. You should still tell them, but be prepared for bad news. To them, it seems that fitting sporty brakes must automatically make you drive like Colin McRae - the clear implication is that if you need better brakes, you've either also uprated the engine (and not told them?), or you simply drive on the limit everywhere. Shame. We just like to know our cars will stop quickly. That, actually, might be another reason why they don't like better brakes - you stop better, but does the old dodderer behind you? Crunch.

Uprating the brakes will be a complete waste of time if you're a cheapskate on tyres. Cheap, no-name tyres (or ones with no tread left) won't always be able to translate extra braking power into actual vehicle-stopping power - they'll give up their grip on the tarmac and skid everywhere. Something like 90% of braking is done by the front wheels - ie the ones you steer with. If you consider that locked-up wheels also don't tend to steer very well, you'll begin to see why top brakes and lame tyres are a well-dodgy mixture.

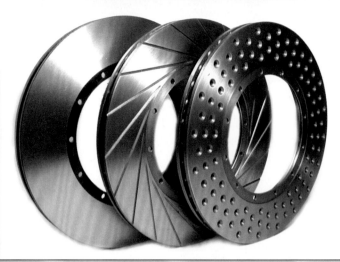

Groovy discs

Besides the various brands of performance brake pads that go with them, the main brake upgrade is to fit performance front brake discs and pads. Discs are available in two main types - grooved and cross-drilled (and combinations of both).

Grooved discs (which can be had with varying numbers of grooves) serve a dual purpose - the grooves provide a 'channel' to help the heat escape, and they also help to de-glaze the pad surface, cleaning up the pads every time they're used. Some of the discs are made from higher-friction metal than normal discs, too, and the fact that they seriously improve braking performance is well-documented.

Cross-drilled discs offer another route to heat dissipation, but one which can present some problems. Owners report that cross-drilled discs really eat brake pads, more so than the grooved types, but more serious is the fact that some of these discs can crack around the drilled holes, after serious use. The trouble is that the heat 'migrates' to the drilled holes (as was intended), but the heat build-up can be extreme, and the constant heating/cooling cycle can stress the metal to the point where it will crack. Discs which have been damaged in this way are extremely dangerous to drive on, as they could break up completely at any time. Only fit discs of this type from established manufacturers offering a useful guarantee of quality, and check the discs regularly.

Performance discs also have a reputation for warping (nasty vibrations felt through the pedal). Is this fair? Well, the harder you use your brakes (and we could be talking serious abuse), the greater the heat you'll generate. Okay, so these wicked discs are meant to be able to cope with this heat, but you can't expect miracles. Cheap discs, or ones which have had a hard time over mega-thousands of miles, will warp. So buy quality, and don't get over-heroic on the brakes.

Performance pads can be fitted to any brake discs, including the standard ones, but are of course designed to work best with heat-dissipating discs. Unless your Nova's got an over-boosted Calibra turbo lump under the bonnet, don't be tempted to go much further than 'fast road' pads - anything more competition-orientated may take too long to come up to temperature on the road. Remember what pushbike brakes were like in the wet? Cold competition pads feel the same, and old dears always step off the pavement when your brakes are cold!

Lastly, fitting all the performance brake bits in the world is no use if your calipers have seized up (this is a common problem on early models, which had Delco calipers - if you can source some later ATE calipers from a scrapyard, you'll be doing yourself a favour). If, when you strip out your old pads, you find that one pad's worn more than the other, or that both pads have worn more on the left wheel than the right, your caliper pistons are sticking. Sometimes you can free them off by pushing them back into the caliper, but this could be a garage job to fix. If you drive around with sticking calipers, you'll eat pads and discs. You choose.

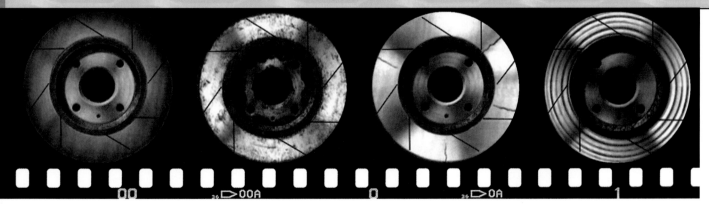

Brake discs and pads

01 Loosen the wheel bolts, jack up the corner of the car you're working on, and take off the wheel. Make sure you've got an axle stand under a solid part of the car in case the jack gives out. Have a look in *'Wheels & tyres'* for more info on jacking up. First job is to tap out the roll-pins which secure the pads - tap from the inside, outwards.

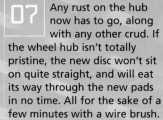

06 It should be possible to remove the disc without unbolting the caliper (okay, it's only two more bolts, but they're tight, Allen-headed, and tucked round the back).

07 Any rust on the hub now has to go, along with any other crud. If the wheel hub isn't totally pristine, the new disc won't sit on quite straight, and will eat its way through the new pads in no time. All for the sake of a few minutes with a wire brush.

08 Like the hubs, the new discs must be clean before fitting - give 'em a wipe over with meths, or a squirt of brake cleaner. Your new discs probably are not identical, and should only be fitted with the grooves facing a certain way (this is the left front). Check your paperwork - our new multi-grooved discs were supplied by Red Dot Racing Ltd, with matching pads. Cheers, chaps!

Achtung!
Brake dust from old pads or shoes may contain asbestos. Wear a mask to avoid inhaling it.

02 Once the first pin is removed, you'll be able to unhook the pad retaining springs. Make a quick mental note how these go - you'll be refitting them later.

03 When the other pin's removed, the old pads should come out. Ours were well stuck in there, and a fair bit of tapping and prising was needed to free them off.

04 To make room for your new pads, the caliper piston has to be pushed back inside the caliper. This isn't as easy as it sounds, because the piston may be partly seized - it's a common problem. You can lever it back in with a screwdriver, but this marks the disc. We used a pair of adjustable spanners - clamp one round the handle of the other, and twist.

05 Now to remove the old disc. Not much holding it on, is there? Just one screw? Don't forget - when the wheel's bolted up, it clamps the disc in place. If the screw's rusted itself in, it could be tricky to remove - ultimately, you might need to hire or borrow an impact driver. Ours came off easily - honest.

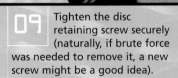

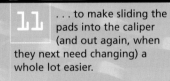

09 Tighten the disc retaining screw securely (naturally, if brute force was needed to remove it, a new screw might be a good idea).

10 Smearing a bit of copper grease on the pad backplates shows you're serious about not having annoying squealing brakes. These pads already have an anti-squeal coating, so we're putting a little grease on the metal edges . . .

11 . . . to make sliding the pads into the caliper (and out again, when they next need changing) a whole lot easier.

12 Give the pad pins a good clean-up with emery paper (and a smear of copper grease) before fitting. If the pins or springs have seen better days (or any bits were missing), get a new pin/spring kit - available v. cheap from outlets such as Halfords.

Remember!
It's a good idea to have your brake mods MOT-tested once you've fitted new discs and pads, and you might even be able to 'blag' a free brake check at your local fast-fit centre if you're crafty! Brakes are a serious safety issue, and unless you're 100% confident that all is well, demo-ing your car's awesome new-found stopping ability could find you in the ditch…

Remember!
New pads of any sort need careful bedding-in (over 100 miles of normal use) before they'll work properly - when first fitted, the pad surface won't have worn exactly to the contours of the disc, so it won't actually be touching it, over its full area. This will possibly result in very under-whelming brakes for the first few trips, so watch it - misplaced over-confidence in your brakes is a fast track to hospital…

Cool coloured **stoppers**

One 'downside' to fitted massive multi-spoked alloys is that - gasp - people can see your brakes! So don't be shy about it - paint some of the brake bits so they look the biz, to match (or clash completely) with your chosen colour scheme. Red is the colour inspired by the racing/touring-car boys, but isn't the only choice.

Novas don't have rear discs, but painting the brake drums is acceptable under the circumstances - but then, do you paint 'em black, to de-emphasise them, or in your chosen colour for the fronts? It's all tough decisions, in modifying. If you're really sad, you can always buy fake rear discs… For the less-sad among you, Vauxhall performance specialists may be able to sell you a rear disc brake conversion kit - pricey, but maybe necessary if there's now a 2-litre lump up front. A rear disc conversion's going a bit far, just to have red calipers front and rear - and remember, the rear brakes don't do much actual stopping…

Painting the calipers requires that they're clean - really clean. Accessory stores sell aerosol brake cleaner, which (apart from having a distinctive high-octane perfume) is just great for removing brake dust, and lots more besides! Some kits come complete with cleaner spray. Many of the kits advertise themselves on the strength of no dismantling being required, but we don't agree. Also, having always successfully brush-painted our calipers, we wouldn't advise using any kind of spray paint.

We know you won't want to hear this, but the best way to paint the calipers is to do some dismantling first. The kits say you don't have to, but trust me - you'll get a much better result from a few minutes' extra work. We took off the new brake pads and disc we'd just fitted - stopping halfway through the new disc fitting process would have been a really sound move, but nobody thinks that far ahead.

Painting calipers

01 Get the wire brush out, and attack the rusty old caliper to get rid of all the loose muck. If the caliper's black with brake dust, try not to breathe much of it in.

Tricks 'n' tips
If you have trouble reassembling your brakes after painting, you probably got carried away and put on too much paint. We found that, once it was fully dry, the excess paint could be trimmed off with a knife.

02 Squirt on your brake cleaner (our Folia Tec kit came with its own can), giving the caliper a good dose, and get wiping as soon as possible. Spraying alone will only loosen the muck, and a good scrub is the only answer. If you don't get it spotless, you'll get black streaks in the paint later, which looks really cack.

03 If your hand isn't too steady, or you're using a big brush, you'll need to mask up some bits - like the bleed screws, for instance. Only paint what you can see with the wheel back on. Most caliper paint comes in two tins, which you mix together - if yours is like this, remember it goes off fast (do all four brakes in the same morning/afternoon). It's best to do more than one coat, we found. Wait 'til the paint's totally dry (like overnight, or longer) before reassembling.

Painting drums

At least there's no dismantling with drums - get the rear end jacked up, wheels off (see *'Wheels & tyres'* if you need jacking info) and just get stuck **01** in with the wire brush, sandpaper (to smooth the surface) . . .

. . . then it's spray on the brake cleaner and wipe thoroughly. Wiping is important - don't rely **02** on the spray alone, as you won't get the surfaces clean.

You definitely don't want any paint in the wheel bolt holes, nor where the wheel hubs touch the drum. Masking-up shouldn't be necessary if your hand is steady. Painting the drums is much easier than the fiddly calipers. Use a thicker, better-quality brush than the one they give you in the kit - you'll get a much smoother paint **03** finish on the drums. Let off the handbrake and turn the drum half a turn every so often until the paint's dry. Nobody likes the runs, after all.

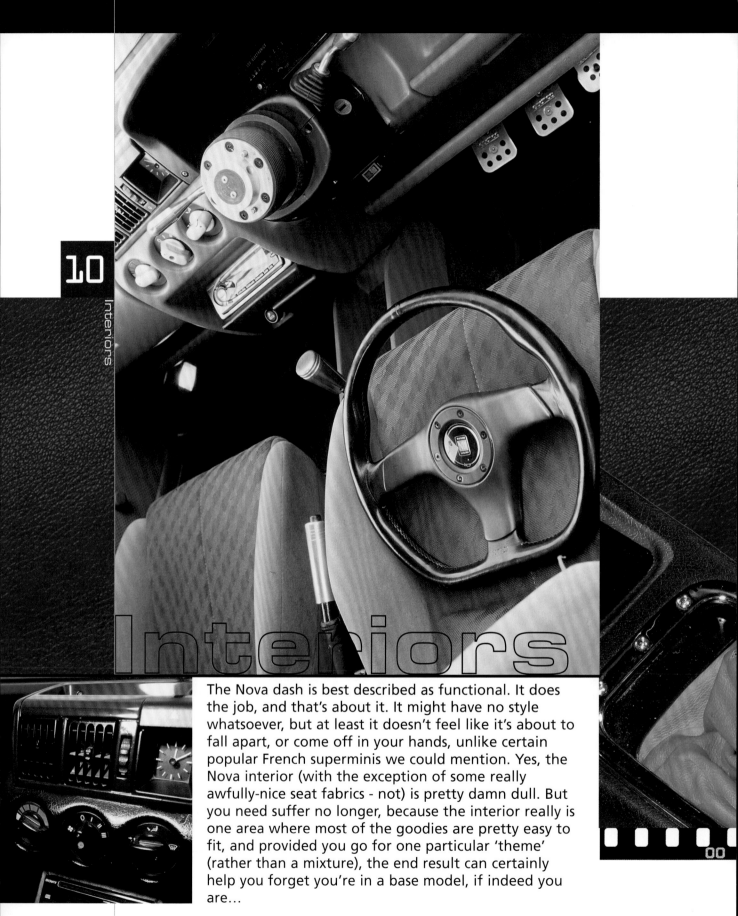

Interiors

The Nova dash is best described as functional. It does the job, and that's about it. It might have no style whatsoever, but at least it doesn't feel like it's about to fall apart, or come off in your hands, unlike certain popular French superminis we could mention. Yes, the Nova interior (with the exception of some really awfully-nice seat fabrics - not) is pretty damn dull. But you need suffer no longer, because the interior really is one area where most of the goodies are pretty easy to fit, and provided you go for one particular 'theme' (rather than a mixture), the end result can certainly help you forget you're in a base model, if indeed you are...

To be fair to the Nova, not many standard interiors are anything to shout about, particularly when you compare them with the sort of look that can easily be achieved with the huge range of product that's out there. As with the exterior styling, though, remember that fashions can change very quickly - so don't be afraid to experiment with a look you really like, because chances are, it'll be the next big thing anyway. Just don't do wood, ok? We've a feeling it's never coming in, never mind coming back…

Removing stuff
Take it easy and break less

Many of the procedures we're going to show involve removing interior trim panels (either for colouring or to fit other stuff), and this can be tricky. It's far too easy to break plastic trim, especially once it's had a chance to go a bit brittle with age. Another 'problem' with the Nova is that the interior trim is pretty well-attached (and the designers have been very clever at hiding several vital screws), meaning that it can be a pig to get off. On Mk 2 models especially, there's more than

a few Torx screws - invest in a set or Torx keys (like Allen keys), otherwise you'll come across one screw that won't come out using any other type of screwdriver. We'll try and avoid the immortal words 'simply unclip the panel', and instead show you how properly, but inevitably at some stage, a piece of trim won't 'simply' anything.

The important lesson here is not to lose your temper, as this has a highly-destructive effect on plastic components, and may result in a panel which no amount of carbon film or colour spray can put right, or make fit again. Superglue may help, but not every time. So - take it steady, prise carefully, and think logically about how and where a plastic panel would have to be attached, to stay on. You'll encounter all sorts of trim clips (some more fragile than others) in your travels - when these break, as they usually do, know that many of them can be bought in ready packs from accessory shops, and that the rarer ones will be available from a Vauxhall dealer, probably off the shelf. Even fully-trained Vauxhall mechanics aren't immune to breaking a few trim clips!

Door trim panel

You'll find plenty of excuses for removing your door trim panels - fitting speakers, re-trimming the panel, de-locking, even window tinting, so we'd better tell you how.

01 The first bit's easy - unclip and remove the trim around the door lock handle.

02 Open the window, by whatever means you have. We'll assume you've got wind-up windows, in which case work the edge of a piece of (clean) cloth/rag into the gap between the handle and the plastic disc, from underneath. Using a 'sawing' action, work the cloth side to side, and release the spring clip which secures the handle. With a little patience, this does work - just watch where the spring clip goes!

03 Alternatively, use this special window winder tool (no, don't panic, it's available v. cheap from Draper - tool code WWT) which makes removing the winder handles so much easier, and makes you look all professional.

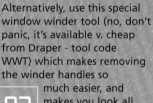

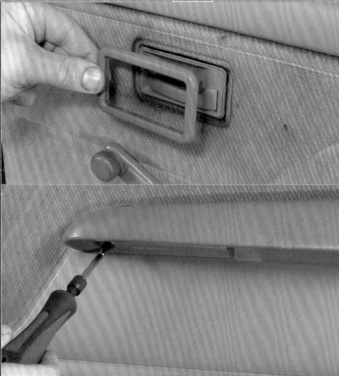

05 . . . and two more below the armrest (all cross-heads too - none of your Torx rubbish on this job).

06 All that's left now is to prise the edges of the panel, to release the push-in clips behind. Use something flat and wide-bladed for this (not a skinny screwdriver), as there's less chance of damaging the panel. You'll probably break a clip or two, no matter how careful you are.

07 Now the trim panel's free to come off. Unless, of course, there's any aftermarket speakers been fitted, in which case they'll need your attention too (removing speaker screws, disconnecting speaker wiring).

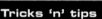

Tricks 'n' tips

Find something like an old ice-cream or margarine tub to keep all the little screws and bits in, as you take them off. This approach is far superior to the chuck-them-all-on-the-floor method most people use, until they lose something vital.

04 Now there's a row of screws to remove along the base of the door . . .

01 Prise out the nasty plastic clip at the lower corner . . .

02 . . . then remove one or two screws from the back end of the door sill trim panel . . .

03 . . . and peel away the rubber door seal, to free the front edge of the panel.

Rear side **panels**

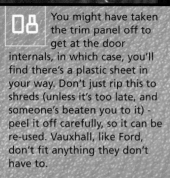

04 Carefully unclip the base of the B-pillar trim panel . . .

05 . . . then release the side panel from its remaining clips by feeding your hand in behind for a gentle prise, and it should come away without too much damage. Unclip the seatbelt plastic guide, then feed the belt out through the slot at the top of the panel.

08 You might have taken the trim panel off to get at the door internals, in which case, you'll find there's a plastic sheet in your way. Don't just rip this to shreds (unless it's too late, and someone's beaten you to it) - peel it off carefully, so it can be re-used. Vauxhall, like Ford, don't fit anything they don't have to.

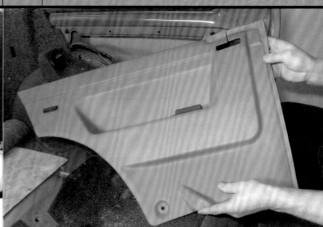

Mk 2 dash bits

01 For those of you with Mk 1s, we apologise, but there's always the Haynes Nova manual to fall back on. We figured the Mk 2 owners needed our help more. We're concentrating on the driver's side of the dash - the first place you might want to colour-code. The standard speaker grille just unclips . . .

02 . . . and you've got to get it off, to reach the screw securing the vent underneath . . .

03 . . . which, after a brief struggle, pulls out like this.

04 What about the light switch panel, to the right of the clocks? Well, it's a mare to remove - but not impossible. With the instrument surround removed (as described in the white dials section), the light switch is the main problem. Use a very small screwdriver, poked in the base of the switch knob, to release its securing tag, and pull the knob off.

05 What GM genius came up with the light switch design? We'd like to shake his throat. Just an absurdly difficult thing to remove - you will swear lots. The correct way is to make up two tools, with a 5 mm 90° bend at the ends - we tried two junior hacksaw blades, but they break a lot. Hook the bent ends in as shown, and the switch lugs are supposed to release.

06 With the switch removed, you can see the two lugs you're trying to free up. We cheated, and used a small screwdriver to release one side of the switch at a time. This is a bit brutal, but that was just the mood we were in, after struggling with it for ages.

07 And why exactly have we gone to all this trouble? To get at this one screw, which Vauxhall chose to hide behind the switch.

08 Your problems aren't even over with the silly hidden screw. The panel wiring plugs are nuclear bomb-proof, and are a real pig to disconnect. We could get to not liking this car very much. The trick with the plugs is to examine them closely, and use a small screwdriver to prise back the retaining lugs. This is one panel you don't want to take off twice.

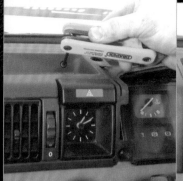

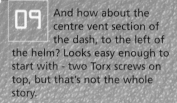

09 And how about the centre vent section of the dash, to the left of the helm? Looks easy enough to start with - two Torx screws on top, but that's not the whole story.

10 Prise out the left-hand vent . . .

11 . . . and there's another of those now-famous Vauxhall hidden (crosshead) screws. Why put two in clear view, and hide the third?

12 Off it comes, for disconnection of the wiring plugs behind. Now the entire top part of the dash is at your mercy, for a timely spot of colour-coding.

Centre console

Our console's the most basic there is, on a Mk 2 Nova, but removing's the same on almost any model. First, there's

01 a square plastic cover (or several) to prise up . . .

02 . . . for access to the screws underneath.

Now, our console just lifts away. With a longer console, you may have to unclip the gear lever gaiter, and pull the handbrake lever fully on, to get the console to come out. Posh Novas have their electric window switches in the console - prise out the switches and

03 disconnect the wiring plugs. If the console's not even loose, it means there's more screws concealed under more plastic covers which you haven't spotted yet. Good luck.

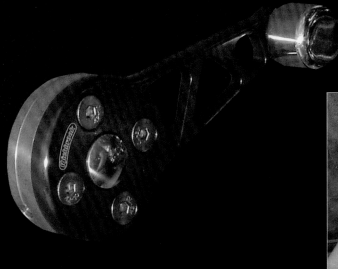

Window
winders

01 Removing the old winder handles is covered in removing your door trim panel (okay, you can feel smug if yours are electric). Before you can fit these tasty Richbrook winders, you have to pull them to bits - no challenge for a confident Maxer. Slide the handle base onto the splines (use the handle to check it's at the right angle), then tighten the Allen screw.

02 Now fit the chunky alloy handle to the base, and secure with four more Allen screws. Dead easy.

Door trim top section

03 Now tell me that chunky chrome item's not miles better than wobbly grey plastic. You can't, can you.

01 Just because something isn't meant to be removed, doesn't mean it can't be modded. Take the lovely grey vinyl top of our door trim - please, take it. After discovering it's not easy to remove, we decided to blast it with Folia Tec spray, in place. All it means is a bit of masking. Lots of cleaning prep, too - this is a 'high-traffic' area. The result? Looks cool-as.

Anything but black?

The interior trim on the Nova at least hides its age well, and doesn't rattle much. And that's about it - for a lover of elephant-hide grey, it's heaven, but for more normal people, it's something else. Fortunately, there's plenty you can do to personalise it, and there are three main routes to take:

1) Spray paint - available in any colour you like, as long as it's... not black. This Folia Tec stuff actually dyes softer plastics and leather, and comes in a multi-stage treatment, to suit all plastic types. Don't try to save money just buying the top coat, because it won't work! Special harder-wearing spray is required for use on steering wheels. Ordinary spray paint for bodywork might damage some plastics, and won't be elastic - good primer is essential. Make sure you also buy lots of masking tape.

2) Adhesive or shrink-fit film - available in various wild colours, carbon, ally, and, er... walnut (would YOU?). Probably best used on flatter surfaces, or at least those without complex curves, or you'll have to cut and join - spray is arguably better here. Some companies will sell you sheets of genuine carbon-fibre, with peel-off backing - looks and feels the part (nice if you have touchy-feely passengers).

3) Replacement panels - the easiest option, as the panels are supplied pre-cut, ready to fit. Of course, you're limited then to styling just the panels supplied.

If you fancy something more posh, how about trimming your interior bits in leather? Very saucy. Available in various colours, and hardly any dearer than film, you also get that slight 'ruffled' effect on tighter curves.

Get the cans out

For our red/grey theme, we found that silver Folia Tec interior spray was the best way to lift the grey interior out of the ordinary - but that's just us, and for our chosen look. For variety, we fitted red dials, sprayed the column stalks red, and finally had the glovebox lid covered in red alcantara, to match our door trim panels.

Any painting process is a *multi-stage* application. With the Folia Tec system (thanks to Eurostyling for supplying ours), many of you apparently think you can get away just buying the top coat, which then looks like a cheap option compared to film - WRONG! Even the proper interior spray top coat won't stay on for long without the matching primer, and the finish won't be wear-resistant without the finishing sealer spray. You don't need the special foaming cleaner - you could get by with a general-purpose degreaser, such as meths. Just watch the grey/black plastic doesn't suddenly turn white - if it does, you're damaging the finish! This might not be too important to you, as it's being sprayed over anyway, but if you take out the grey too far on a part that's not being sprayed all over, you'll have to live with a cacky-looking white-grey finish to any non-painted surface...

Providing you're a dab hand with the masking tape, paint gives you the flexibility to be more creative. For instance, you could try colour-matching the exterior of the car - but will ordinary car body paint work on interior plastics? Course it will, as long as you prep the panels properly.

Choice of paint's one thing, but what to paint? Well, not everything - for instance, you might want to avoid high-wear areas like door handles. Just makes for an easier life. The glovebox lid and instrument panel surround are obvious first choices, as are the ashtray and fusebox lid. The centre console's not lighting anyone's fire in standard Vauxhall grey, so hit it with some spray too. Any panels which just pop out are targets, in fact (lots less masking needed) - just make sure whatever you're dismantling was meant to come apart, or it'll be out with the superglue instead of the cans.

Don't be afraid to experiment with a combination of styles - as long as you're confident you can blend it all together, anything goes! Mix the painted bits with some tasteful carbon-fibre sheet or brushed-aluminium film, if you like - neutral colours like this, or chrome, can be used to give a lift to dash bits which are too tricky to spray.

Painting **trim**

01 To make certain your chosen paint won't peel when the masking comes off, you need to get a bit brutal (no going back if you change your mind). You need some Scotchbrite, which is a bodyshop-spec scouring pad, available in several grades. Try a bodyshop or motor factors - it's not dear, and it's great for roughing-up any surface before spraying, giving the paint a 'key'. Cheaper alternatives may be available in Tesco!

02 Clean up the surface to be sprayed, using a suitable degreaser - we used meths in the end, having tried some thinners initially (this started taking off the black). You must use something fairly evil, to get off any silicone-based products you or the previous owner may have used, as these are death to paint adhesion. If you're not going to paint the whole thing, don't degrease the whole thing, or you might ruin the finish on the black bits.

03 Mask up the bits you don't want sprayed, as necessary - you can never do too much masking. Give the job a final wipe over with solvent, then apply a mist coat of primer - essential to help the paint 'stick' to the plastic. With the Folia Tec system we used, they make their own primer - if you're using ordinary spray as a topcoat, use a plastic primer (available in Halfords).

04 Now for the colour coat - keep shaking the tin between passes, and don't bottle-out halfway across, or the can's nozzle will spit paint on, leaving nasty blobs in the finish. Also, don't try to cover the job in one coat, nor spray too close. You'll be a natural in the end - practise on some scrap card until you've mastered the technique (it's all in the wrist, y'know). Allow time for each coat to dry (a few minutes) before banging some more on.

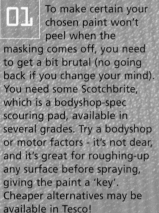  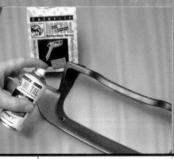

Cheating - ready-made panels

05 Once you're happy that there's even coverage, let the last top coat dry, then slap on the sealer coat or lacquer. This final coat is intended to improve wear-resistance (not much good if your carefully-applied paint rubs off in a few weeks, is it?). You should only need a light coat to finish the job.

06 Of course, there's more to trim painting than a new colour, and more effects you can go for. Take this Color-It Metal effect spray from MHW, which really does what it says on the tin, and produces quite an effective shiny metal effect on plastic. Whatever your chosen final coat, stick to the general rules of good prep and primer, and anything goes.

A far easier route to the brushed-ally or carbon look, pre-finished ('here's some we did earlier') panels are available from suppliers. Dash kits are available for the Mk 1 Nova from companies like Dash Dynamics, and offer a simpler way of livening-up the dull Nova dash. Did we say simple? It's sometimes not too obvious where the various kit bits are supposed to go! A trial fitting isn't a bad idea, before peeling off the backing. Make sure your chosen trim piece is lined up nice and square, and keep it square as you press it on - the adhesive's usefully-sticky, meaning it will stay stuck whether you get it right or wrong. Still, it's easier by far than trying to mask up and spray the edges of the vents, which is what you'd have to do otherwise.

Filming your **Nova**

If you fancy creating a look that's a bit more special than plain paint colours, film is the answer - but be warned - it's not the easiest stuff in the world to use, and so isn't everyone's favourite. If you must have the brushed-aluminium look, or fancy giving your Nova the carbon-fibre treatment, there really is no alternative (apart from the lazy-man option of new panels, of course).

01 Cut the film roughly to size, remembering to leave plenty of excess for trimming - it's also a good idea to have plenty to fold around the edges, because thin film has a nasty habit of peeling off, otherwise.

02 Next, we gently warmed up both the panel, and the film itself. Just following the instructions provided, and who are we to argue?

03 Peel off the backing, being careful that the film stays as flat as possible. Also take care, when you pick the film up, that it doesn't stick to itself (our stuff seemed very keen to do this!).

04 Stick the film on straight - very important with any patterned finish. Start at one edge or corner, and work across, to keep the air bubbles and creases to a minimum. If you get a really bad crease, it's best to unpeel a bit and try again - the adhesive's very tacky, and there's no slide-age available.

05 Work out the worst of the air bubbles with a soft cloth - get the stuff to stick as best you can before trimming, or it'll all go horribly wrong. To be sure it's stuck (especially important on a grained surface), go over it firmly with the edge of your least-important piece of 'plastic' - ie not a credit card.

06 Once the film's laid on, it's time for trimming - which (you guessed it) is the tricky bit. We found it's much easier to trim the tricky bits once the film's been warmed up using a hairdryer or heat gun, but don't overdo it! Make sure you've also got a very sharp knife - a blunt one will ripple the film, and may tear it (one good thing about film is that blood wipes off it easily!).

07 To get the film to wrap neatly round a curved edge, make several slits almost up to the edge, then wrap each sliver of film around, and stick on firmly. If the film's heated as you do this, it wraps round and keeps its shape - meaning it shouldn't try and spring back, ruining all your hard work.

Bum notes

There are limitations to using film, and the quality of the film itself has a lot to do with that. We had major problems doing any kind of job with one particular make of brushed-aluminium-look film - it was a nightmare to work with, and the edges had peeled the next day. Buying quality film will give you a long-lasting result to be proud of, with much less skill requirement and lots less swearing. But it still pays not to be too ambitious with it.

Gear knob jobs

01 Begin by pulling off that nasty Vauxhall knob. Anyone who doesn't agree that this is a good idea - get your coat. It'll take some pulling off (try twisting, or even heating, to loosen it first).

02 One of the nastiest rubber gaiters we've ever had the pleasure of ridding a car of. Removing it's so easy, we didn't even get to damage it in the process - it just unclips from the mounting lip, and lifts off over the now-naked gear lever.

03 That mounting lip comes in very handy if, like us, you've got a new gaiter with an elasticated base. This Richbrook silver leather job is cool enough to look out of place in our still-standard Nova interior. That won't last long, though.

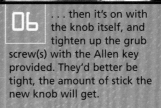

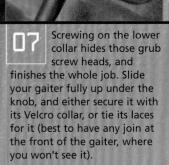

04 That new gaiter will look miles better when it's had the Momo gear knob treatment. First out of the packet are the rubber mounting sleeves - find one that's a snug fit over the end of the lever, and squidge it on there.

05 Don't forget to slip on the gear knob's lower collar now, if yours has one . . .

06 . . . then it's on with the knob itself, and tighten up the grub screw(s) with the Allen key provided. They'd better be tight, the amount of stick the new knob will get.

07 Screwing on the lower collar hides those grub screw heads, and finishes the whole job. Slide your gaiter fully up under the knob, and either secure it with its Velcro collar, or tie its laces for it (best to have any join at the front of the gaiter, where you won't see it).

Handbrake
knobs & gaiters

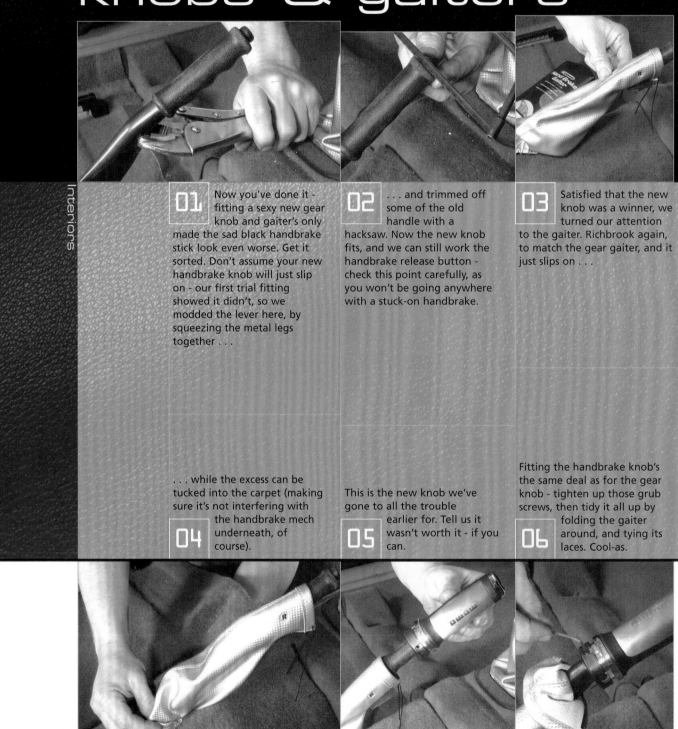

01 Now you've done it - fitting a sexy new gear knob and gaiter's only made the sad black handbrake stick look even worse. Get it sorted. Don't assume your new handbrake knob will just slip on - our first trial fitting showed it didn't, so we modded the lever here, by squeezing the metal legs together . . .

02 . . . and trimmed off some of the old handle with a hacksaw. Now the new knob fits, and we can still work the handbrake release button - check this point carefully, as you won't be going anywhere with a stuck-on handbrake.

03 Satisfied that the new knob was a winner, we turned our attention to the gaiter. Richbrook again, to match the gear gaiter, and it just slips on . . .

04 . . . while the excess can be tucked into the carpet (making sure it's not interfering with the handbrake mech underneath, of course).

05 This is the new knob we've gone to all the trouble earlier for. Tell us it wasn't worth it - if you can.

06 Fitting the handbrake knob's the same deal as for the gear knob - tighten up those grub screws, then tidy it all up by folding the gaiter around, and tying its laces. Cool-as.

The personal touch –
re-trimming

Okay, so you're definitely not happy with how the inside of your Nova looks, but you're not sold on any of the off-the-shelf options for tricking it up, either. You know how you want it to look, though, so get creative!

There are any number of upholstery companies in Yellow Pages, who will be able to create any look you want (we got one in our own back yard, almost - Pipers of Sparkford, Somerset, and very helpful lads they are, too). If your idea of Nova heaven is an interior swathed in black and purple leather, these guys can help. Don't assume that you'll have to go to Carisma, to get a car interior re-trimmed - they might well be the daddies at this, but any upholsterer worth the name should be able to help, even if they normally only do sofas!

Of course, if you're even slightly handy with things like glue and scissors, you might be inspired to get brave and DIY. An upholsterers will still be a useful source for materials (and maybe advice too?).

Door trim **panels**
What applies to seats can also be applied to your door cards. If you're gonna DIY, practice on something old first.

If you've had your seats trimmed, you'll obviously choose the same stuff for your doors - but here's a tip. Say you've gone for some nice bucket seats, in maybe a red-and-black pattern cloth. Would be nice to match your seats to the door panels here, too, wouldn't it? So how about doing what we did for another of our project cars, and contacting the seat manufacturer for a few square metres of the actual cloth they use to make the seats? Should match then, shouldn't it? Hand material and cash to your upholstery experts, with cash, and wait. Or do it yourself.

Carpeting the back end

The Nova's a cheap car - it shouts it from everywhere you look, but especially in the boot area. Not much good if your boot and back seat are going to be home to a kicking ICE install, is it? All that cheap-looking plastic must be dealt with somehow.

01 We're not keeping the rear shelf in our Nova - the sub enclosure we've got planned will be fully on display. That means the shelf side supports can go - and they're attached to the boot side trim panels, so out they come. First, prise out the plastic plugs (three of these) . . .

02 . . . then remove the five bolts under the shelf side support.

03 Prise out the boot light, and disconnect the wiring . . .

. . . and, once the seat belt's been unhooked from the top, the side panel's ready for our special attention. The first job in our case was making a tidy job of slicing off the shelf supports - a hacksaw blade or very sharp knife will do, but we had the luxury of a Dremel.

It's amazing how just sticking some cheap carpet over a cheap plastic panel gives it such a luxury look. Carpet comes in any colour you like, so don't be shy - just 'cos we've picked grey box cloth doesn't mean you can't be more adventurous. Cut it roughly to shape, then spray the carpet and the panel with spray glue . . .

. . . and stick it on. Apart from ensuring it's stuck to all the curves and bulges, trimming and folding over the edges is the worst bit. Here, we're making a diagonal cut to make a neat job of a corner.

It's also important not to carpet over important features, such as this opening for accessing the rear lights. See what a neat job we've made of slicing the carpet, ready for folding the edges? Anyone would think we did this for a living.

04 **05** **06** **07**

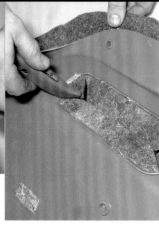

Making an MDF
rear side panel

It's not impossible to fit a set of speakers straight into the stock side panel, but you'll do a neater job of carpeting your own custom-made MDF alternative. With the side panel removed as described earlier,

01 flip it over onto the MDF, and mark its outline . . .

02 . . . then get jiggy with it, and cut out the required shape.

Not surprisingly, it's a good fit, first time. Except - it won't go flat against the inside. To make up the inch-or-so gap at the top edge (under the window), we screwed on a length of

03 aluminium flange. When the panel's carpeted later, you won't see the metal.

04 As before, trim up the carpet roughly to the right shape, then get busy with the glue (of course, trying not to inhale).

05 More carpeting skills - on a corner like this, trim diagonally across to get a neat folded edge for gluing . . .

06 . . . and here, we're making sure that metal flange we added gets the carpet treatment too. Now we've got a tidy panel, sturdy enough to take almost any speaker we choose to cut into it (see the ICE section).

Achtung!
MDF dust is nasty stuff to breathe in. Wear a mask when you're cutting, drilling or sanding it.

Under neon light

So how much of a poser are you? How'd you like to show off all this shiny chequer floor and sexy pedals to full effect, in the midnight hour? You need some neons, baby! Yeah!

Bum notes

It appears that interior neons have recently been declared illegal, and this means, in the first place, you're unlikely to find anywhere that even sells them any more. Exterior neons have been illegal from day one. If you fit interior neons, make sure they're at least easily switched off, should you get pulled. Remember that driving at night with a brightly-lit interior makes it even harder to see out. Neons are best used for show purposes.

01 There's not a great deal to this, really - decide where you want 'em, where you're going to get a live and an earth (and a switch, if necessary), then fit 'em. We wanted our neons up under the dash, to light up the footwells. The first thing to do is offer one in place - remember, it would be sort-of useful if your feet don't hit them as you work the pedals…

02 One of the most convenient places for mounting footwell neons is on the driver's/passenger's oddments shelves - these are only held in by two screws.

03 Sit the neon under your shelf, mark the holes either end, and drill yourself a pair of holes.

04 To make extra-sure your neons don't fall off, try sticking them in place with double-sided tape. But use some self tappers as well, or small nuts and bolts, like us. Okay, so neons don't exactly weigh lots, but take some pride in the job.

05 That's the 'mechanical' side of fitting dealt with - how about the electrical stuff? Join the two black wires together, using a ring terminal, and fit the ring terminal to a good earth point. This can be one you make by drilling a hole in the car's metal body, and fitting a self-tapping screw, or look in the section on fitting the starter button for another earth-point solution.

06 Join the neon red wires together into a spade terminal, and run it to one side of your new switch. In our case, one of two kill switches we're fitting to an alloy plate we've made, which fits to the front of our very basic centre console. Mount the switch somewhere you can get at it quickly (remember what we said earlier about the legal issues here).

07 All we need now is a live feed, to run from the other side of the switch. This means either poking about with a test light and your Haynes wiring diagrams for an existing wire to splice into, running one into the car from the battery, or making an auxiliary fusebox of your own (refer to the security section).

Are your dials all white?

Red dial kit

White or coloured dial kits aren't that difficult to fit, but you will need some skill and patience not to damage the delicate bits inside your instrument panel - the risk is definitely worth it, to liven up that dreary grey Nova dash, anyway.

Just make sure you get the right kit for your car, and don't start stripping anything until you're sure it's the right one - look carefully. Most dial kit makers, for instance, want to know exactly what markings you have on your speedo and rev counter. If they don't ask, be worried - the kit they send could well be wrong for your car, and might not even fit. There seems to be two basic dial layouts for a Nova - cars with a rev counter have one kit, while those without have another.

01 If you haven't yet removed the steering wheel - don't! You don't really need to for this. The surround comes off first, held by a total of four Torx screws, one at each corner. This is the procedure for a Mk 2 Nova - getting the clocks out of a Mk 1 car isn't quite the same as this, but the Haynes Nova manual tells you all.

02 Four screws down, and the surround comes off in our hands.

07 . . . then unhook and remove the cover. Put it somewhere away from small children with sticky fingers - if the 'glass' isn't kept clean, your efforts with the dials will be a total waste of time.

08 On the bigger clocks (speedo and tacho), the first job is pulling out the needle stop with pliers. Bet you didn't even know you had one. Put it somewhere safe. The stop is actually in two parts, but ours came out in one (best to keep it that way).

09 Next, on the speedo, you've got to pull its knob off. Don't worry, it won't feel a thing - just don't lose it, or you'll make it very unhappy.

10 On this basic Nova, we've really got it easy - not only are there just three dials to do, you don't even have to slice off the old ones. Fitting is just a case of sticking the new one on top. Okay, so it's not quite that easy - hook the needle through the centre hole in the dial, and slide the dial up the needle . . .

Tips 'n' tricks

Before peeling off the backing, and sticking the dials in place, have a trial run at it. Fitting the dials over the needles isn't easy when you first try - with practice, it ain't so bad!

03 Now there's three more (crosshead) screws holding the clocks in - one in the centre, and one more in each lower corner.

04 The clocks are almost free to come out now, but first there's the speedo cable to disconnect - it pulls off, but hold down the catch with your thumb as you pull. To give yourself more slack in the cable, open the bonnet and trace the cable up from the back of the gearbox to the bulkhead. Carefully push a bit more cable through into the car.

05 All that's left now is the instrument wiring plug, which releases after squeezing together the lugs at either end.

06 Move the clocks to somewhere clean (where you won't easily lose any of the fiddly small bits). First job is to prise off the lens/cover, using your trusty small screwdriver to unclip the lugs . . .

. . . then make sure the dial goes under the round hub at the top of the needle. Notice we've kept the dial face curved in our fingers - this stops the sticky pads on the back from sticking to everything while you're lining it up.

11

Line the dial up with the mileometer and trip meter, and also check that the holes for the needle stop are lined up. When you're happy, press the dial on like you mean it. Check there's no bits of sticky tape (used in the packaging) left on the dial face, too.

12

Now you can re-unite the speedo with its knob, then swing the needle up with one finger while you refit the needle stop.

13

The lesser dials are way easier to fit than the speedo, but don't try to rush it. With white dials, you might want to paint the white needles, or (d'uh) they won't show up. Choose your colour, then slip some paper under the needle while you're painting it on.

14

Rev counter

Those of you who already have a rev counter (or tacho), ignore this bit. Or perhaps not - you might want a tidy little tacho mounted somewhere more helpful than in the instrument podule. If so, we're here to help. Having one separate gauge mounted on the A-pillar, centre of the dash or centre console adds hugely to the racing look - so how smart would three look?

If you don't want to give yourself a hard time, choose extra gauges which are easy to wire in - rev counter, voltmeter, water temperature, that kind of thing. Oil pressure and temperature gauges need dedicated sender units fitted, which makes things trickier (though not impossible). Then again, if you're just going for the look, who cares if they actually work or not?

01 A bit like doing the starter button, the most-fun part of fitting new dials is figuring out where they'll go. Getting them working is the boring bit. The podule to the right of the Mk 2 Nova clocks looks favourite, so we took our new tacho's mounting bracket, and marked up some holes.

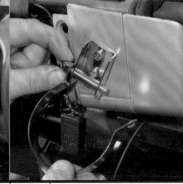

02 This is the finest bit of 'free-form' drilling you'll ever see. You might want to take a bit more care than this - there's not many Mk 2 Novas in scrap yards, for spare dash bits. Sticking on a piece of masking tape before marking/drilling helps stop the drill bit wandering off.

03 With the holes where we want, screws are next - self-tappers, secured behind by two 'speed clips' or 'U-nuts' - a flat 'nut' designed for just this purpose.

04 Lastly, there's the clamp for the gauge itself, which secures using a through-bolt. Simple.

05 The only other hole we'll need is one to feed the gauge wiring through - as this is plastic, for once we won't need a grommet on the wiring hole.

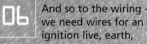

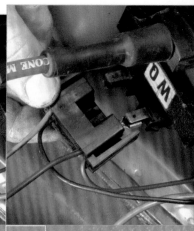

06 And so to the wiring - we need wires for an ignition live, earth, tacho signal and instrument lighting. On Novas having a tacho as standard, the tacho signal wire is green, and on the instrument wiring plug - lesser Novas go without. Everything else is here, though - earth is brown, ignition live is black, and gauge lighting is grey/green. Trim a little wire insulation off . . .

07 . . . and you're ready to twist on the wires from the new gauge, for soldering. Our tacho wiring was black for earth, red for live, and - wait a minute - two green wires? That's helpful - not. One green's from the gauge's bulb (lighting), and the other is the tacho signal. Nothing like making it foolproof, is there?

08 We keep mentioning the tacho signal wire, but haven't shown you where to get one - yet. Down at the front of the passenger-side inner wing, you'll find the ignition coil. Take off the wiring plug at the base, and you'll see several spade terminals - the bottom right one isn't used . . .

09 . . . but it is now. Get a piece of wire long enough to reach round the engine, and into the car, and crimp on a spade connector. Feed the new spade and wire in through the ignition coil wiring plug, and fit the new spade to the bottom right terminal. Finish by reconnecting the coil wiring plug, and feed the new wire into the car. One tacho signal feed.

10 Now the wires are ready, let's give them a gauge to connect to. You can get anodised bezels (trim rings) for most gauges, which you press on (hard) first - we didn't bother with ours, and went straight for slotting the gauge into its chrome holder . . .

11 . . . which in turn sits neatly into the clamp we fitted earlier, then the wires can be poked down the hole we made in our switch podule (sorry, technical term there).

12 Tighten the clamp bolt, and the new gauge is already looking sweet. Let's see if we can get it to work now.

13 The 'strip and solder' method of splicing new wires - here, we're fitting the ignition live feed (black to red). Wrap some tape round the soldered joint, and it's a reliable connection. All that's left is to fire the engine up, and see if it works. Of course.

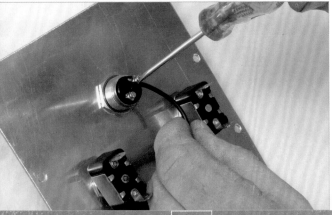

Starter button

Like to have a racing-style starter button on your Nova? Read on! A very cool piece of kit, and not too bad a job to wire up - the most difficult bit's deciding where to mount the button (somewhere easy to get at, but still in full view so's you can impress your passengers!).

The idea of the racing starter button is that the ignition key is made redundant, beyond switching on the ignition lights (it'd be a pretty negative security feature, if you could start the engine without the key at all).

This is one job where you'll be messing with big wires, carrying serious current - more than any other electrical job, don't try and rush it, and don't skimp on the insulating tape. Do it properly, as we're about to show you, and there's no worries. Otherwise, at best, you'll be stranded - at worst, it could be a fire.

01 Our basic Nova was pretty featureless at the front of the centre console, so we trimmed up an alloy plate to fit over it, and mounted the button (and two kill switches, for neons) into the plate. The first black wire (sometimes this is a green wire) at the button goes to a good earth, which we'll figure out in a minute . . .

As we mentioned earlier, we need a good earth for that first black wire from the button. You could tap into an existing earth wire (they're pretty much all brown ones, on the Nova), but we wanted to show you something different. Having checked up behind the dash first, we went through the bulkhead with our trusty drill . . .

02 . . . the other black wire which gets connected to the switch is from the starter button relay. Make sure both screw connections are tight, or the car's going nowhere.

03 The white wire from the relay is an ignition live (which we'll take from the ignition switch itself, later on). The white wire has an in-line fuse - connect the fuse holder to the relay using the spade terminals provided.

04 The relay and fuse holder must be mounted out of the way, up under the dash. Obviously, you must be able to get at the fuse, if it blows (which they often have a nasty habit of doing). One self-tapping screw should do for the relay.

05 As we mentioned earlier, we need a good earth for that first black wire from the button. You could tap into an existing earth wire (they're pretty much all brown ones, on the Nova), but we wanted to show you something different. Having checked up behind the dash first, we went through the bulkhead with our trusty drill . . .

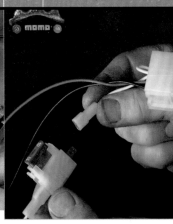

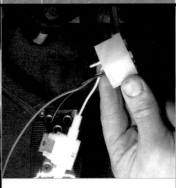

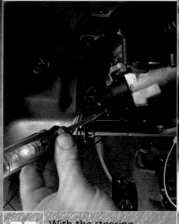

06 . . . and poked through a small bolt, secured by one nut on the inside. Now, with a ring terminal fitted to our black wire, we slip it over our new 'earth bolt', and secure it with another nut (this shot was taken with the driver's vent removed). The beauty of this is - we can add extra wires as we need new earths.

07 With the steering column shrouds removed (covered in fitting the Momo wheel), we have full access to the ignition switch. Check that the car's out of gear, then, using a test light, turn the ignition switch until you find which wire's live only when the starter's working, and which is live only when the ignition's on (warning lights on).

08 Before you go any further, now would be a great time to disconnect the battery. The ignition switch wiring is a prime source of volts, and we'll be chopping those wires about some. Better if they're not carrying voltage at the time, really.

09 On our car, the starter-live wire was black and red. Cut this wire an inch or two from the back of the switch, and tape the short end from the switch up. Leaving it cut like this means the ignition key will no longer start the engine, which is the whole point of a starter button.

Now join the other end of the black/red wire to the blue wire from the relay. We used a bullet-type joiner - whatever you use, make a solid, safe connection (insulate it with tape or heat-shrink afterwards).

We found that one of the black wires at the ignition switch was the ignition-live we needed. Rather than cut and join it (which might create problems with other circuits, if you don't do a very good job), we used the 'strip-and-solder' method. Use a knife to trim off a little black insulation all round the wire . . .

. . . then bare the end of the white wire, twist it round the bared section of black, and use solder to make the joint permanent. No ordinary soldering iron we've got here - this is a butane-powered iron (these are great for soldering larger wires, which can take ages to get hot with electric irons).

Don't forget to insulate the soldered joint afterwards - the last thing you want is an ignition switch fire. Stick the battery back on, and give the new button a try. When you're happy it all works, go back and make a neat job of all the wiring - loom it with tape, fix it in place with cable-ties, that sort of thing. Boring but important.

10 **11** **12** **13**

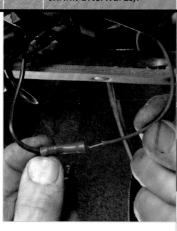

Boring flooring?

Alright, so carpets have always been a dull colour because they have to not show the dirt - when was the last time you heard of a car with white carpets? What goes on the floor needn't be entirely dull, though, and can still be easy to clean, if you're worried.

Ripping out the old carpets is actually quite a major undertaking - first, the seats have to come out (you might be fitting new ones anyway), but the carpets and underfelt fit right up under the dashboard, and under all the sill trims and centre console, etc. Carpet acts as sound-deadening, and is a useful thing to hide wiring under, too, so don't be in too great a hurry to ditch it completely. Unless, of course, your Nova is having a full-on race/rally style treatment, in which case - dump that rug!

Chequerplate is the current fashion in cool flooring, and it's easy to see why it'll probably have an enduring appeal - it's tough but flexible, fairly easy to cut and shape to fit, has a cool mirror finish, and it matches perfectly with the racing theme so often seen in the modified world, and with the ally trim that's widely used too.

Tips 'n' tricks
If you're completely replacing the carpet and felt with, say, chequerplate throughout, do this at a late stage, after the ICE install and any other electrical work's been done - that way, all the wiring can be neatly hidden underneath it.

Chequer mats

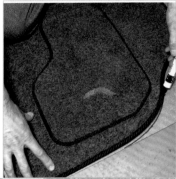
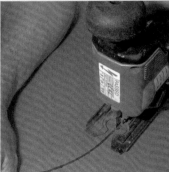
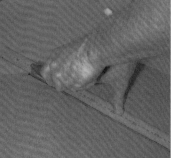
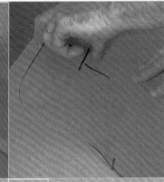

01 The halfway-house to a fully-plated interior is to make up your own tailored mats (hell, you can buy ready-mades if you're not allowed to play with sharp knives). Unless you buy real ally chequer, what you'll get is actually plastic, and must be supported by mounting it on hardboard. Take one of the lovely 'Granny' mats your car might have come with, and use it as a template to mark the shape onto the hardboard (you could always make a template from some thin card).

02 With the shape marked out, it's time for the jigsaw - next to a cordless drill, this has to be one of the most useful tools ever invented for the modder.

03 To make the hardboard fit better into the footwells, score it at the bend where it goes up under the pedals . . .

04 . . . then carefully 'fold' the hardboard back to the required shape - trust us, this will make your new chequer mats fit superbly.

05 Not unlike this in fact. Try your hardboard mat in place, and trim the corners and edges as necessary to get it fitting as flat as poss.

06 Now you can use your hardboard as a template, for cutting out the chequer. Try to make the chequer fractionally bigger overall than the hardboard, so you don't see the wood edge (you shouldn't anyway, if your board is a tidy fit). Stick the chequer to the board, using some decent glue - spray glue's convenient, but usually not quite up to the job. You can't beat good old brush-on Evo-Stik (and no, we're not being paid to say that).

07 Do it right, and you too can have a floor like this - looks sweet, and the mats don't slip. Sorted.

Wheely cool

A new steering wheel is an essential purchase in personalising your Nova. It's one of the main points of contact between you and the car, it's sat right in front of you, and the standard ones are dull and massive!

Don't be tempted to fit too small a wheel - Novas never had power steering, and a tiny-rimmed steering wheel will make manoeuvring very difficult, especially with phat tyres.

One bit of good news is that, once you've shelled out for your wheel, it may be possible to fit it to your next car, too. When you buy a new wheel, you usually have to buy a boss (or mount) to go with it - the mounts are less pricey, so one wheel could be fitted to another completely different car, for minimum cost.

A trick feature worth investigating is the detachable wheel/boss. This feature comes in handy when you park up and would rather the car was still there when you come back (something most people find a bonus). It's all very well having a steering wheel immobiliser or steering lock, but I doubt many thieves will be driving off in your car if the steering wheel's completely missing! Also, removing the wheel may remove the temptation to break in and pinch… your wheel!

Fitting a sports wheel

01 First, a confession. It's not absolutely essential to remove the steering column shrouds to fit your new wheel, but taking them off gives you more scope for violence getting the old wheel off. And you might want to spray them, anyway. There's four screws underneath . . .

02 . . . and one more each side, behind the steering wheel (turn the wheel to get at them) . . .

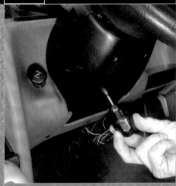

03 . . . then the lower half of the shroud comes away. The top half's a trickier prospect - it doesn't seem to want to come off, but can be persuaded with a little careful pulling, and bending of the plastic. Just make sure bending doesn't turn into breaking. We left ours on 'til the wheel was off, but you can do it sooner.

04 Novas have it easy, with no modern airbags to worry about. Prise out the horn push . . .

05 . . . then simply pull the red and black wires from their connectors.

>>

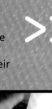

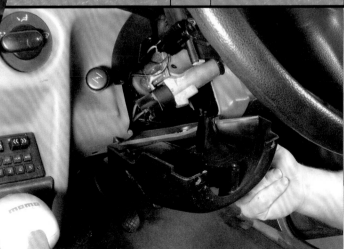

The wheel nut has a locking collar around it, to prevent it coming undone (though why they bothered is a mystery, when you see how tough it is getting the wheel off). We're tapping the collar down with a chisel, but you'll probably try a screwdriver.

06

Getting the old wheel off is a real grotty job. Undoing the nut's no problem, but hold onto the wheel to stop it turning - don't just let the steering lock take the strain, as you might bust it. Before you go much further, make sure that the steering wheel's straight - as confirmation, look to see that the front wheels are pointing straight-ahead.

07

If you're lucky, the wheel will now pull off. We struggled with ours - Vauxhall wheels have notoriously tight splines. In our fully-equipped workshop, we turned to this small puller, specially designed for the job. Don't tug the wheel from side to side - you'll wreck the column bushes. Better to smack the wheel off from behind, if you can.

08

Just to give hope to those of you who are struggling, Vauxhall wheels do come off eventually. Well, this one did, anyway.

09

Any new (non-Vauxhall) wheel will also need a new boss (well, we all feel like a new boss at times). The first job is to fit your new wheel to the boss, prior to fitting. Make sure the 'TOP' mark is (duh) at the top, then line up the screw holes . . .

10

. . . and fit a couple of Allen screws. This isn't final fitting - we're only fitting the wheel now, to give us something to hang onto while the big steering wheel nut's tightened (the nut actually secures the new boss). Confused? Don't be - it'll all make sense in a sec.

11

The most vital part of this operation is to make sure the front wheels are still straight. The next most vital bit is to get the wheel onto its splines straight. Get either wrong, and the boss has to come off again. So don't get it wrong.

12

On with the lockwasher and steering wheel nut, and start tightening. The correct torque for this is 'only' 15 Nm, but don't be fooled. As you tighten the nut, it draws the boss onto the splines, so you must actually have several 'go's at it, to be sure it's fully seated. A wobbly wheel, we don't need.

13

14 Now the boss is fixed on, the wheel can come off again. Why? Well, we haven't got the horn yet, for starters.

15 Before wiring-up the horn button, don't forget to bend up the tabs on the lockwasher under the steering wheel nut. Could save your life.

16 The horn button is an earth switch. The earth path comes from the steering column, through the new boss. To get it to the horn button, we need a contact plate, which is the circular metal item we're fitting now. Comes with its own wire, and everything (yellow/green, in this case).

17 Now take your horn button, and fit the wire from the contact plate, and the one from the wheel boss (black on our car). Doesn't matter which way round the wires go - pressing the button just completes the earth circuit, and fires the horn.

18 Clip the horn button into the contact plate - the spring round the centre of the plate holds the button in place, and ensures a good contact with the button. If, after fitting, the horn doesn't work, chances are there's a loose or dirty connection on the boss or contact plate. But let's think positive - it will work.

19 Now at last the wheel can go on for real. Offer it in place, lining up the screw holes . . .

20 . . . then fit and tighten - this time, all of them, and securely. Grab that rim and go for a spin - see what it feels like, to really be in control of your Nova. Now the fifth wheel looks as good as the one at each corner.

Pedalling your Nova

A tasty race-equipment touch to your modded machine, pedal extensions really look the part when combined with full chequerplate mats, or alloy footwells - available in several styles and (anodised) colours. Not sure how well the anodising will wear, though... The only other issue with pedals is the clutch and brake must have rubbers fitted - this is first of all sensible (so your feet don't slip off them at an awkward moment) and it's also a legal requirement. Don't buy extensions without.

Achtung!
Check your insurance company's position regarding pedal extensions. A while ago there was a big fuss after a couple of cars fitted with pedal extensions crashed, which resulted in pedal extensions being withdrawn from sale at a lot of places.

01 The old pedal rubbers just peel off - but wait. We found later that we could've left them on, and it might've been better if we had. The rubber's not very thick, and gives a flat base for the extensions to mount on - better than the lumpy metal underneath. Even we can learn something.

02 The next job is to hold the extension up in place, and work out where to drill the mounting bolt holes. You'll soon find there's no-go areas for drilling - e.g. don't go too close to the pedal arm, or you won't be able to fit the nut to the mounting bolt. You must have at least two holes per pedal. Mark the positions with a pen or scriber . . .

03 . . . and if you're drilling the metal, use a centre-punch to mark the hole centre, or the drill will skate all over the place.

04 The block of wood behind the pedal arm's just to stop the pedal sinking while we drill, but it also saves the carpet from getting holed, if we go too far. Put some paper down, to catch the metal swarf.

You too can have pedals like these. Smart, eh? If your clutch pedal's out of line with the brake (too high or too low), adjust your clutch with a little help from your Haynes Nova manual. It's all in the details.

05 One Allen-headed bolt, one nut behind, and we're one step nearer footwell heaven. Do them up tight - loose pedals is a fast track to the hospital ward.

06 Most pedal extension kits come with dire warnings about keeping the pedal spacing the same as before - so we're saying the same. Having the 'stop' and 'go' pedals too close could also mean a trip to hospital, so be smart. The throttle pedal's tricky on a Nova, though - fit the extension too far to the right, and it'll catch on the carpet.

07

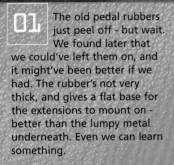

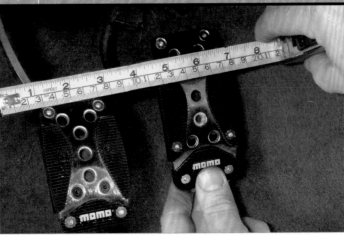

Are you **sitting stylishly?**

The perfect complement to your lovingly-sorted suspension, because you need something better than the standard seats to hold you in, now that you can corner so much faster... and they look brutal, by way of a bonus. Besides the seat itself, remember to price up the subframe to adapt it to the mounting points in your car. Most people also choose the three- or four-point harnesses to go with it (looks a bit daft to fit a racing seat without it), but make sure the harness you buy is EC-approved, or an eagle-eyed MOT tester might make you take 'em out.

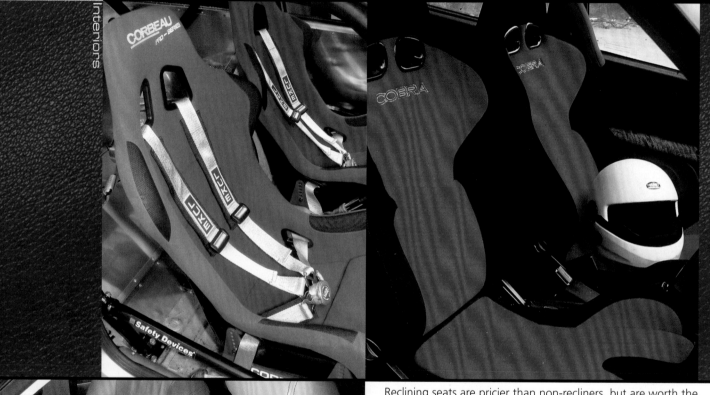

Reclining seats are pricier than non-recliners, but are worth the extra. With non-adjustable seats, how are your mates meant to get in the back? Through the tailgate? Or maybe there is no back seat... You can get subframes which tilt, so that non-reclining seats can move forward. Non-reclining racing seats should be tried for fit before you buy.

An alternative to expensive racing seats would be to have your existing seats re-upholstered in your chosen colours/fabrics, to match your interior theme. You might be surprised what's possible, and the result could be something truly unique. If you've got a basic model, try sourcing GTE or GSi seats from a breakers (haggle if the side bolsters are worn away - a common fault). A secondhand interior bought here will be a lot cheaper than buying new goodies, and you know it'll fit easily (all Novas are the same underneath) - but - it won't have that unique style. Specialist breakers may be able to supply something more rad, such as a wicked leather interior from a top-spec Cavalier/Calibra - might take some persuading to get it in, though!

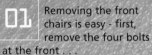

01 Removing the front chairs is easy - first, remove the four bolts at the front . . .

02 . . . and lift off these mounting clamps.

03 Slide the seat forwards, and pull out the metal stop-pegs from the rear of the seat rail . . .

04 . . . then slide the seat all the way back, and off the rails. Getting rid of those nasty grey chairs, I'd look happier than he does.

Removing
seats

Removing the rear seats isn't any harder - fold the backrest down, and there's a **05** screw each side, in the corner . . .

06 . . . then fold the seat cushion forwards, and there's another screw on the seat hinge, in front.

07 The seat cushion's held on by a pair of self-tapping screws - two per seat half. Away with those Granny-grey seats!

Fitting new Corbeaus

01 We had a bit of a challenge fitting our Corbeau Pro-Series seats - because they were too sporty! Being proper race buckets, they don't come with Nova subframes, which gave us some head-scratching. It was pretty obvious some home-made metal would be needed, so first we unclipped the plastic covers from the Nova seat runners . . .

02 . . . before doing some mods of our own, with a few sturdy strips of metal, and a large mig welder. Don't try this at home - it's a lot less grief to get seats which come with proper Nova subframes (which just bolt to the seats, and to your existing runners). But we like a challenge.

03 Our welding efforts finished up looking like this - and boy is it strong (as it needs to be). Remember - any seats, including ones you might grab at a scrapyard, must be really securely mounted. Bodging is not an option.

04 The seat mounting brackets give plenty of scope for height adjustment, but you'll need to set them pretty accurately for reaching the wheel and pedals. Of course, being pros, we checked all this before welding-in our subframes.

05 You could always drill more than one set of holes, to give you fore-and-aft adjustment on your seats. Just use decent nuts 'n' bolts to pin them to the mounting brackets.

06 Finally we get to see a seat. Trust me - these babies grab you and don't let go. Can't reach the stereo controls? Too bad - you'll have to wait 'til you get out.

07 The final step in fitting is setting the seat height, which you do easily enough by deciding which of the many sets of holes you'll use in the seat mounts. Do those sturdy Allen screws up tight, and the only thing moving in that seat will be your eyes.

How strapped are you?

It's true that not everyone likes racing harnesses, but anyone like that's just boring, or should probably eat less pies. Besides, you don't fit sexy race seats and then not fit race belts, do you?

The only problem with harnesses is caused by where you have to mount them. Even with a three-point harness, you end up using one of the rear seat belt mounts, and it seriously reduces your ability to carry bodies in the back seats (webbing everywhere). The MOT crew say that, if you've got rear seats, you must have rear seat belts fitted, so you either 'double-up' on your rear belt mounts (use the same mounting bolts for your harnesses and rear belts), or you take the back seats out altogether. Removing the rear seats leaves the rear deck free for chequerplate, speakers, roll cages - whatever you like.

It's just important to understand how fundamental harnesses can end up being, to the whole look of your car - there's almost no half-measures with race belts, so you've got to really want 'em.

One thing you must **not** do is to try making up your own seat belt/harness mounting points. Vauxhall structural engineers spent plenty of time selecting mounting points and testing them for strength. Drilling your own holes and sticking bolts through is fine for mounting speakers and stuff, but you're heading for an interview with the Grim Reaper if you try it with seat belts. The forces in a big shunt are immense. We're not convinced either that the practice of slinging harnesses round a rear strut brace is kosher, from the safety angle - the poxy strut braces available are so flimsy (they're usually ally) you can bend them in your hands. Nuts to trusting my life to one of those!

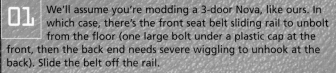

01 We'll assume you're modding a 3-door Nova, like ours. In which case, there's the front seat belt sliding rail to unbolt from the floor (one large bolt under a plastic cap at the front, then the back end needs severe wiggling to unhook at the back). Slide the belt off the rail.

02 Up top, there's a plastic cover over the belt upper mounting, which flicks off, revealing a reassuringly-large bolt underneath.

03 Remove the rear side panel as described earlier, and you'll have no trouble spotting the belt reel. Held on by just one bolt, it's soon ready to be consigned to the bin.

Removing seat belts

Removing the rear seat belt is similar to the fronts - there's the large upper **04** bolt . . .

 . . . one on the floor (fold the rear seats for **05** access) . . .

 . . . and then the belt reel itself, which is tucked behind the rear shelf side support (which we removed to cover with carpet, earlier in this **06** section).

 To make room for the harness rear mounts, the rear belt buckles should also be unbolted from the floor. Keep the bolts - you'll be needing them again. **07**

Harnesses

01 Fitting the new harnesses is a walk in the park, compared to taking out the naff old belts. The harnesses clip onto 'eyes', which you screw in, in place of the old seat belt bolts.

02 The only trick is tightening the eyes sufficiently to be safe - they must go in all the way down to the shoulder. Use an adjustable spanner to help with final tightening, as shown.

03 Hooking-on the new harness is made very easy by the spring-loaded tag which you pull back. These are some quality Luke harnesses, looking very saucy in red, supplied by our friends at Corbeau seats.

04 Oh, so that's what the big holes in the tops of the seats are for... Feed the belts through . . .

05 . . . and clip onto the eye you've fitted to the front lower seat belt mount, on the inside of the door sill.

06 On most cars, the other front mounting is your seat belt stalk in the centre - on the Nova, the belt stalk is on the old front seat. Which we've just removed. So - if it's good enough for Vauxhall, let's get the drill to our seat mounting bracket, and make a hole for our last eye (again, proper subframes might have seat belt mountings built-in).

07 Besides your new eye, you'll need a nut to fit it, and you'll probably find that just any nut won't do - it has to be a fine-pitch thread, or it won't go on the eye. When you're at your local nut 'n' bolt specialists, try and get a nut with a (blue) Nyloc insert, which will stop the nut working loose. This is a safety harness we're talking about, after all.

08 Don't be shy about tightening the eye and its bolt, either. Do it right, and you can clip on that last bit of harness, safe in the knowledge that you're, er... safe.

ICE

Headset

The cheaper your Nova, the nastier your standard head unit's going to be. Of course, by the time an Nova's passed through several owners, it's pretty unlikely to still have a standard Vauxhall radio in anyway, but if all you've got is a hole, don't feel too bad. Standard sets are fine if all you want to do is aimlessly listen to the radio with your arm out the window, but not - definitely not - if you want to impress your mates with the depth and volume of your bass.

Or, of course, if you want to listen to CDs. It's got to go - and there's plenty of decent headsets out there which will give you a night-and-day difference in sound quality and features. The headset is the heart of your new install - always go for the best you can afford. Ask the experts which features matter most, if you're building a full system.

Our Alpine 7874RB headset was supplied by Optima of Bristol, and is pretty typical of the current single-CD state of the art - looks decent, good sound, plenty of features. The peak of in-car entertainment, so to speak.

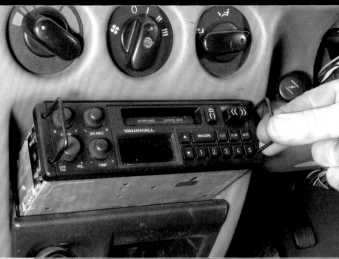

01 First, the old set's got to be shifted. Resist the urge to just crowbar the thing out of the dash - you'll be needing two of the standard radio removal tools to do the job with less damage. And you could always sell it, or keep it, to stick back in when you sell the car?

02 Next, the standard cage has to go, and this isn't exactly a pushover. Normally, a little light work with a screwdriver, and out she comes - but not on this baby. There's a cunningly-placed screw right at the back of the cage to undo first, y'see.

03 Now we can set to with the screwdriver, prising out the locating lugs . . .

ISO plug wiring **colours**

Black plug (power/earth)
Red - 12V permanent live
Yellow - radio memory live
Black - earth
Blue - Remote/P-cont
Orange - dimmer

Brown plug (speakers)
White pair - front left
Grey pair - front right
Green pair - rear left
Purple pair - rear right

Having ISO plugs makes life much easier - one does power, the other speakers (the power one has red, yellow and black leads, among others). Plug in the power one, and all your lives and earths are taken care of. If you're in no-ISO-plug hell, buy a universal ISO converter, and wire it in yourself, using the Haynes wiring diagrams as a guide to the standard stereo wiring.

In body styling, we upgraded the grotty standard Nova aerial to a cool beesting, which had its own built-in amplifier, needing a 12-volt live feed. Our Alpine headset wiring loom provides a spare live feed - once its ISO plug's been connected, this comes from the car's standard wiring.

04 . . . then the cage can be persuaded out, and - what's this? The standard wiring's plugged into the cage itself. Weird. It looks like someone's been here before us, and converted the normal Vauxhall stereo wiring to ISO standard, saving us a job. You can normally buy ISO converter leads for older cars, but the Nova's an exception.

06 How easy do you want it? Plug it in!

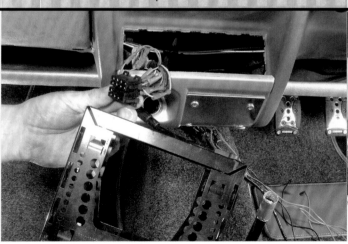
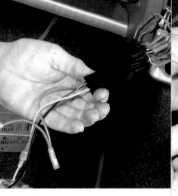
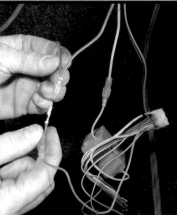

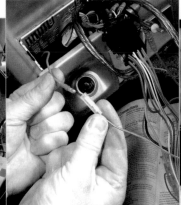
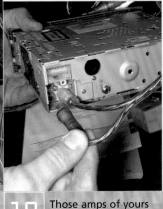

07 We're running our rear mid speakers off the headset, but want to improve the sound by using our own oxygen-free speaker wire. All we do is use the Alpine instructions to check which wire colours do rear left and right, trace the wires through our ISO plug to the Vauxhall wiring the other side, then chop and crimp on our new (sexy blue) speaker wire.

08 Before we get too carried away connecting up wires, now's a good time to introduce the new set's cage into the equation. From behind the dash, feed in every wire that's going to be connected to the headset (which includes any RCA leads, CD changer lead, P-cont/remote wire, and so on), and slip the cage loosely into place.

09 If you're running amps in your system, you'll need a remote or P-cont lead, to switch them on (see the section on amps). The headset has a P-cont output wire, usually blue or blue/white. Any ordinary bit of wire will do for this - from the headset, feed it round the car to your amps.

10 Those amps of yours also need a signal to work from, and that's what the RCA outputs on the headset provide. If your set's got more than one pair of connections (pre-outs), these may be marked 'front', 'rear' or 'sub'. Use whichever set makes sense for location and type of amped speakers you're running. Connect red lead-to-red connection, white lead-to...

And this is the headset main wiring plug going on. This is where all your power, earth and speaker wiring comes in, from the ISO plugs. It's a bit vital to the plot, this plug, so make sure it clips in tight.

11

If listening to the radio has any part in your life, you'll be needing an aerial connection any time soon. Most good sets come with an aerial adaptor plug, if your lead doesn't fit straight off.

12

If you can, test that everything's working at this point, before pushing the unit right into its cage. If all's well, push the headset home until it clicks. If it gets stuck, take the set out, and un-bunch all the wiring by hand. Do not force it in, or you could end up having a very bad day. Success? Now get out the instruction manual again, and set those levels properly. Enjoy.

13

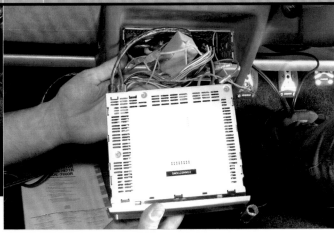

The standard items in the Nova speak volumes (hur-hur) about any car manufacturer's desire to build things down to a price - ie spend as little as poss. What does it cost Vauxhall for the speakers in a Nova? If it's more than a fiver a set, they're being robbed. Low on power, and with nasty paper cones which disintegrate after a few years, fitting ANY aftermarket speakers is going to be an upgrade. But we don't want to give you that - how about showing you how to fit some tasty components?

Boss - the name's familiar, if you've ever shopped at the budget end of the market. But do not be fooled - Boss make several ranges, and until now, we've only seen the very cheapest range in the UK (for more info, check the DD Audio website). These very tasty-looking items very obviously come from their more expensive range - so let's see if the sound matches the looks...

Front
speakers

The best place for your front components is in the doors. Trouble is, Novas don't have speakers there as standard, which makes life a bit tricky. But not impossible. Using the holes we drilled for fitting the central locking, it was easy feeding decent speaker wire through into the door. First job completed.

01

Now - where's the woofer going? The tweeter can fit pretty much anywhere on the door panel, but getting the big speaker fitted so it misses the window winder could be fun. Then there's door internal bits, like the window and its mech, and even the door check strap to consider. When the door's shut, is the speaker 'blanked' by the end of the dash?

02

Finally, we decided to put it here, at the base of the door (just above where the door pocket will be). We don't need all four speaker mounting holes, so we're marking two at the base . . .

03

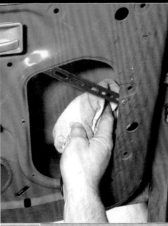

04 . . . before drilling the required holes. If all this is too much work for you, check to see what upgrades you might be able to get for the dash-mounted speakers (bet they won't sound as good as our approach, though).

05 Before the speaker goes in for good, we ought to do something to make it sound even better. Like sound-deadening the door. The market leader in deadening is Dynamat - but - it comes at a price. What else is out there? Brown Bread. Sounds dead. Clean up the door panel with some decent solvent . . .

06 . . . then cut it, and get it onnn. Don't get too carried away in your quest for sonic perfection, but don't skimp on it, either.

07 You mainly want to deaden the large 'floppy' areas of the door which will vibrate, but some deadening round the speaker will help too. Two things about this stuff - use it warm (warm it up with a heat gun, on a cold day), and watch your fingers (the metal foil edges are sharp!).

Mmm - perhaps we aren't as clever as we thought. Our tweeter's not going to sit right back in the door, where our hole is - there's a door **12** in the way. Mark that metalwork . . .

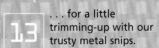

13 . . . for a little trimming-up with our trusty metal snips.

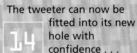

The tweeter can now be fitted into its new hole with **14** confidence . . .

. . . and pinned to the panel from behind, with this clever mounting **15** bracket.

08 Use proper speaker terminals on the ends of your speaker wire, and remember - the convention is striped/writing wire is speaker positive (bigger terminal of the two). Notice we've also put heatshrink on the terminals - insulating against possible contact with metal door bits is a good plan, even if you just use tape.

09 The last part of our cunning speaker mounting plan was to use a metal strip across the top, for a third mounitng point. Not an ideal way to mount a speaker, and some more sound deadening would be an idea, but it should work fine.

10 The speaker's in the door, but there's no hole in the door trim panel for it. Much eyeing-up and checking with the panel later, we had the speaker position roughly marked. Out came the old school compasses, for a proper circular-type hole . . .

11 . . . then Stanley (with a sharp new blade) was pressed into service to do the actual cutting. While we were there, we also marked and cut the hole for the tweeter, which will sit above it in the door panel.

The final chapter in the front components story is fitting the crossover. We love these units, which look like something out of Star Trek, and way too good to hide - so put them on display, just above the door pockets.
16 With the funky cover removed, mark them for position . . .

. . . then drill and screw, and clip that cool chrome cover back in place.
17

Of course, we needed another small hole in our door trim, to feed the speaker wiring through to the crossover. But you don't want to see another hole being drilled. Instead, here we are, connecting up the tweeter wiring. Ensure that the speaker wiring inside the door's done neatly, secured with tape or ties, otherwise the window mech might chew it up.
18

The crossovers take the main input from the headset, and 'filter' the sound, splitting it into the best frequencies for the woofer and tweeter. Make sure you connect the speaker wires to the right outputs, and observe the convention for pos and neg connections.
19

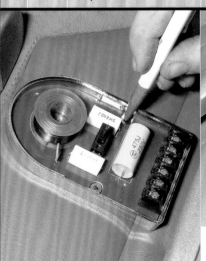

01 First job with a new ready-made shelf is to mark the speaker positions. Not tricky.

Rear speakers

If we're talking about a set of 6x9s, rear shelf-mounting is the simplest option. If you don't want to butcher your standard shelf (always a flimsy item), either make a new one from MDF (using your stock shelf as a template), or buy a ready-made acoustic 'stealth' shelf. Either way, make hiding your new speakers a priority - tasty speakers on display in the back window could soon mean no rear window, and no speakers...

While shelf mounting offers top quality sound and an easy life, 3-door Novas also have another top spot for speakers - the rear side trim panels. Providing you don't go for mahoosive units with huge, heavy magnets, you just cut a suitable-sized hole in the panel, and mount your speaker in from behind. The experts say you shouldn't really panel-mount 6x9s (though there's no harm trying it), so instead we chose some 6-inch mids to provide our 'rear fill' on the sound.

Remember that the length of wire to each speaker should be the same (as near as poss), or you might find the speakers run slightly out of phase. Crimp on the right terminals, and connect up your speakers. For max neatness, use P-clips screwed along the edge of the shelf. To remove the shelf more easily, fit some bullet connectors in the speaker wiring, or ask your ICE dealer for a Neutrik connector plug.

02 With a speaker outline marked, remove the wood from the rest of the shelf, and drill a nice big hole somewhere inside the outline... then get busy with the jigsaw.

03 Use the speaker mounts (or even the speakers themselves) as a template to drill the mounting holes . . .

04 . . . then screw on the speakers. Don't forget that 6x9s can be run off the headset, to provide a little 'rear fill' - if you have them amped-up, you might find that the sound's too biased to the back of the car.

05

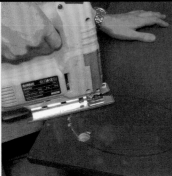

Achtung!
MDF dust is nasty stuff to breathe in. Wear a mask when you're cutting, drilling or sanding it.

Side trim panel mounting

We'd already made up some tidy substitutes for the old side trim panels, from carpeted MDF (see interiors) - not only does this look better, it makes fitting any speakers miles easier (and the sound'll probably be better, too). Using our Boss instructions as a guide to the hole size, it's out with the old compasses again . . .

01

. . . then bring on the jigsaw, and make us a speaker-sized hole. How did people ever fit speakers before the jigsaw? Badly, I suspect.

02

Being extremely careful that drill doesn't slip and ruin your day (as well as your speakers), drill round the edge for the mounting screw holes . . .

03

. . . then fit the surround and screw the whole lot to the panel.

04

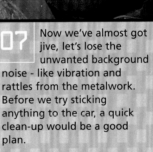

05 Connect up the speaker wire, remembering it's the larger terminal that's positive (and the writing/striped wire that goes to it) . . .

06 . . . then flip the panel back over and fit the grille. Not essential (especially with cones as sexy-looking as these), but useful if you don't trust your passengers to keep their fingers to themselves.

07 Now we've almost got jive, let's lose the unwanted background noise - like vibration and rattles from the metalwork. Before we try sticking anything to the car, a quick clean-up would be a good plan.

08 We know that Dynamat and Brown Bread are both good tin-deadening options here, but how about an alternative, suggested by our friends at Optima in Bristol? Roofing weatherstrip, from a builder's merchants. It's not sexy, and you might want two layers of it, but it is cheap - and it works. Who's gonna know? No-one ever sees it!

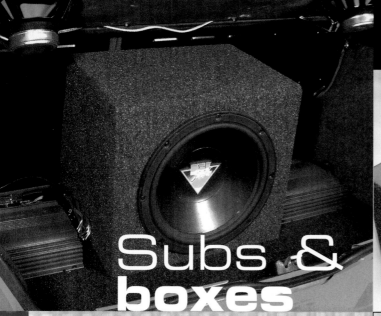

Subs &
boxes

No system's complete without that essential deep bass boom and rumble. Don't muck about with bass tubes - get the real thing to avoid disappointment. So you lose some of your boot space - so what? Is getting the shopping in an issue? We think not.

Most people opt for the easy life when it comes to boxes, at least until they're ready for a full-on mental install. The Nova at least has a roomy boot, so standard boxes will fit easily. Making up your own box isn't hard though, especially if you were any good at maths and geometry. Oh, and woodwork. Most subs come with instructions telling you what volume of box they work best in, but ask an expert (or a mate) what they think - the standard boxes are just fine, and none are pricey. The only real reason to build your own is if you've got an odd-shaped boot (or want something that looks trick).

Standard boxes go out the window when you get greedy with the bass, and want a trick-looking multi-sub install like ours (and ours is way off being the most radical you'll see). Three 12-inch subs where the back seat used to be? We need a custom-made enclosure, and our friends at Optima in Bristol came up with the goods. Making the MDF 'sculpture' look the nuts was a job we entrusted to our tame local car trimmers, Pipers of Sparkford - and the lads done good, with a tasty blend of red alcantara and grey (to match the outside of the car, of course).

The subs deserve a mention, too. Supplied by DD Audio, these are their own-branded subs, made in the land of Uncle Sam. They might not look that special, but you'll love them with your ears, if not your eyes. Made using the highest-quality components, turn this up and no-one needs to apologise.

01 One custom-made sub enclosure, fit for three big subs. We've even got holes the right size, like you'd get with most ready-made boxes. If you're hole-less, try using the template which came with your sub to mark the hole, then get busy with a jigsaw.

02 Don't forget to wire up your sub before fitting it - a very common mistake, caused by being too keen. Most ready-made boxes come fitted with a terminal plate on the side of the box - with these, just run your speaker wire from the sub to the inside of the plate (keep the pos and neg wiring the right way round).

Achtung!
MDF dust is nasty stuff to breathe in. Wear a mask when you're cutting, drilling or sanding it.

03 Our custom-made enclosure doesn't have the luxury of a terminal plate, and we've got to get the wires out somehow - looks like we need a hole (or possibly, three).

04 This is where we find out if our pre-cut holes are actually the right size. Having the box covered in carpet (and the edges folded into the hole) hasn't helped, but at least the sub's not going to be loose.

05 Make sure the sub's logo is lined up correctly (this won't affect the sound, just the pose-value), then drill through the mounting holes round the edge of the sub.

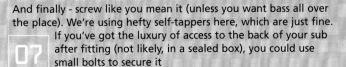

And finally - screw like you mean it (unless you want bass all over the place). We're using hefty self-tappers here, which are just fine. If you've got the luxury of access to the back of your sub after fitting (not likely, in a sealed box), you could use small bolts to secure it

06 Most subs come with some kind of gasket, which helps to seal the box and deaden any unwanted vibes. This chunky rubber item slips over the outer edge of the sub basket.

07

Amplifiers

So, how many amps do we want in our car? One school of thought says each pair of speakers, and each sub, should have an individual amp - by setting the output from each amp separately, you can control each aspect of the sound, before you even need to think about adding a graphic equaliser. You can also better match your speakers to the level of power they need, to work best. Trouble is, running several amps means doubling-up on wiring, and you could end up drawing a monster amount of power from that battery.

Any starter system can be made to seriously kick, using just one 400W four-channel amp - choose the right one carefully (and the components to go with it), and just one will do. With a 'tri-mode' amp, you could run your front components off one pair of channels, bridge the other two for a sub, and run some 6x9s off the head unit. Don't forget that decent modern headsets chuck out fifty-per-channel now, so don't assume you'll need separate amps for everything.

Decide where you'll mount the amps carefully. Amps must be adequately cooled - don't cover it up so there's no airflow, and don't hang it upside-down from your shelf.

Our system set-up uses two small two-channel amps for two of our three subs, with a large four-channel amp in tri-mode for our remaining sub and the front components. The rear mid speakers are run off the headset (well, with all those subs in the back, we didn't need much more power behind us). Again, we're using Boss for the amps (courtesy of DD Audio), and as with all the components supplied for this install, the 'Chaos' amps look the business, with plenty of features. Do they kick? Let's find out.

Achtung!
MDF dust is nasty stuff to breathe in. Wear a mask when you're cutting, drilling or sanding it.

01 First to go on is the live feed. This is one amp connection you should really use a ring terminal on, rather than just stuffing a bare wire into the hole. And insulate any bare metal on the terminal - that live touches anything else, and the results won't be good.

02 Next thing we need is an earth. Don't use skinny wires for earths - ideally, it should be the same-thickness wire as you've used for your live feed. Notice how we've twisted the bared end of the thick earth wire, then folded it over before fitting the amplifier screw terminal. With a wire this thick, make sure there's no stray strands hanging out.

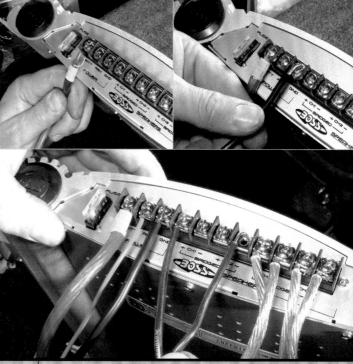

06 . . . while here, we're wiring up the large tri-mode amp for our sub, in bridged mode. In all cases, you must check the manual for the right combination of speaker wires. As with the lives and earths, it's also vital there's no stray bits of wire left poking out.

03 For an earth point, you can use any handy bolt, but seat and seat belt mounting bolts must be re-done up tight, of course. Or you can always make your own hole (just don't go through the fuel tank). We fitted our own bolt behind one of the rear side panels - we could then hook on any number of earth wires, secured with a second nut.

04 Next up, it's the humble P-cont (remote) lead going on. This performs the vital function of carrying the 'switch-on' signal from your headset - without this, you won't hear much. The good news is, this is one time when size doesn't matter - it doesn't carry much current, so the wire can be as skinny as you like.

05 Read the amp's instruction book carefully when connecting any wires, or you might regret it, especially for bridged or tri-mode. Identify your speaker pos and neg/left and right wires, and get them screwed on. This is the wiring for our front speakers . . .

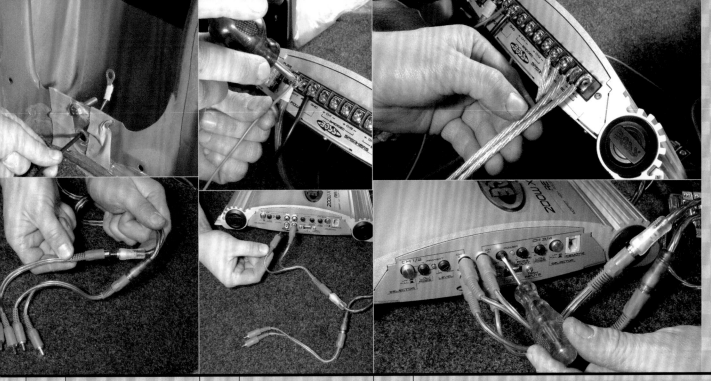

07 To get our large amp to work in tri-mode, we needed to split the RCA input across four channels, using an adaptor lead known as a splitter (cunning, eh?). These plug into each end of the RCA lead, and double the number of outputs.

08 Splitters aren't always clearly marked for left and right channels, so check what you're doing carefully. You can also use splitters to run more than one amp from one RCA lead (but the 'sound quality' experts say you shouldn't).

09 A good tip is to leave the amps loose until after you've set them up - if you can, leave good access to the gain adjustment (volume) screws after final fitting, too. Starting at normal listening volume, with the amp gain turned down, put on a kicking track, then turn the gain up until the speakers just start to distort. Turn the gain down a tad from there, and you've a good basic setting. Amp gain and headset faders can now be tweaked to give a good balanced sound - or whatever tickles your lugholes.

Tricks 'n' tips
Very few systems work 100%, first time. If the amp LEDs don't light up, for instance, are they getting power? Are the P-cont/remote wires connected properly? If the sub doesn't kick, is the amp switch set to bridged or tri-mode, not stereo? Are the low-pass switches in the correct position? RTFM.

Wiring-up

For most people, this is the scariest part of an install - just the thought of masses of multi-coloured spaghetti sticking out of your dash might have you running to the experts (or a knowledgeable mate). But - if you do everything in a logical order, and observe a few simple rules, wiring-up isn't half as brain-numbing as it seems.

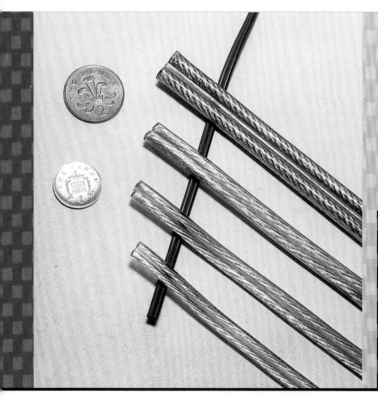

Live feeds

Although a typical head unit can be powered off the standard Vauxhall wiring (the stock wire is good for about 15 amps, tops) running amplifiers means you'll be needing a new live feed, taken straight off the battery.

Get some decent 'eight-gauge' (quite heavy) or 'four-gauge' (getting on for battery cable thickness - serious stuff) wire, and a matching fuseholder. If you're running more than one item off this feed wire, get a distribution block too, which splits the feed up, with a separate fuse for each item - who'd have thought electrical safety can look trick too?

Pub trivia

Hands up, who knows what 'RCA' stands for? We use it every day in ICE-speak, but what does it really mean? Really Clever Amplifier lead? Remote Control Acoustic lead? Well, the answer's a strange one. RCA leads and connectors are also known as 'phono' connectors in the world of TV and hi-fi, and they've been around a long, long time. How long, exactly? We're talking back in the days when you could only get radios - big suckers with valves in them, and long before anyone thought of putting one in a car. RCA actually stands for Radio Corporation of America, who hold the patent on this type of connector and lead. Not a lot of people know that.

Speaker and RCA wiring

As with all wiring, the lesson here is to be neat and orderly - or - you'll be sorry! RCA leads and speaker wires are prone to picking up interference (from just about anywhere), so the first trick to learn when running ICE wiring is to keep it away from live feeds, and also if possible, away from the car's ECUs. Another favourite way to interference-hell is to loop up your wiring, when you find you've got too much (we've all been there). Finding a way to lose any excess lengths of wire without bunching can be an art - laying it out in a zig-zag, taping it to the floor as you go, is just one solution.

Another lesson in neatness is finding out what kinds of cable clips are available, and where to use them. There's various stick-on clips which can be used as an alternative to gaffer tape on floors, and then 'P-clips', which look exactly as their name suggests, and can be screwed down (to speaker shelves, for instance). 'Looming'

your wiring is another lesson well-learned - this just means wrapping tape around, particularly on pairs of speaker wires or RCAs. As we've already said, don't loom speaker wire with power cables (or even with earths).

The last point is also about tidiness - mental tidiness. When you're dealing with speaker wiring, keep two ideas in mind - positive and negative. Each speaker has a pos (+) and neg (-) terminal. Mixing these up is not an option, so work out a system of your own, for keeping positive and negative in the right places on your headset and amp connections. Decent speaker cable is always two wires joined together - look closely, and you'll see that one wire has writing (or a stripe) on, and the other is plain. Use the wire with writing for pos connections throughout your system, and you'll never be confused again. While we're at it, RCA leads have red and white connector plugs - Red is for Right.

01 First step in running a live feed is deciding where best to run the wire into the car - try and go for the most direct route. On the Nova, the ideal spot is behind the battery - refer to fitting an alarm. Carefully make a new hole (seal it up with silicone sealant later) and feed that large wire into the front footwell.

02 Kit yourself out with a decent fuseholder - they not only look good, they're really excellent to use. Get a fuse the same rating as your amp, or the total load on your distribution block - ask a pro for advice. First stage in fitting is remembering to slide the screw end fitting down the large wire, followed, in this case, by a nut.

03 This fuseholder's kinda unusual in how the wire end is attached. Once you've stripped a little insulation off the wire end, splay the strands out, and fold them back over the nut . . .

04 . . . which then screws into the fuseholder body, where the fuse itself lives. Weird. Normally, the wires are clamped using large Allen-headed screws (slightly easier to understand). Fix the fuseholder securely, using the screw holes provided in the base. Don't connect up to the battery until you're ready - this feed is NOT ignition-switched!

05 Here's where your live feed could end up - a distribution block. Split your power off to the amps as you need it - each amp gets its own fuse (downrated from the large one in the holder up front). Excellent electrical safety, trick looks. Pin the wire ends with the chunky Allen grub screws, then fit the plastic cover tight (or lives will touch earths, and sparks will fly).

06 Not an ideal solution, but it works - most people will be familiar with the 'wiring-bulge' along their sills. Unscrew the plastic sill trim panels, and you'll be surprised how much wire can be hidden neatly underneath. Notice that these are the RCA leads and speaker wires for our system - no live feeds here (they're along the other sill).

07 Looming the wires together keeps things neat, but don't pull those cable-ties too tight - it can be useful if the wires lie flat, and bunching them up might work against you. Also, take great care when refitting the screws for the sill trim panels - a screw through your wiring is a good way to kill your system.

Engines

Faster, faster!

So - does your car talk the talk (sounds fast), or does it walk the walk (actually is fast)? There's no shame in just having a fast-sounding car - not everyone can afford mega-performance, which is why bolt-on goodies like induction kits and big-bore exhausts are such big business. Serious engine tuning costs, and not just in the engine parts - your insurance company will throw a wobbly at a gas-flowed head, and might refuse to cover you altogether if you go for that 2.0 litre conversion.

The induction kit and sports exhaust are an essential first choice, and usually it's as far as you can really go before your insurance company disowns you. Both mods help the engine to 'breathe' better, which helps when you go for the accelerator initially, improving the response you feel, while you also get a crowd-pleasing induction roar and rasp from the back box, so everyone's happy.

Now for the harsh and painful truth. On their own, an induction kit and back box will not gain you much extra 'real' power. Sorry, but it's a myth. Time and again, people fit induction kits and back boxes, expecting huge power gains, and those 'in the know' have a quiet chuckle. All these things really do is make the car sound sportier, and improve the response - accept this, and you won't be disappointed. Ask yourself why most insurance companies don't generally increase premiums for the likes of a performance rear box or induction kit. The answer is - because (on their own) they don't make enough difference!

The 'bolt-on' performance goodies have more effect as part of an engine 'makeover' package, and setting-up the engine properly after fitting these parts can make a huge difference. If you're halfway serious about increasing the go of your Nova, talk to someone with access to a rolling road, so you can prove what's been done has actually made a useful gain. If you've spent time and a ton of money on your car, of course you're going to think it feels faster, but is it actually making more power?

Fitting all the performance goodies in the world will be pretty pointless if the engine's already knackered, but it might not be as bad as you think. One of the best ways to start on the performance road is simply to ensure that the car's serviced properly - new spark plugs, HT leads (also dizzy cap/rotor arm on most models), and an oil and filter change, are a good basis to begin from (see your Haynes manual). Correct any obvious faults, such as hoses or wiring plugs hanging off, and look for any obviously-damaged or leaking components, too.

Breathe with me...

Replacement element

One of the simplest items to fit, the replacement air filter element has been around for years - of course, now the induction kit's the thing to have, but a replacement element is more discreet (if you're worried about such things).

While we're at it, don't listen to your mates who tell you to simply take out the air filter completely - this is a really dumb idea. The fuel system's air intake acts like a mini vacuum cleaner, sucking in air from the front of the car, and it doesn't just suck in air, but also dust, dirt and leaves - it's also designed to suck in oil fumes from the engine itself (through the 'breather' connection). Without a filter, all this muck would quickly end up in the sensitive parts of the fuel system, and will quickly make the car undriveable. Worse, if any of it makes it into the engine, this will lead to engine wear. Remember too, that cheaper performance filters can be of very suspect quality - if your new filter disintegrates completely inside six months, it'll do wonders for the airflow, but it'll also be letting in all sorts of rubbish!

Some performance filters have to be oiled before fitting - follow the instructions provided; don't ignore this part, or the filter won't be effective. If the filter won't fit, check whether you actually have the right one - don't force it in, and don't cut it to fit, as either of these will result in gaps, which would allow unfiltered air to get in.

01 This is obviously a Nova with a tiddler of a motor - GTEs and GSis have a totally different air cleaner. Step one in reaching the old element is releasing all the spring clips around the edge of the air cleaner . . .

02 . . . then remove the small screw next to the air cleaner inlet duct . . .

03 . . . and the three long screws in the centre (which actually hold the whole air cleaner on the carb/throttle body).

04 Lift up the air cleaner lid (preferably without taking off the whole unit) - and there she is. One very nasty old element, which doesn't look like it's been changed any time this century.

05 Don't just stick the new filter in - clean out some of the muck that's gathered in the filter box. Use a damp cloth for this, as we don't want the grit and leaves going into the engine, thank you.

06 Stick in your new filter (making sure it's the right way up), put it all back together, and feel the difference. Don't forget to find a prominent spot to display your K&N sticker.

Pancake filter

If your Nova's 'only' got a carb, or happens to be one with single-point injection (1.2i or 1.4i), you may find there's no induction kit you can get for it. So how do you boost its performance, and get that induction kit roar under the bonnet? The old-school answer is a 'pancake' filter, which, like an induction kit, does away with the old air cleaner, in favour of a sweet-looking filter unit which bolts straight to the top of the carb or throttle body. Our filter came from K&N - look under 'custom assemblies' on their website.

01 Dumping that standard air cleaner is one of the best ways to start tidying the Nova engine - as described earlier in this section, take out three screws, and it's almost completely off. There's just a few hoses underneath to pull free, and it's history. The largest of them's the breather hose.

02 Flip - that was fast. It can't be that easy, fitting one of these new filters? What we've done is just place the filter on top, to get an idea where the breather hose will fit. Don't leave breather hoses hanging off (see *Tricks 'n' tips*).

06 Look at that luvverly shiny chrome - just a slight improvement over that black plastic splat you used to have on your engine? Insert your hose into the intended orifice (sure there's a mucky one-liner in there somewhere) . . .

Bum notes
One potential problem of fitting a filter like this is carb 'icing' in cold weather. Your old air cleaner had an automatic warm-air supply system built in, to combat the problem - chuck the air cleaner, and you lose the benefit. Carb icing is caused by water vapour freezing inside the carb, which leads to the engine losing power and maybe stalling in cold weather. Curing the problem's not easy - refitting the warm-air pipe from the exhaust manifold will help, but if you leave it on in hot weather, you'll get fuel vapourisation and pinking. Certain fuel additives might help to reduce icing, and could be the simplest answer.

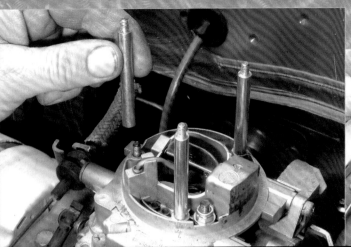

03 This filter's dead easy to dismantle, which makes drilling a hole for the breather hose simple. Like it says in the instructions, make the hole slightly smaller than the hose, so it's a tight fit.

04 The rest of the filter install's easy-peas - it always makes a difference when you buy something that actually seems to have been designed for your car. Screw the mounting posts onto the studs thoughtfully provided on your Nova's carb . . .

05 . . . then slip over the cork gasket. We know the idea's to get as much air in as poss, but not fitting this part will give you a random air leak, which majorly messes up the running of your engine.

Tricks 'n' tips

When fitting a bolt-on filter to a carb, don't leave the breather pipe hanging off (this is the large pipe which pulls off the base of the old air cleaner). Not only could this mean an MOT fail, it will make your Nova run like a Lada on two cylinders (lumpy tickover). Check with your filter supplier whether there's provision to connect the breather pipe into the new filter. The smaller vacuum pipes might have to be plugged to make the car run right, but don't plug the breather pipe!

. . . or second, try taking off one of the hoses completely, looking to see the pipe stub it fits onto under the carb. Now take the end of the first hose, and plug it onto the pipe stub for the second. In theory, this completes the vacuum circuit, and is as good as plugging the ends of both hoses.

07 . . . then mount the filter, and tighten your nuts. Must go and have a lie down now.

08 Just those two small vacuum hoses we removed from below the old air cleaner to deal with now. You might find your car runs okay with them left hanging, but here's a couple of tips to try. First, plug the end of the hose with a bolt the right size . . .

09 is as good as plugging the ends of both hoses.

Induction kit

Kits can usually only be had for Novas with multi-point injection (which means 1.6 GTEs and GSis, and the later 1.4 SRi). With an induction kit, the standard air filter housing and ducting are junked, and the new filter bolts directly to the airflow meter or throttle body. Most kits also feature special air inlet ducting (hoses) to feed the new filter with the coldest possible air from the front of the car - cold air is denser, and improves engine power. Feeding the filter with cold air is in theory good for maximum performance with a hot engine or in hot weather, but in colder conditions with a cold engine, driveability and fuel economy might suffer.

The fuelling arrangements for fuel injection are based largely on the volume of incoming air. If you start feeding the injection system an unusually large amount of air (by fitting an induction kit, for instance), the management system will compensate by throwing in more fuel. This could result in some more power - or the car will drink petrol and your exhaust emissions will be screwed up, inviting an MOT failure. We're not saying 'don't do it', just remember that power gains can be exaggerated, and that there can be pitfalls.

What no-one disputes is that an induction kit, which operates without all the normal ducting provided as standard, gives the engine a real throaty roar when you go for the loud pedal. So at least it sounds fast. Jubbly.

Other air filter-type mods

One old favourite, if you've got an injection Nova with a square filter box and haven't gone for an induction kit, is drilling holes in the air filter box. Only drill the air filter box below the level where the filter element sits, or the air going into the engine won't be filtered. Making your airbox look like a Swiss cheese won't make the car faster, but it does give you the nice throaty induction roar at full throttle.

Carb conversions

Carb models have actually got it best of all for extracting more go, and there's no power-sapping cat to worry about. Check your Yellow Pages for a carburettor specialist, and see what can be done by increasing the jet sizes first. In the end, you'll probably need a different carb (and maybe a different inlet manifold) for major oomph. Ones to go for? Try the Weber 32/34 DMTR (fitted to 1.5 and 1.6 litre Fiat Strada/Regata models) or the 32/34 DMTL (Land Rover 90 & 110) - but check with a carb expert before parting with cash at a scrap yard. Any carb off an old car is bound to need attention, and the throttle/choke cables probably won't just go straight on.

Finally...

Once you've fitted your new filter or induction kit, even if you don't take the car to a rolling road for setting up, at least take it to a garage and have the emissions checked - any minor adjustments should ensure that the engine will, if nothing else, still tick over okay, and should ensure an MOT emissions pass.

Adjustable fuel pressure regulator
(power boost valve)

Only available for Novas with multi-point injection (1.4 SRi and the 1.6 litre models), these valves allow the fuel system pressure to be increased over the standard regulator valve. Contrary to what you might think, they don't actually provide much more fuel (this is regulated separately by the injection ECU).

The effect of increasing the injection pressure is to improve the injector spray pattern, which helps the fuel to burn more efficiently, and has the effect of increasing engine power while actually reducing emission levels.

To see the true effect of these valves, they must be set up using emission test gear and ideally a rolling road - merely turning the pressure up to the maximum level might not produce the desired effect. Fitting one of these valves involves breaking into the high-pressure fuel line, which is potentially dangerous for the inexperienced - also, if the valve is poorly fitted (or the fuel lines are in poor condition), you could end up with fuel spraying out under pressure onto a hot engine. Make sure you know what you're doing - take great care when dealing with petrol, and watch carefully for any sign of fuel leakage after fitting, even if this is done by a professional.

No quicker but it looks nice

Looks are just as important as performance. No hot hatch is 'finished' without making it look sweet. Details to the engine bay as well as your interior and exterior mods are an important factor, especially if you were thinking about getting your motor featured in top magazines. Every one does it, and you're next.

First up - try cleaning the engine, for heaven sake! How do you expect to emulate the show-stopping cars if your gearbox is covered in grot? Get busy with the degreaser (Gunk's a good bet), then get the hosepipe out. You can take it down to the local jetwash if you like, but remember your mobile - if you get carried away with the high-power spray, you might find the car won't start afterwards!

When it's all dry (and running again), you can start in. Get the polish to all the painted surfaces you reasonably can, and don't be afraid to unbolt a few of the simpler items to gain better access.

We're assuming you've already fitted your induction kit, but if not, these nicely do away with a load of ugly plastic airbox/air cleaner and trunking, and that rusted-out exhaust manifold cover, in favour of decent-looking product. Take off the rocker cover (or engine cover), and paint it to match your chosen scheme (heat-resistant paint is a must, really, such as brake caliper paint), set off with a funky oil filler cap. A strut brace is a tasty underbonnet feature, especially chromed. Braided hose covers (or coloured hose sets), ally battery covers and bottles, mirror panels - all give the underbonnet a touch of glamour.

Braided hoses

01 Unroll your braiding, check the length against your freshly-removed hose, and trim it roughly to length - you might need something heftier than scissors for this.

02 Now expand the braiding to the right size using a suitable blunt object. Like a screwdriver handle, we mean - what were you thinking of? Once the braiding's roughly the right size, you can slip your pipe in (lovely). Smooth out the braiding round the bends, as it tends to gather up and look naff otherwise, then trim up the ends.

03 Slide a new Jubilee clip over the braiding at one end, then slip one of the coloured end fittings over the clip. Repeat this process at the other end of your chosen hose, and it'll be ready to fit back on. When you're sure the hose is fully onto its fitting, tighten the hose clip securely to avoid embarrassing leakage.

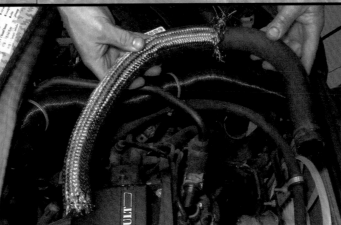

You's a hose

There are many ways to add detail and colour to otherwise boring components. Spraying your hoses is just one of those ways. Only apply paint that is suitable for engine bay use, as temperatures get very high under the hood. The good folk from ABC Design supplied our paint.

01

Choose the most visible hoses first, and be careful undoing the hose clips - there could be coolant or fuel in there. Don't even think about spraying the hoses in place - do you really want to colour-code the entire underbonnet area? Give the pipe a good clean to thoroughly degrease it - any oil or silicone-slippery stuff, and the paint won't stick.

02

 Achtung!

The engine must be completely cold before you start. Even if you've only done a quick lap, it would be dangerous to attempt doing anything with a remotely warm engine, as the fluids inside the pipe are often a lot hotter than they appear. Be warned!

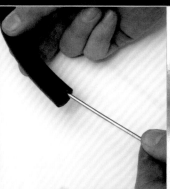

03 A preferred way of spraying, to ensure maximum coverage, is to hang the pipe from above. Use a stiff piece of wire inserted into the end of the hose (NOT poked through the hose) to hold onto.

04 Apply the paint in three or four light layers until pipe is evenly covered. You'll also have to wait a while (ideally, leave overnight) before that hose can go back on.

05 Given enough time to dry, this hose paint's really good stuff - doesn't crack or flake off. But we wouldn't advise going ballistic with the pressure washer, once the hose is back on - the paint might not be quite that good.

06 Tighten all hose clips securely - coolant leaks are not cool, and fuel leaks could be deadly. If you've lost any coolant, the system will need topping-up once you're done - you'll want a 50-50 mix of antifreeze and water, not just plain water.

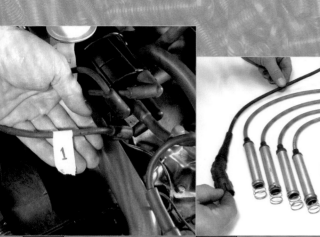

01 Brighten up the underbonnet, and maybe (if you believe what it says on the tin) make your car go better too? Gotta be worth a punt, to find out. First, make sure the ignition's off - take out the key, to be certain. Mark the old leads for position with tape, and work on one lead at a time here - pull one end off the spark plug, then trace it through and unclip from the distributor.

02 Lay the new leads out, and choose the lead closest in length to the one you've just pulled off. Always pays to check the leads look right, before you get too far in - and don't wreck the box they came in, when you open it up. Our leads, though right for our Nova engine, were all far too long. The shortest lead is the 'king' lead for the ignition coil (on the inner wing).

03 When you're happy with your choice of lead, give it a squirt of WD-40 inside to keep the damp out, then push it onto the plug - it should click positively into place. Clip the lead across the front of the engine, and onto the right location on the distributor - this is where you'll get confused if you don't do the leads one by one.

Achtung!
Switch off the ignition and remove the key before starting this job. You don't want to be on the wrong end of 40,000 volts.

Coloured
HT leads

04 The last lead's the easiest to get right - the 'king' lead goes from the distributor centre terminal to the coil on the inner wing.

05 And here's some we did earlier. Don't like red? Well, they also come in blue, yellow…

Silicon heaven

All Novas with fuel injection have an engine management system with a 'computer' at its heart, known as the ECU, or Electronic Control Unit. The ECU contains several computer chips, at least one of which has programmed onto it the preferred fuel/air mixture and ignition advance setting for any given engine speed or load - this information is known as a computer 'map', and the system refers to it constantly while the car's being driven. Obviously, with the current trend towards fuel economy and reducing harmful exhaust emissions, the values in this 'map' are set, well, conservatively, let's say (read 'boring'). With a little tweaking - like richening-up the mixture, say - the engine can be made to produce more power, or response will be improved, or both. At the expense of the environment. Oh well.

Companies like Superchips offer replacement computer chips which feature a computer map where driveability and performance are given priority over outright economy (although the company claims that, under certain conditions, even fuel economy can be better, with their products). While a chip like this does offer proven power gains on its own, it's obviously best to combine a chip with other enhancements, and to have the whole lot set up at the same time. By the time you've fitted an induction kit, four-branch manifold, big-bore pipe, and maybe even a fast-road cam, adding a chip is the icing on the cake - chipping an already-modified motor will liberate even more horses, or at least combine it with

majorly-improved response. Vauxhall tuning specialists are best placed to advise you on the most effective tuning mods.

Another feature programmed into the ECU is a rev limiter, which cuts the ignition (or fuel) progressively when the pre-set rev limit is reached. Most replacement chips have the rev limiter reset higher, or removed altogether. Not totally sure this is a good thing - if the engine's not maintained properly (low oil level, cambelt changes neglected), removing the rev limiter and running beyond the red line would be a quick way to kill it. But a well-maintained engine with a rally cam fitted could rev off the clock, if the ECU would let it, so maybe not a bad thing after all...

Now the bad news

Chipping is often thought of as an easy, 'no-tell' route to increased performance and driveability - after all, the ECU is well-buried inside the car, not on show under the bonnet, so who's gonna know? Needless to say, the insurance companies have been wise to this trick for a long time. A sure way to tell whether a 'performance' product does what it says on the tin is to see what it'll do to your premium - telling them you're fitting a sports ROM chip will cost. Big-time. But, in the event of a claim, if they suspect your car's been 'chipped', rest assured, they will make efforts to find out, because if you haven't told them about it, it means they save on paying out. What's an insurance assessor's salary for one day, compared to the thousands you could be claiming in case of an accident or theft? Do it by all means, but at least be honest.

Engine tuning

So you've done the filter/induction kit and exhaust box - what's next, short of going for a complete engine swap? If you've got a sports back box, try a performance exhaust manifold up front - or better still, a full system for the best gains. If your 1992-on Nova is strangled by a 'cat', there's the option of a de-cat pipe (but remember that the car's not MOT-able with one of these fitted, so isn't strictly legal for use on the road).

A new camshaft's often a juicy way to pep up a standard motor, but the standard Nova cam's pretty good, so unless yours is knackered (common Vauxhall ohc failing, with worn followers too), all you'll achieve by fitting one is moving the power further up the rev range. But - treat your Nova to a skimmed, gas-flowed, big-valve cylinder head (and a fast road cam) and it'll really start to percolate. Incidentally, some 1.4 litre cylinder heads are actually more restrictive than either the 1.2 or 1.3, so fitting a standard 1.4 head to a 1.2 engine might not be much of an upgrade.

Most young Nova owners wait 'til they've built up some no-claims bonus on their insurance, and go for a bigger Vauxhall engine. Easiest to fit, and offering useful performance gains over a basic 1.2 or 1.4 lump, is the 1.6 engine from the Nova GTE or GSi. Better still, find a 1.6 16-valve motor from a Corsa GSi or new-ish Astra. Apart from splicing-in the injection system wiring (and you

might also need the fuel tank, to get the injection's fuel pump), this is a reasonable DIY prospect.

If you're gonna change an engine, though, why not make it worthwhile, and get 2.0 litres of throbbing power under your bonnet? Not quite such an easy DIY project, some 'modification' of the engine bay's needed, as well as custom-made driveshafts - try PVD (Performance Vauxhall Developments) for a conversion kit. Vauxhall tuners such as Courtenay, Blydenstein or ASW Motorsport are worth consulting on this (besides any mates who've had the job done, and Nova internet forums).

And finally tonight - the bad news. Any major engine mods means telling those nice suits who work for your insurance company, and it's likely they'll insist on a full engineer's report (these aren't especially expensive - look one up in the Yellow Pages, under 'Garage Services' or 'Vehicle Inspection').

Exhausts

It's gotta be done, hasn't it? Your rusty old exhaust lacks the girth to impress, and doesn't so much growl as miaow. Don't be a wimp and fit an exhaust trim - they'll fool nobody who really knows, and they certainly won't add to your aural pleasure (oo-er). Sort yourself out a decent back box upgrade, and even a timid 1.0 Nova can begin to cut it at the cruise.

What a back box won't do on its own is increase engine power - although it'll certainly sound like it has, provided you choose the right one, and fit it properly. Check when you're buying that it can be fitted to a standard system - you'll probably need something called a reducing sleeve for a decent fit, which is a section of pipe designed to bridge the difference between your small-diameter pipe and the larger-diameter silencer. Try and measure your standard pipe as accurately as possible, or you'll have major problems trying to get a decent seal between the old and new bits - don't assume that exhaust paste will sort everything out, because it won't.

Fashion has even entered the aftermarket exhaust scene, with different rear pipe designs going in and out of style. Everyone's done the upswept twin-pipe 'DTM' style pipes, while currently the trend in single pipes is massive Jap-style round exits, or fat oval (or twin-oval) designs. If you must have the phattest Nova on the block, you can't beat a twin-exit system (from someone like Powerflow), even though it'll probably mean losing your spare

Know your enemy - this is what your cat looks like inside. Is it any wonder they restrict gas flow?

wheel in the fitting process. Well, when was the last time you had a puncture? And what are mobiles and breakdown cover for, anyway?

If you've got a capacity-challenged Nova, you might need to lightly modify even your standard rear bodywork/bumper to accommodate a bigger rear pipe; if you're going for a bodykit later, your back box will have to come off again, so it can be poked through your rear valance/mesh.

You'll see some useful power gains if you go for the complete performance exhaust system, rather than just the back box. Like the factory-fit system, the sports silencer again will only work at its best if combined with the front pipe and manifold it was designed for! Performance four-branch manifolds alone can give very useful power gains. Watch what you buy, though - cheap exhaust manifolds which crack for a pastime are not unknown, and many aftermarket systems need careful fitting and fettling before you'll stop it resonating or banging away underneath. A sports rear box alone shouldn't attract an increased insurance premium, but a full system probably will.

Novas after February 1992 are lumbered with a catalytic converter (or 'cat'), which acts like a restrictor in the exhaust, inhibiting the gas flow and sapping some engine power (maybe 5 to 10%). Various specialist exhaust companies market replacement sections which do away with the cat (a 'de-cat pipe'), and get you your power back. As the Nova didn't always have a cat, you could just buy the relevant standard front section of exhaust for a pre-cat model (from your local fast-fit centre), and save yourself some dosh. Unfortunately, by taking off or disabling the cat, your car won't be able to pass the emissions test at MOT time, so you'll have to 're-convert' the car every 12 months. This fact, arguably, means that the car is illegal on the road with a de-cat pipe fitted - you'd have no defence for this, if questions were asked at the roadside, and potentially no insurance if the unthinkable happens. Sorry, but we have to say it...

One other point to consider, if your Nova's been slammed to the floor - will your big new sports system be leaving behind a trail of sparks as it scrapes along the deck? Shouldn't do, if it's been properly fitted, but will the local multi-storey be out-of-bounds for your Nova, from now on? And - pub trivia moment - you can actually be done for causing damage to the highway, if your exhaust's dragging. Well, great.

You probably couldn't give a stuff if your loud system's a very loud major public nuisance, but will that loud pipe start interfering with your sound system? If you rack up many motorway miles, you might find the constant drone of a loud pipe gets to be a real pain on a long trip, too...

Fitting a sports back box

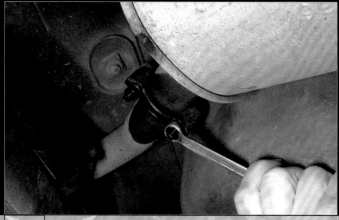

01 First we've got to survey the whole under-Nova situation. It helps to remove the nearside rear wheel for this, but it's not absolutely essential. Jack up the back end of the car - have a look in *'Wheels & tyres'* for more info on jacking up. A quick squirt of WD-40, and it's time to tackle the exhaust clamp nuts . . .

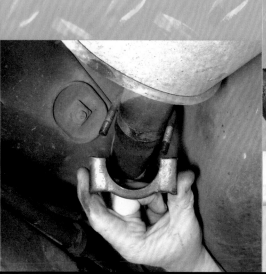

02 . . . which shouldn't present much of a challenge. If the pipes look rusty as hell, you know you'll be in for a fight getting the old box off.

03 Before you can really start separating the rusty old box, there's the rear mounting to remove. This is just a hooked-on rubber mounting - some more lube, and a little prising sideways with a large screwdriver might be needed. Working a stubborn joint apart usually entails trying to twist one section against the other (swearing at it is also essential).

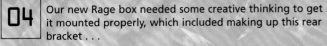

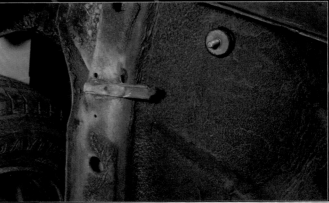

04 Our new Rage box needed some creative thinking to get it mounted properly, which included making up this rear bracket . . .

05 . . . and drilling a hole through the boot floor, to take this bolt (which is the top half of our new rear mounting).

06 Although our box came with two reducing sleeves (to enable easy fitting to a standard front pipe), neither of them were much use to us. What we needed was a sleeve with a bend in it, to turn the box into the correct position. In the end, we chopped a curved section from a scrap exhaust - not the easiest job to fit, then . . .

07 . . . but when you get an end result like this, a little extra effort's got to be worth it. Look at the pipe on that.

Safety and **tools**

Safety

We all know that working on your car can be dangerous - and we're not talking about the danger of losing your street cred by fitting naff alloys or furry dice! Okay, so you'd be hard-pushed to injure yourself fitting some cool floor mats or a tax disc holder, but tackle more-serious mods, and you could be treading dangerous ground. Let's be honest - we have to put this safety section in to cover ourselves, but now it's in, it would be nice if you read it…

Burning/scalding

The only way you'll really burn yourself is if your car's just been running - avoid this, and you won't get burned. Easy, eh? Otherwise, you risk burns from any hot parts of the engine (and especially the exhaust - if you've got one, the cat runs very hot), or from spilling hot coolant if you undo the radiator hoses or filler cap, as you might when you're braiding hoses.

Fire

Sadly, there's several ways your car could catch fire, when you think about it. You've got a big tank full of fuel (and other flammable liquids about, like brake fluid), together with electrics - some of which run to very high voltages. If you smoke too, this could be even worse for your health than you thought.

a Liquid fuel is flammable. Fuel vapour can explode - don't smoke, or create any kind of spark, if there's fuel vapour (fuel smell) about.

b Letting fuel spill onto a hot engine is dangerous, but brake fluid spills go up even more readily. Respect is due with brake fluid, which also attacks paintwork and plastics - wash off with water.

c Fires can also be started by careless modding involving the electrical system. It's possible to overload (and overheat) existing wiring by tapping off too many times for new live feeds. Not insulating bare wires or connections can lead to short-circuits, and the sparks or overheated wiring which results can start a fire. Always investigate any newly-wired-in kit which stops working, or which keeps blowing fuses - those wires could already be smouldering…

Crushing

Having your car land on top of you is no laughing matter, and it's a nasty accident waiting to happen if you risk using dodgy old jacks, bricks, and other means of lifting/supporting your car. Please don't.

Your standard vehicle jack is for emergency roadside use only - a proper trolley jack and a set of axle stands won't break the overdraft, and might save broken bones. Don't buy a cheap trolley jack, and don't expect a well-used secondhand one to be perfect, either - when the hydraulic seals start to fail, a trolley jack will drop very fast; this is why you should always have decent stands in place under the car as well.

Steering, suspension & brakes

Screwing up any one of these on your car, through badly-fitted mods, could land you and others in hospital or worse. Nuff said? It's always worth getting a mate, or a friendly garage, to check over what you've just fitted (or even what you've just had fitted, in some cases - not all "pro" fitters are perfect!). Pay attention to tightening vital nuts and bolts properly - buy or borrow a torque wrench.

To be absolutely sure, take your newly-modded machine to a friendly MOT tester (if there is such a thing) - this man's your ultimate authority on safety, after all. Even if he's normally a pain once a year, he could save your life. Think it over.

Even properly-fitted mods can radically alter the car's handling - and not always for the better. Take a few days getting used to how the car feels before showing off.

Wheels

Don't take liberties fitting wheels. Make sure the wheels have the right stud/bolt hole pattern for your car, and that the wheel nuts/bolts are doing their job. Bolts which are too long might catch on your brakes (especially rear drums) - too short, and, well, the wheels are just waiting to fall off. Not nice. Also pay attention to the bolt heads or wheel nuts - some are supposed to have large tapered washers fitted, to locate properly in the wheel. If the nuts/bolts "pull through" the wheel when tightened, the wheel's gonna fall off, isn't it?

Asbestos

Only likely to be a major worry when working on, or near, your brakes. That black dust that gets all over your alloys comes from your brake pads, and it may contain asbestos. Breathing in asbestos dust can lead to a disease called asbestosis (inflammation of the lungs - very nasty indeed), so try not to inhale brake dust when you're changing your pads or discs.

Airbags

Unless you run into something at high speed, the only time an airbag will enter your life is when you change your steering wheel for something more sexy, and have to disable the airbag in the process. Pay attention to all the precautionary advice given in our text, and you'll have no problems.

One more thing - don't tap into the airbag wiring to run any extra electrical kit. Any mods to the airbag circuit could set it off unexpectedly.

Exhaust gases

Even on cars with cats, exhaust fumes are still potentially lethal. Don't work in an unventilated garage with the engine running. When fitting new exhaust bits, be sure that there's no gas leakage from the joints. When modifying in the tailgate area, note that exhaust gas can get sucked into the car through badly-fitting tailgate seals/joints (or even through your rear arches, if they've been trimmed so much there's holes into the car).

Tools

In writing this book, we've assumed you already have a selection of basic tools - screwdrivers, socket set, spanners, hammer, sharp knife, power drill. Any unusual extra tools you might need are mentioned in the relevant text. Torx and Allen screws are often found on trim panels, so a set of keys of each type is a wise purchase.

From a safety angle, always buy the best tools you can afford - or if you must use cheap ones, remember that they can break under stress or unusual usage (and we've all got the busted screwdrivers to prove it!).

DO Wear goggles when using power tools.

DO Keep loose clothing/long hair away from moving engine parts.

DO Take off watches and jewellery when working on electrics.

DO Keep the work area tidy - stops accidents and losing parts.

DON'T Rush a job, or take stupid short-cuts.

DON'T Use the wrong tools for the job, or ones which don't fit.

DON'T Let kids or pets play around your car when you're working.

DON'T Work entirely alone under a car that's been jacked up.

Legal modding?
No such thing!!

The harsh & painful truth

The minute you start down the road to a modified motor, you stand a good chance of being in trouble with the Man. It seems like there's almost nothing worthwhile you can do to your car, without breaking some sort of law. So the answer's not to do it at all, then? Well, no, but let's keep it real.

There's this bunch of vehicle-related regulations called Construction & Use. It's a huge set of books, used by the car manufacturers and the Department of Transport among others, and it sets out in black and white all the legal issues that could land you in trouble. It's the ultimate authority for modifying, in theory. But few people (and even fewer policemen) know all of it inside-out, and it's forever being updated and revised, so it's not often enforced to the letter at the roadside - just in court. Despite the existence of C & U, in trying to put together any guide to the law and modifying, it quickly becomes clear that almost everything's a "grey area", with no-one prepared to go on record and say what is okay to modify and what's not. Well, brilliant. So if there's no fixed rules (in the real world), how are you meant to live by them? In the circumstances, all we can promise to do is help to make sense of nonsense…

Avoiding roadside interviews

Why do some people get pulled all the time, and others hardly ever? It's often all about attitude. We'd all like to be free to drive around "in yer face", windows down, system full up, loud exhaust bellowing, sparks striking, tyres squealing - but - nothing is a bigger "come-on" to the boys in blue than "irresponsible" driving like this. Rest assured,

if your motor's anywhere near fully sorted, the coppers will find something they can nick you for, when they pull you over - it's a dead cert. Trying not to wind them up too much before this happens (and certainly not once you're stopped) will make for an easier life. There's showing off, and then there's taking the pee. Save it for the next cruise.

The worst thing from your point of view is that, once you've been stopped, it's down to that particular copper's judgement as to whether your car's illegal. If he/she's having a bad day anyway, smart-mouthing-off isn't gonna help your case at all. If you can persuade him/her that you're at least taking on board what's being said, you might be let off with a warning. If it goes further, you'll be reported for an offence - while this doesn't mean you'll end up being prosecuted for it, it ain't good. Some defects (like worn tyres) will result in a so-called "seven-day wonder", which usually means you have to fix whatever's deemed wrong, maybe get the car inspected, and present yourself with the proof at a police station, inside seven days, or face prosecution.

If you can manage to drive reasonably sensibly when the law's about, and can ideally show that you've tried to keep your car legal when you get questioned, you stand a much better chance of enjoying your relationship with your modded beast. This guide is intended to help you steer clear of the more obvious things you could get pulled for. By reading it, you might even be able to have an informed, well-mannered discussion about things legal with the next officer of the law you meet at the side of the road. As in: "Oh really, officer? I was not aware of that. Thank you for pointing it out." Just don't argue with them, that's all…

Documents

The first thing you'll be asked to produce. If you're driving around without tax, MOT or insurance, we might as well stop now, as you won't be doing much more driving of anything after just one pull.

Okay, so you don't normally carry all your car-related documents with you - for safety, you've got them stashed carefully at home, haven't you? But carrying photocopies of your licence, MOT and insurance certificate is a good idea. While they're not legally-binding absolute proof, producing these in a roadside check might mean you don't have to produce the real things at a copshop later in the week. Shows a certain responsibility, and confidence in your own legality on the road, too. In some parts of the country, it's even said to be a good idea to carry copies of any receipts for your stereo gear - if there's any suspicion about it being stolen (surely not), some coppers have been known to confiscate it (or the car it's in) on the spot!

Number plates

One of the simplest mods, and one of the easiest to spot (and prove) if you're a copper. Nowadays, any changes made to the standard approved character font (such as italics or fancy type), spacing, or size of the plate constitutes an offence. Remember too that if you've moved the rear plate from its original spot (like from the tailgate recess, during smoothing) it still has to be properly lit at night. You're unlikely to even buy an illegal plate now, as the companies making them are also liable for prosecution if you get stopped. It's all just something else to blame on speed cameras - plates have to be easy for them to shoot, and modding yours suggests you're trying to escape a speeding conviction (well, who isn't?).

Getting pulled for an illegal plate is for suckers - you're making it too easy for them. While this offence only entails a small fine and confiscation of the plates, you're drawing unwelcome police attention to the rest of your car. Not smart. At all.

Sunstrips and tints

The sunstrip is now an essential item for any modded motor, but telling Mr Plod you had to fit one is no defence if you've gone a bit too far. The sunstrip should not be so low down the screen that it interferes with your ability to see out. Is this obvious? Apparently not. As a guide, if the strip's so low your wiper(s) touch it, it's too low. Don't try fitting short wiper blades to get round this - the police aren't as stupid as that, and you could get done for wipers that don't clear a sufficient area of the screen. Push it so far, and no further!

Window tinting is a trickier area. It seems you can have up to a 25% tint on a windscreen, and up to 30% on all other glass - but how do you measure this? Er. And what do you do if your glass is tinted to start with? Er, probably nothing. Of course you can buy window film in various "darknesses", from not-very-dark to "ambulance-black", but being able to buy it does not make it legal for road use (most companies cover themselves by saying "for show use only"). Go for just a light smoke on the side and rear glass, and you'd have to be unlucky to get done for it. If you must fit really dark tints, you're safest doing the rear side windows only.

Some forces now have a light meter to test light transmission through glass at the roadside - fail this, and it's a big on-the-spot fine.

Single wiper conversion

Not usually a problem, and certainly not worth a pull on its own, but combine a big sunstrip with a short wiper blade, and you're just asking for trouble. Insufficient view of the road ahead. There's also the question of whether it's legal to have the arm parking vertically, in the centre of the screen, as it obscures your vision. Probably not legal, then - even if it looks cool. Unfortunately, the Man doesn't do cool.

Lights

Lights of all kinds have to be one of the single biggest problem areas in modifying, and the police are depressingly well-informed. Most people make light mods a priority, whether it's Morette conversions for headlights or Lexus-style rear clusters. If they fit alright, and work, what's the problem?

First off, don't bother with any lights which aren't fully UK-legal - it's just too much hassle. Being "E-marked" only makes them legal in Europe, and most of our Euro-chums drive on the right. One of our project cars ended up with left-hand-drive rear clusters, and as a result, had no rear reflectors and a rear foglight on the wrong side (should be on the right). Getting stopped for not having rear reflectors would be a bit harsh, but why risk it, even to save a few quid?

Once you've had any headlight mods done (other than light brows) always have the beam alignment checked - it's part of the MOT, after all. The same applies to any front fogs or spots you've fitted (the various points of law involved here are too many to mention - light colour, height, spacing, operation with main/dipped headlights - ask at an MOT centre before fitting, and have them checked out after fitting).

If Plod's really having a bad day, he might even question the legality of your new blue headlight bulbs - are they too powerful? Keeping the bulb packaging in the glovebox might be a neat solution here (60/55W max).

Many modders favour spraying rear light clusters to make them look trick, as opposed to replacing them - but there's trouble in store here, too. One of the greyest of grey areas is - how much light tinting is too much? The much-talked-about but not-often-seen "common sense" comes into play here. Making your lights so dim that they're reduced to a feeble red/orange glow is pretty dim itself. If you're spraying, only use proper light-tinting spray, and not too many coats of that. Colour-coding lights with ordinary spray paint is best left to a pro sprayer or bodyshop (it can be done by mixing lots of lacquer with not much paint, for instance). Tinted lights are actually more of a problem in daylight than at night, so check yours while the sun's out.

Lastly, two words about neons. Oh, dear. It seems that neons of all kinds have now been deemed illegal for road use (and that's

interior ones as well as exteriors, which have pretty much always been a no-no). If you fit neons inside, make sure you rig in a switch so you can easily turn them off when the law arrives - or don't drive around with them on (save it for when you're parked up). Distracts other road users, apparently.

ICE

Jungle massive, or massive public nuisance? The two sides of the ICE argument in a nutshell. If you've been around the modding scene for any length of time, you'll already know stories of people who've been done for playing car stereos too loud. Seems some local authorities now have by-laws concerning "music audible from outside a vehicle", and hefty fines if you're caught. Even where this isn't the case, and assuming a dB meter isn't on hand to prove the offence of "excessive noise", the police can still prosecute for "disturbing the peace" - on the basis of one officer's judgement of the noise level. If a case is proved, you could lose your gear. Whoops. Seems we're back to "do it - but don't over-do it" again. If you really want to demo your system, pick somewhere a bit less public (like a quiet trading estate, after dark) or go for safety in numbers (at a cruise).

Big alloys/tyres

One of the first things to go on any lad's car, sexy alloys are right at the heart of car modifying. So what'll interest the law?

Well, the first thing every copper's going to wonder is - are the wheels nicked? He'd need a good reason to accuse you, but this is another instance where having copies of receipts might prove useful.

Otherwise, the wheels mustn't rub on, or stick out from, the arches - either of these will prove to be a problem if you get stopped. And you don't need to drive a modded motor to get done for having bald tyres…

Lowered suspension

Of course you have to lower your car, to have any hope of street cred. But did you know it's actually an offence to cause damage to the road surface, if your car's so low (or your mates so lardy) that it grounds out? Apparently so! Never mind what damage it might be doing to your exhaust, or the brake/fuel lines under the car - you can actually get done for risking damage to the road. Well, great. What's the answer? Once you've lowered the car, load it up with your biggest mates, and test it over roads you normally use - or else find a route into town that avoids all speed bumps. If you've got coilovers, you'll have an easier time tuning out the scraping noises.

Remember that your new big-bore exhaust or backbox must be hung up well enough that it doesn't hit the deck, even if you haven't absolutely slammed your car on the floor. At night, leaving a trail of sparks behind is a bit of a giveaway…

Exhausts

One of the easiest-to-fit performance upgrades, and another essential item if you want to be taken seriously on the street. Unless your chosen pipe/system is just too damn loud, you'd be very unlucky to get stopped for it, but if you will draw attention this way, you could be kicking yourself later.

For instance - have you in fact fitted a home-made straight-through pipe, to a car which used to have a "cat"? By drawing Plod's attention with that extra-loud system, he could then ask you to get the car's emissions tested - worse, you could get pulled for a "random" roadside emissions check. Fail this (and you surely will), and you could be right in the brown stuff. Even if you re-convert the car back to stock for the MOT, you'll be illegal on the road (and therefore without insurance) whenever your loud pipe's on. Still sound like fun, or would you be happier with just a back box?

It's also worth mentioning that your tailpipe mustn't stick out beyond the very back of the car, or in any other way which might be dangerous to pedestrians. Come on - you were a ped once!

Bodykits

The popular bodykits for the UK market have all passed the relevant tests, and are fully-approved for use on the specific vehicles they're intended for. As long as you haven't messed up fitting a standard kit, you should be fine, legally-speaking. The trouble starts when you do your own little mods and tweaks, such as bodging on that huge whale-tail spoiler or front air dam/splitter - it can be argued in some cases that these aren't appropriate on safety grounds, and you can get prosecuted. If any bodywork is fitted so it obscured your lights, or so badly attached that a strong breeze might blow it off, you can see their point. At least there's no such thing as Style Police. Not yet, anyway.

Seats and harnesses

Have to meet the UK safety standards, and must be securely bolted in. That's about it. It should be possible to fasten and release any seat belt or harness with one hand. Given that seat belts are pretty important safety features, it's understandable then that the police don't like to see flimsy alloy rear strut braces used as seat harness mounting points. Any other signs of bodging will also spell trouble. It's unlikely they'd bother with a full safety inspection at the roadside, but they could insist on a full MOT test/engineer's report inside 7 days. It's your life.

While we're on the subject of crash safety, the police also don't like to see sub boxes and amps just lying on the carpet, where the back seat used to be - if it's not anchored down, where are these items gonna end up, in a big shunt? Embedded in you, possibly?

Other mods

We'll never cover everything else here, and the law's always changing anyway, so we're fighting a losing battle in a book like this, but here goes with some other legalistic points we've noted on the way:

a It's illegal to remove side repeaters from front wings, even to create the ultimate smoothed/flushed motor. Sorry.

b All except the most prehistoric cars must have at least one rear foglight. If there's only one, it must be fitted on the right. We've never heard of anyone getting stopped for it, but you must also have a pair of rear reflectors. If your rear clusters ain't got 'em, can you get trendy ones? Er, no.

c Fuel filler caps have to be fitted so there's no danger of fuel spillage, or of excess fumes leaking from the top of the filler neck. This means using an appropriate petrol-resistant sealer (should be supplied in the kit). Oh, and not bodging the job in general seems a good idea. Unlikely to attract a pull, though.

d Front doors have to retain a manual means of opening from outside, even if they've been de-locked for remote locking. This means you can't take off the front door handles, usually. It seems that rear door handles can be removed if you like.

e Tailgates have to have some means of opening, even if it's only from inside, once the lock/handle's been removed. We think it's another safety thing - means of escape in a crash, and all that.

f You have to have at least one exterior mirror, and it must be capable of being adjusted somehow.

g If you fit new fog and spotlights, they actually have to work. No-one fits new lights just for show (or do they?), but if they stop working later when a fuse blows, relay packs up, or the wiring connectors rust up, you'd better fix 'em or remove 'em.

h Pedal extensions must have rubbers fitted on the brake and clutch pedals, and must be spaced sufficiently so there's no chance of hitting two pedals at once. This last bit sounds obvious, but lots of extension sets out there are so hard to fit that achieving this can be rather difficult. Don't get caught out.

i On cars with airbags, if you fit a sports wheel and disconnect the airbag in the process, the airbag warning light will be on permanently. Apart from being annoying, this is also illegal.

j Pace-car strobe lights (or any other flashing lights, apart from indicators) are illegal for road use. Of course.

k Anything else we didn't think of - is probably illegal too. Sorry.

Any questions? Try the MOT Helpline (0845 6005977). Yes, really.

Thanks to Andrew Dare of the Vehicle Inspectorate, Exeter, for his help in steering us through this minefield!

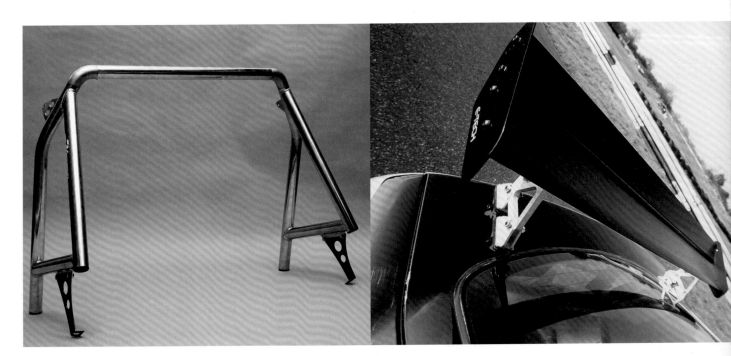

Thanks to:

We gratefully acknowledge all the help and advice offered from the following suppliers, without whom, etc, etc. Many of those credited below went way beyond the call of duty to help us produce this book - you know who you are. Cheers, guys! Roll the credits...

ABC Design Autostyling Ltd
(AutoArt & MHW)
www.abcdesignltd.com

Autopoint Car Care
(accessories)
01934 712612

Avo UK Ltd (coil overs)
01604 708101
www.avouk.com

Avon Custom Engineering
01934 876250
www.avoncustom.co.uk

Brown & Geeson (Momo)
01268 764411
www.brownandgeeson.com

Burnley Motors
(Bat Motorsport Body Kit)
0151 709 5818
www.batmotorsport.co.uk

Cooper Avon Tyres
01225 703101
www.coopertire.com

Corbeau Seats
01424 854499
www.corbeau-seats.co.uk

DD Audio UK Ltd (ICE)
01934 644400
www.ddaudiouk.co.uk

Demon Tweeks (accessories)
01978 664466
www.demon-tweeks.co.uk

Draper Tools (tools)
023 8026 6355
www.draper.co.uk

Eurostyling (Folia tec)
01908 324950
www.eurostyling.com

Halfords
08457 626 625

House of Kolor
(paint)
01302 341788
www.houseofkolor.com

K & N Filters
(induction kits)
01925 636950
www.knfilters.co.uk

Microscan Alarms
www.microscanalarms.co.uk

Novatech (fuel filler cap)
01753 696216
www.novatechmotorsport.co.uk

Optima (ICE)
01179 770060
www.optima-bristol.co.uk

L A & R W Piper
(upholsterers)
01963 441431
www.trimmers.fsnet.co.uk

Quad Conversions
01132 504527
www.quadconversions.com

Rage Products Ltd
(exhausts)
0870 8400091
www.rageproducts.com

Raid (accessories)
01664 823792
www./raid-rdi.com

Red Dot Racing
(brake discs & pads)
020 8888 2354
www.reddotracing.co.uk

Richbrook (sport auto accessories)
020 8543 7111
www.richbrook.co.uk

Ripspeed at Halfords
0845 609 1259

Venom Motorsport Ltd
(number plate recess)
01254 814444
www.venommotorsport.com

Wolfrace Wheels (UK) Ltd
01621 843770
www.wolfrace.co.uk

A special thank you to:
Bryn Musselwhite

Editorial Director	Matthew Minter
Designer	Simon Larkin
Page Build	James Robertson
Workshop	Paul Buckland Pete Trott Trevor Young
Editor	Ian Barnes
Project Co-ordinator	Carole Turk
Production Control	Kevin Heals

Haynes Car Manuals

Haynes Car Service and Repair Manuals are available from car accessory retailers.
For further information or to find your nearest stockist, call **01963 442030** or visit **www.haynes.co.uk**

Haynes Manuals